ROOTS OF
THE AMERICAN
WORKING CLASS

ROOTS OF
THE AMERICAN
WORKING CLASS

Susan E. Hirsch

The Industrialization of Crafts
in Newark, 1800–1860

University
of Pennsylvania
Press
1978

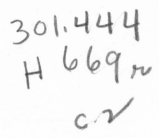

Library of Congress Cataloging in Publication Data

Hirsch, Susan E.
  Roots of the American working class.

  Includes index.
  1. Skilled labor—New Jersey—Newark—History.
  2. Labor and laboring classes—New Jersey—Newark
  —History. 3.   Newark, N. J.—Social conditions. I. Title.
HD8085.N63H57   301.44'42'0974932   78-51784
ISBN 0-8122-7747-3

To my mother and father

Contents

Tables

Figures

Acknowledgments

As this project has matured, I have received aid and encouragement from many friends and colleagues. I owe a special debt to Sam Bass Warner, Jr., who has given me unstintingly of his time since this project's inception, and who has helped me to appreciate many of the wider implications of my research. Milton Cantor and Lewis Erenberg read an earlier version of the manuscript and made many valuable suggestions for its improvement. I also want to thank Clyde Griffen for his encouragement, Beth Roberts for her editorial assistance, and Erik Austin for his aid in the computer analysis.

In researching the manuscript, I was aided by the staffs of the New Jersey State Archives, the New Jersey Historical Society, the Newark Public Library, and the Princeton University Library. Grants from the University of Michigan and the University of Virginia have supported part of the research and writing. The quantitative data on Newark's craftsmen is on file with the Center for Political Studies in Ann Arbor, Michigan. I want to thank Linda Condon and Carla Vaughn for typing the manuscript.

Introduction

Although the last fifteen years may well be called the age of "history from the bottom up," our understanding of the roots of the American working class is limited because the effect of industrialization on workers in the early nineteenth century remains obscure. Industrialization changed more than habits of work. It was one of the few forces to reshape both the physical environment and the social system in its own image, radically altering urban class structure and culture in the sense of values and life styles.[1] The relative paucity of research on this topic, however, has left the procedure and its results in some dispute.

This book approaches the history of the effects of industrialization on the social system by concentrating on skilled craftsmen in one city—Newark, New Jersey—and analyzing their work, their life styles and values, and the interest groups they formed. The roots of the American working class are clearly visible by the 1850s in Newark. Craftsmen there did not experience industrialization as a cataclysm that left no tradition unchanged nor any power in their hands. They accepted mechanization without Luddite protest, but they also created a union movement that was consciously hostile to capitalist employers as oppressors and which maintained some control over their work. Craftsmen, however, shared some basic values and customs with other classes, as when they preferred to follow Victorian family norms of male dominance and the nonworking wife and child rather than to increase family income. Moreover, workmen rarely aired their economic grievances in the political arena; they did not perceive the political structure as amenable to working-class action. But as the crafts were industrialized, workers created their own leisure activities and formed an exclusive social group, mixing little with employers or other entrepreneurs outside of work. The unity of Newark's working class was far from complete, however, because craftsmen were able to shape their homes and exercise some control over their work; not all workers experienced industrialization; and mass immigration brought together antagonistic ethnic groups in the labor force. A working class developed in Newark, but workers' consciousness of themselves as a separate class was not always strong.

This analysis of workers in the first half of the nineteenth century differs widely from those of traditional labor historians. In the past, labor historians have disagreed over whether a working class arose in the nineteenth century: they have equated the existence of a working class with expressions of class consciousness within the political parties or the union movement, but they have differed over what criteria to use to gauge that consciousness.

John R. Commons was the first to deny the formation of the working class in the early nineteenth century, since he interpreted neither the political parties nor the trade union movement as class conscious. In his pioneering study of the labor movement, *A History of Labour in the United States,* Commons described commercialization and industrialization as affecting crafts by causing a change in the relationship of the worker to capital and hence to the means of production.[2] According to Commons, however, workers reacted to the consequent exploitation by forming group-conscious unions demanding wage increases for small numbers of craftsmen and not class-conscious unions that attacked capitalism. Working-class consciousness was absent because craftsmen accepted the doctrine of individualism; they maintained their belief in capitalism and the liberal democratic state. Craftsmen believed in individualism, according to Commons, because America's easily obtainable land formed a safety valve allowing them to escape being permanent proletarians.

While the myth of the West as safety valve for dissatisfied urban workers has been demolished to the satisfaction of most historians, many still deny the existence of working-class consciousness in the early nineteenth century.[3] More recent studies have proffered the decided propensity of poor and manual workers for transiency as a reason for their lack of clearly expressed class action—mobility bred powerlessness.[4] Others have stressed the effect of occupational mobility or the accumulation of property in alleviating discontent, although they have differed on whether spectacular instances of these or generalized modest improvements were the moderating factor.[5]

The first major monograph on labor in the early nineteenth century, Norman Ware's *The Industrial Worker, 1840–1860,* propounds a very different interpretation, however.[6] Ware follows the traditional Marxian view of industrialization, interpreting this period as a time of economic disequilibrium, popular agitation, loss of status by craftsmen, and exploitation of manual workers. Ware proposes that the preindustrial class structure was overturned by the formation of an industrial working class as a self-conscious entity that had its own political program and value system as well as solidarity at the work place. Paralleling this development was the emergence of a capitalist class monopolizing the means of production and the wealth these created. Craftsmen lost status when the independence of self-employment became unattainable, and the plight of Northern workingmen brought forth "heroic opposition," according to Ware, in the union movement (which met his criteria for class consciousness, if not Commons') and in utopian socialist groups. William Sullivan painted a similar portrait of labor in Pennsylvania. In *The Industrial Worker in Pennsylvania, 1800–1840,* he catalogued the variety of workers' experiences in different industries, but he insisted on the general decline in autonomy and living standards and the rise of class consciousness.[7]

Some non-Marxist historians at first gave further credence to Ware's view by describing the Jacksonians, the Locofocos, and the Workingmen's Parties of the 1820s and 1830s as the political component of a working-class movement, an expression of the solidarity of this new class in society.[8] The Whig Party, on the other hand, was described as the political vehicle of the capitalist class. More recently, however, political historians have attacked the idea that political activity expressed class identification in the pre–Civil War period.[9] They have noted that some Workingmen's Parties aligned with the Whigs, and they have found that the political groups thought to have been working-class included many nonworkers and were not aligned with the union movement. No large-scale political expression of a working class has been found, and the differences between the major parties are not readily related to class divisions.

Students of American economic history also have labored to assess the validity of the Marxian picture of the effects of industrialization, specifically the alleged impoverishment suffered by workers. They have investigated the trend of real wages by searching for wage data and cost of living indices. Although the economic historians' models of wage and price behavior are ever more sophisticated, a consensus has not been reached on the trend of real wages between 1800 and 1860. In *Manpower in Economic Growth,* Stanley Lebergott estimated that real wages were unchanged from 1800 to 1819, rose moderately from 1819 to 1850, and were unchanged again from 1850 to 1860. More recently, Jeffrey Williamson has argued that real wages for unskilled workers rose at a rate of 1.21 percent per annum between 1820 and 1860, and that skilled workers did even better.[10] This is a much greater increase than Lebergott estimated, but, regardless of technique, most recent studies insist that general immiseration did not result from industrialization; if anything, real wages rose.

Recently, social historians focusing on the urban populace have questioned the assumptions of traditional labor historians. Today, historians define class not simply in terms of reactions to industrialization, such as the existence of "class conscious" political or union movements, but in terms of the ways in which workers' values and life styles shaped the industrial world. They are studying the culture of work, leisure activities, family patterns, and other aspects of daily life to understand how the consciousness of workers in the industrial world differed from that of preindustrial workers.

In *The Private City*, Sam Bass Warner, Jr. described how industrialization, by organizing workers into large groups in the factories, taught workers cooperation.[11] As workers began to appreciate the value of cooperation they not only formed unions but also new types of mass organizations for leisure, such as guard units, sports teams, and volunteer fire companies, which created some working-class social solidarity.

Several other scholars have supplemented Warner's work on Philadelphia, exploring more fully the changing life style of urban workers in the nineteenth century by focusing on the critical issue of leisure and its meaning. Artisans had made no sharp division between work and leisure, but workers began to value diligent, continuous labor and to restrict leisure activities when the industrial elite challenged preindustrial customs, and fear of poverty made the old habits seem harmful. Bruce Laurie has documented the persistence of preindustrial work and leisure habits among Philadelphia journeymen in an era of industrialization.[12] Paul Faler has demonstrated that only very limited job actions were supported by all Lynn shoemakers because of the split between those who accepted the new industrial morality of hard work, thrift, and sobriety and those who clung to preindustrial work habits.[13] Herbert Gutman has posited that throughout the nineteenth and early twentieth centuries the migration to American cities of people from rural and preindustrial backgrounds maintained the division between the workers who had internalized industrial values and those to whom the new ways were an anathema.[14] Nineteenth-century workers were not unified in their attitudes toward work and leisure, and the cultural conflict sometimes undermined their solidarity on economic issues. Larger studies combining the new social history with the concerns of labor history are not numerous, however. Alan Dawley's study of shoemakers, *Class and Community: The Industrial Revolution in Lynn,* is one of the first to combine an interest in workers' political consciousness with an examination of their values and life styles.[15]

Thus far, historians have examined only a few aspects of the urban class structure. Herbert Gutman has shown that the industrial elite in some cities did not dominate society immediately but was challenged by an older bourgeoisie that often supported the workers.[16] This calls into question the assumption made by Ware and others that the capitalist class was a united group by mid-century. There has been no extensive investigation besides Ware's, however, of how and when the class structure changed during industrialization. The lack of clarity on this important topic is especially unfortunate because so many recent studies in urban and social history are based on assumptions about class structure in nineteenth-century cities.[17]

This study of Newark analyzes the transition from a preindustrial to an industrial class structure. Any class shares a way of life, and the emergence of a common value system and life style is basic to the development of class consciousness. But in order to understand this development it is important to distinguish between the concepts of class and status. Most studies of American workers fail to make this distinction although much of the complexity of workers' consciousness was a function of the divergence between the class and status structures and of the intricacy of both.

The social rank, or status, of individuals or groups is based on widely-held community values that may include other than economic criteria. The basis for status may change drastically as society's evaluation of roles and attributes is altered by such factors as economic development or ideological and religious movements. There were many status differences among American workers as industrialization proceeded since wealth and ethnic identity became important criteria of status. The wealthier worker had more status than the poorer one, and the native-born more than the immigrant. Michael Feldberg has shown, for instance, that in Philadelphia a status struggle between workers of different ethnic and racial groups surfaced over such issues as job competition and control of neighborhoods, and led to repeated violence.[18]

A person's class, unlike his status, depends solely on his relationship to the means of production.[19] If the producer owns his tools and materials, he receives the profits of his labor and is independent of others. If he merely works with the capital owned by another, he is dependent and engaged in an unequal contest to keep the wealth he produces. Classes are not static entities but are created and destroyed at critical junctures when the relationships embodied in production change. Industrialization transformed artisans into wage workers by stripping craftsmen of their tools and of sufficient capital for self-employment. Consciousness of class arises from shared experience, but it is also shaped by old traditions and institutions. Newark's journeymen formed unions to fight their employers when they lost their old independence because their new situation was oppressive and because it violated their traditional artisan values.

In preindustrial Newark, an artisan class that included all craftsmen—apprentices, journeymen, and masters—was an important component of the class structure. Craftsmen had much status and power in local society; they were allied with a commercial class of merchants and professionals, and were above the class of laborers. Industrialization caused a split within the old artisan class between employers and employees and brought a new class structure and a new status structure to local society. The former artisan class was destroyed by industrialization since various craftsmen were affected in different ways by the process. Those craftsmen who were employers joined merchants and professionals to form a capitalist class, while journeymen and apprentices aligned with other wage workers. Few journeymen managed to rise to self-employment within their industry, and most of the few who switched their occupations remained employees. The paucity of occupational mobility among craftsmen strengthened the division between employers and employees. Economic development altered the status structure as craft skill ceased to be an important status attribute, while wealth became more influential. This change in status attributes favored the employer over the employee and thus reinforced class cleavages, but others did not. The native-born had always felt superior to the immigrant, the Protestant to the Catholic. But as mass immigration began in the 1840s and 1850s, religious and ethnic differences became more deep and divisive in American cities. Industrialization had created the jobs that, in part, spurred immigration, and as the industrial labor force became heterogenous in cultural background, the working class was split by bitter status divisions.

In order to understand the interrelation of industrialization with class, culture, and social status in the early nineteenth century, it is necessary to focus on craftsmen in a local urban milieu. Industrialization was not a "national experience" for many decades since it did not proceed at the same pace in every area, and any but a local focus may obscure its effects. Many labor historians, studying the union movement on the national level, have paid too little attention to local social structure to relate the growth of unions to changes in the culture of workingmen. The relationships between specific individuals, local industries, and perceived communities offer the best keys to determining the effects of industrialization on the life style and values of workers and on the class and status structures. This suggests the fruitfulness of case studies melding the concerns of social and urban historians with the traditional interests of labor historians.

Industrialization began in America in the textile industry of New England, in rural mills employing primarily female and child labor. Consequently, labor historians have focused on these mills and their workers when investigating early industrial labor.[20] But the typical manufacturing worker in the early nineteenth century was a male artisan who lived in a town or city. Many preindustrial cities were already manufacturing centers filled with skilled craftsmen making a variety of products for urban and rural dwellers alike.[21] Prior to 1840 the majority of working males did not labor in large factories, and even thereafter some crafts maintained many of their traditional forms and customs.[22] But, by 1840, industrialization had altered production techniques and employer-employee relations in many crafts common to American cities, large and small. By 1860, a revolution had affected the conditions of work in urban America.

Craftsmen in Newark were representative of these early industrial workers, and their history explains much about the effect of industrialization on class and culture in the larger manufacturing towns of the United States. Newark evolved from a preindustrial town into an industrial city in less than forty years—between 1820 and 1860—and the transformation of the local social structure was striking because most Newarkers worked in the manufacturing sector of the economy. By 1860 Newark had become the leading industrial city in the nation. It was the eleventh largest city, with 74 percent of its labor force employed in manufacturing, and sixth in the nation in the value of its manufacturing products.[23] Throughout this period the city's economy included a multitude of diverse crafts and industries. In this study, eight crafts—blacksmithing, carpentry, hatting, jewelry making, leather making, saddle making, shoemaking, and trunk making—were examined in detail to provide an instructive variety of comparisons between craftsmen experiencing various stages of industrialization.[24] By 1860 each craft had had a unique experience with industrialization, and they differed significantly in extent of mechanization, wage level, percentage of women employed, and the average size of a shop. In 1826 those working at these eight crafts comprised 52 percent of all Newarkers who had an occupation; in 1860 the employees in these eight crafts were 38 percent of the "hands employed" in Newark.[25]

Exposing the relationship between changes in the shop and changes in life style and values requires not only a strong focus on community but also a precise definition of industrialization. Industrialization is often characterized in purely economic terms, such as the ratio between capital and labor, but only a broader definition will elucidate how the conditions, expectations, and meaning of work changed for craftsmen. Information from industrial censuses, the U.S. Censuses of Manufacture, business directories, and newspapers is complete enough after 1830 to allow for such a classification of crafts. The data will not support a purely quantitative model of industrialization, but they can be used in a three-stage model that defines industrialization as a process linking two ideal types, the traditional craft and the modern factory-based industry. The amount of task differentiation and the types of mechanization define the three stages of industrialization. That is, crafts can be categorized by how skilled the workers were, whether workers owned their tools, and their chances for self-employment.

This definition is used to relate changes in the shop to the life styles and values of the work force in the eight crafts mentioned above. The U.S. Censuses of Population and Newark city directories include information about the families, residences, households, wealth, age, sex, nativity, and mobility of craftsmen. These data reveal the behavior and the values of all workers, not just those of the elite of articulate activists. Analyzing this information about craftsmen by the stage of industrialization they were experiencing reveals the transformations in culture caused by industrialization as well as those customs and values that were resistant to change. By 1860, the roots of the American working class may be seen in Newark's craftsmen, who struggled for control of their jobs at the work place, not at the ballot box, and who shaped their families, neighborhoods, and social organizations according to their distinctive combination of preindustrial, industrial, and ethnic values.

ROOTS OF
THE AMERICAN
WORKING CLASS

CHAPTER 1

The Artisan
in Preindustrial
Newark, 1800–1830

For almost one hundred and fifty years after its founding in 1666, Newark remained an agricultural township of New Jersey, cut off from the nearest city, New York, by vast salt marshes and three large rivers. Communication and commerce were circumscribed further because the bay of Newark was blocked by a sandbar that hampered navigation. The town center, on the banks of the Passaic River, was still little more than a crossroads in 1800, and the natural setting of the village muted the division between town and country. The Puritans from New Haven who first settled Newark had laid out several, broad tree-lined streets and a Common in the New England manner, and by 1800 most houses still had at least enough land for vegetable plots. The streets were unpaved, and local streams and wells supplied an adequate amount of clean water. Dogs and hogs roamed freely, and sheep grazed on the Common. Small shops supplied local needs; hat, jewelry, shoe, and hardware stores lined Broad Street for just one block between Bank and Market Streets.[1]

Although most Newarkers were farmers, the rudiments of manufacturing had begun. Local craftsmen produced many articles for home consumption. These goods were manufactured in the traditional manner—in small shops where each craftsman made the entire product by hand, be it a hat, a watch, or a tool. Two groups of craftsmen, shoemakers and carriagemakers, produced for a market that was wider than the local farm population. The colonial tradition of shoemaking was one of itinerant shoemakers traveling from farm to farm or practicing farming part-time, but in Newark a new, more sedentary pattern had developed by 1800. Master shoemakers organized substantial numbers of farmers to make shoes as a winter occupation on a putting-out basis. The masters supplied the materials, directed the work, paid piece rates to the farmers, and marketed the product.[2] The farmers were not very skillful craftsmen, so they formed production teams of three persons: one to sew uppers, one to sole, and another to finish.[3]

Newark's master shoemakers claimed a large part of the Southern market for shoes, and to maintain and extend this market the master shoemakers and other entrepreneurs supported road and bridge building projects to link the town with New York City. After the War of 1812 the steamboat provided regular crossings of the Hudson, improving access greatly; the master shoemakers became tied to New York's transportation and credit facilities. As the years passed and demand for their product grew, the workers spent more time at shoemaking and less at farming. Many became quite skilled, and journeymen were differentiated from apprentices. By 1826, over 35 percent of Newark's labor force worked at shoemaking, either as masters, journeymen, or apprentices.[4] They produced a full range of footwear from cheap goods to expensive custom work.

The existence of the shoe industry distinguished Newark from other agricultural towns in several ways. Most importantly, the labor force became skilled in industrial tasks. This attracted other industries, such as saddle and harness making, in which similar skills of leather working were needed. In 1821, Smith and Wright of Bridgeport, Connecticut, moved their saddle and harness factory to Newark. Their firm was the nucleus of an industry that became basic to Newark's economy, and by 1863 their plant was the largest saddle and harness factory in the country. It had been the first to institute the division of labor with a fixed scale of piecework rates.[5] Secondly, the existence of the shoe industry created a demand for leather, stimulating the local leather making industry. By mid-century, Newark had become the nation's leading center of leather production.[6]

The expansion of the manufacturing sector of the economy transformed Newark and its population. By 1826, farming was the primary occupation of only 81 of the more than 1,700 adult males in Newark; over 80 percent of the labor force were employed in some form of manufacturing.[7] Their activities were quite diverse: thirty-four distinct crafts were practiced in the town, and there were printing offices, distilleries, breweries, grist mills, and various factories and foundaries as well. This diversification of the local economy did not coincide, however, with any change in the methods of production used in the crafts, except for the three-person teams in shoemaking. Relatively few men were employed in each craft, and these worked in small groups—the average mechanic's workshop contained only eight men. Newark's economy had changed radically but it remained a preindustrial one.

Accompanying these enlarged occupational opportunities was a slow, steady growth in the population; by 1826 there were 8,017 people in Newark, an increase of 1,500 since 1820. This population growth had little immediate effect on the social structure. In preindustrial Newark few institutions including large numbers of people; most inhabitants were sub-sumed in networks of small groups like the workshops and their families. The family was perhaps the most important institution in ordering local society because there were so many young people—over half of the popu-lation was under twenty-one years of age. Large families were the norm, and the system of production led to even larger households since appren-tices and sometimes journeymen lived with their masters. In 1826, the aver-age household in Newark contained over eight people.[8] The apprenticeship system kept both children and unmarrieds within a family and under the traditional supervision of the head of the household. The colonial Puritans who settled Newark held that the head of the household was responsible for the welfare and the behavior of all members of his household; the family was the first unit of discipline and governance in the society, and the head of the household represented his dependents and employees in the com-munity.[9] In the first decades of the nineteenth century, Newarkers contin-ued to demand that the heads of households control the young.[10] The order imposed by the family was strengthened because there was work enough to keep teenage boys busy. The growing demand for Newark's products led masters to take on many apprentices, and nearby farms provided seasonal employment for the boys as well.

Besides the family and the workshop, churches provided the only other network of group experience. There were six churches in Newark in 1826 representing four denominations: Presbyterian, Methodist, Episcopalian, and Baptist. Newark's Catholics were not numerous enough to have founded their own church, and they experienced some intolerance.[11] The power of religion in Newark derived, however, not from the size of the vari-ous congregations but from the pervasiveness of Protestant values. As New-ark's population had grown, factional disputes had led to the founding of new denominations, beginning in 1719 when the original Congregational Church was converted to Presbyterianism.[12] Dutch and Scandinavian immi-grants also added religious diversity, and the early denominational differ-ences melted into a strict Protestantism, which defined a common code of acceptable social behavior.

On certain parts of that code all were agreed. No labor was to be per-formed on the Sabbath, for instance, and drunkenness was a sin. "Teetotal-ism," however, was not in vogue in Newark or the rest of the country. Most Americans believed that men needed drink to make them strong and able to work, although liquor was kept from women and children; some saw no conflict between going to church and taking a drink on Sunday.[13] Because of the general acceptance of the code, the vices of the large cities—prostitu-tion, theaters, grog shops, and the like—were unknown in Newark.

People disagreed, however, over the breadth of the Protestant code. There were strict Sabbatarians in Newark who condemned those adults who, in their eyes, desecrated the Sabbath by attending horse races, by drinking at taverns, or even by strolling along the river or the streets; children who played on the Sabbath were equally guilty.[14] In 1819, concerned Newarkers formed the Newark Moral Society to combat the evils of Sabbath breaking, intemperance, and profanity.[15] They believed that it was their duty as Christians to warn culprits and try to persuade them to reform, and they called on all heads of households to control those persons "under their care and government." To combat vice, heads of families were requested to begin to catechize the juveniles in their households on Sunday evenings as the Presbyterians had done in the past. In other towns in the Northeast similar disagreements over the limits of the social code were occurring, and the formation of private organizations became a common response. That of Andover, Massachusetts, proclaimed that the founders "had associated not only to benefit themselves and those around them, but to save *their children* from the corrupting influences."[16] Newarkers, like other Americans, generally rejected government action when an individual or private response was possible.

Since there was little immigration from abroad in the early nineteenth century, cultural homogeneity existed unthreatened in Newark. The only large minority was the black population, and they were Protestant too. In 1826, 511 black people lived in Newark; 31 of them were slaves who were too old to have been freed by New Jersey's system of gradual emancipation. The domination of both social and religious life by Newark's Protestant churches linked the town to the culture of rural New Jersey. Farmers could send their sons to Newark for apprenticing without worrying about the corrupting effects of city life.[17]

Outside the church, the family, and the workshop, there were few institutions ubiquitous enough to perform a major role in forging social unity. Clubs, fraternities, and the like were scarce, and none were affluent enough to have their own quarters; Newark's few taverns served as local meeting places for any gathering of much size.[18] There was one mutual benefit society, the Ladies' Shoe and Men's Pumpmakers Benevolent Society, formed by the shoemakers who relied on an uncertain national market.[19] A craftsman producing for purely local consumption had more control over his livelihood and less need for a system of mutual security. The Ladies' Shoe and Men's Pumpmakers Benevolent Society was not a trade union, but an organization that included employer and employee alike and protected its members from life's vicissitudes, especially death and unemployment, through an insurance arrangement. Benevolent societies were common in American cities in the early nineteenth century. They were formed on the basis of occupation, neighborhood, race, and ethnicity.[20] There was no network of benefit societies in Newark, however, because of the small scale and preindustrial nature of the economy within which most craftsmen worked.

The only inclusive institution for adult men was the local government. Newark was still governed by the town meeting and the officers it elected annually. Most years the town met only once, however, and the main order of business and expense concerned the poor.[21] Other than maintaining roads, policing the roamings of sheep, hogs, and dogs, and taxing the local residents to support the poor, the government did little to impinge on the life of the average citizen. Concerned citizens sometimes proposed incorporation to meet the other needs of the town ignored by the meeting; in 1819, according to one citizen, these included the regulation of markets, the assize of bread, the provision of a night watch and street lighting, the regulation of sidewalks, and aid for the fire companies. But in the 1820s, private effort, not public, continued to be the norm. The night watch was supported by individual subscription, and there were three volunteer fire companies of sixty to seventy men each.[22] Newark was not large enough to have generated the urban problems, such as crime or sewage, that necessitated organized communal effort through government. The town meeting made an exception for the children of the poor by establishing a Free School for them.[23] The major objective of the School was to inculcate the social code; the children learned to read from the Bible, and the value of moral and religious principles was stressed along with basic subjects. Only when an issue as vital as the moral health of the community was combined with that of poverty could local antipathy to government action be overcome. Since the meeting and its officers did so little, government did not serve as a strong focus for identity or allegiance.

By the 1820s the central structure of local society, the source of values and ideology, was the artisan class. The traditional American artisan class included craftsmen who possessed various amounts of wealth and received different incomes; some craftsmen were self-employed, and some worked for others. "Mechanic" was the term Newarkers used to describe artisans, and its meaning included master, journeyman, and apprentice. The artisan class was part of a preindustrial American class structure and was not comparable to any class in our later industrial society. The different statuses within this class were not barriers to advancement but clearly-defined stages of transition for the individual, and the unity of the artisan class originated in the expectation of its lowest members that with age, experience, and hard work they could rise to the highest level as self-employed master craftsmen. The wages in some crafts were higher than others, and tailors and shoemakers were often poor while tanners or silversmiths might be wealthy (since their businesses required greater capital and generated higher profits); but independence and skill were the artisan's chief virtues, and these were possessed by all mechanics.[24] American artisans formed a social class in much the same way as traditional European craftsmen had. Sons often followed their fathers' crafts, and close business, marriage, and social ties knit the community of mechanics together.[25] The American artisan class differed from the European, however, in one crucial respect—the absence of guilds. American mechanics were individualists who could join or leave their craft at will, and whose unity was not formalized.

The traditional methods of production were the basis for the unity of the artisan class. Most production took place in the home and was the focus of household activities. Each craftsman could make his product in its entirety, although his female relatives often helped him by doing any light hand sewing involved or by waiting on customers. The craftsman used only hand tools, and no nonhuman power source aided him. And the skills he possessed were so great that they could be learned only in a long apprenticeship. A master usually took his apprentices into his home for the teenage years and supervised them as a parent would, while teaching them all the secrets of the craft. Journeymen who lacked the capital to set up their own shops were nonetheless fully skilled and owned their tools.[26] In Newark in the 1820s, most craftsmen worked within this framework. Some of the shoemakers were less skilled and therefore without the same independence, but, even in shoemaking, boys were trained in apprenticeships and workers owned their tools.

The distinctions between master, journeyman, and apprentice did not override their common interest in keeping prices up and the market well stocked with their wares. The expansion of the market caused by the increase in the local population made harmony the key to prosperity for all. Masters could pass the cost of wage increases on to consumers easily since competition from goods made in other areas was slight. Journeymen and masters had no reason to dispute wages, and in the expanding market journeymen could see future opportunities for themselves as masters-to-be.

In the 1820s, serving an apprenticeship was the norm for Newark boys. The vitality of Newark's crafts drew many boys to the town as apprentices; there were always notices in the newspaper calling for new apprentices and offering rewards for the return of runaways. Most apprentices began their term at age fourteen or fifteen when they committed themselves in an indenture, and masters desired those "well recommended for sobriety and industry."[27] Some boys were apprenticed earlier, and many who left home to live with their master's family experienced intense homesickness at first.[28] This was their first step toward autonomy; they exchanged the supervision of parents for the control of one who would educate them for work.

Apprenticeship was a vital element in the unity of the artisan class, because, along with craft skills, boys learned the values and expectations of mechanics during their term of indenture. Throughout America, artisans believed in work as a duty, but they also enjoyed it and were proud of what they accomplished. Practicing a craft was a way of life that stressed "industry."[29] Henry Clark Wright, a hatter who became an abolitionist, summed up the value craftsmen placed on their work when he said, "Those who are ashamed to work with their hands ought to be ashamed to live."[30] Parents and masters inculcated the value of work even in the youngest children, as Lucy Larcom, once a New England mill girl, explained: "We learned no theories about 'the dignity of labor,' but we were taught to work almost as if it were a religion; to keep at work, expecting nothing else."[31] Mechanics and farmers alike labored from sun up to sun down, but work was not an onerous burden to either. Wright, for instance, attributed much of his enjoyment of life to the habits of self-reliance and the respect for labor his parents taught him. "We were taught," he said, "to find the sources of comfort and happiness within ourselves, and never to rest content to be appendages to individuals or to society"[32] Most importantly, however, mechanics could be proud of the product of their labor. The delight in craftsmanship was genuine, as Wright said: "I felt real satisfaction in being able to make a hat, because I loved to contemplate the work when finished, and because I felt a pleasure in carrying through the various stages."[33]

The importance of work in the mechanic's value system appeared clearly in the provisions Newarkers made for the local poor. Until 1810 the poor were bound out like apprentices, a practice that embodied the idea that all must work to help support themselves. Because of abuses in this system, the town voted in 1810 to build a poor house where the produce raised by the inmates would help pay for their support. In 1813 the first allotment was made for the schooling of poor children in order to help them escape dependency by fitting them for labor. By 1828 there were three free schools for poor children—one each for white males, white females, and "colored children."[34]

The artisan life was not as severe as it might seem, however, because the artisan valued leisure as well as work. While artisans rejected indolence, they freely mixed work and play. A constant pace of unceasing labor was the ideal not of the mechanic but of the machine.[35] The artisan was bound to neither the machine nor the clock, and could set his own pace. Many masters and journeymen would stop to drink whiskey or other alcoholic beverages several times a day, and the apprentices were sent to fetch the refreshments from the tavern. Apprentices learned to mix work and play, although their formal indentures often forbade their frequenting taverns or engaging in other "vices."[36] By the 1820s religious leaders were making concerted efforts to persuade masters of the deleterious effect of this custom. To save both journeymen and apprentices from intemperance, Newark's ministers sought to convince masters to ban liquor because "The too common practice of indulging apprentices with liquors, at stated hours of the day, has imperceptibly beguiled thousands to ruin."[37] In other towns, such as the shoemaking center of Lynn, Massachusetts, a similar campaign was waged to boost temperance among mechanics, but such arguments were far from uniformly accepted.[38] Besides such daily breaks for sociability and refresh-

ment, other time for leisure arose from the seasonal nature of much preindustrial work and the frequent slow periods in business. Consequently, such
holidays as fishing trips and impromptu festivities—sleigh rides, for instance—were part of the typical routine.[39] Both work and leisure lacked the
regimented quality that rule by the clock has since given them.

Mechanics prided themselves on their intelligence as well as their independence, and they based their demand for status in local society on their
intellectual as well as manual skills. In the 1820s, mechanics in many cities
formed educational associations to further develop those skills.[40] They
sought to expose craftsmen to the latest scientific theories so they might
apply that knowledge to make improvements in their crafts and to discuss
pertinent social and economic questions. The Newark Mechanics Association for Mutual Improvement in the Arts and Sciences was formed in 1828
by 114 men from various crafts.[41] It held regular meetings and provided a
series of lectures each year on diverse topics: "Would the abolition of the
system of credit in book accounts be advantageous to the community";
"The nervous system and its connection with the intellectual character of
man"; and "Is it politic in the Government of the United States to encourage emigration" were among those offered in 1833.[42]

Apprenticeship fostered the image of the intelligent mechanic, because
the apprentice was schooled for his future station as a master. Moses
Combs, who began Newark's wholesale shoe industry in the 1790s, opened
the first night school for his apprentices. A Newark indenture in hatting
made in 1829 specified that the apprentice was to be given "three quarters"
of night schooling as well as training in his craft. In the 1820s, to supplement the night school, Newarkers established a library for apprentices; it
was open in the evenings and was intended to further the apprentices' secular and moral education. Although it had a membership fee of twelve and
one half cents, 306 apprentices applied for membership.[43]

In the preindustrial era, Newark's craftsmen had the privileges and respect that were later the property solely of the bourgeoisie. The master mechanics, both skilled and self-employed, were the pillars of the community.
The journeymen and apprentices, as future masters, shared in their prestige, much as the children of the wealthy or successful share that of their
parents today. Newark's craftsmen formed a harmonious group who had
pride in themselves and who were prosperous by the standards of the day.
Because of the poor condition of Newark's harbor, the wealthy commercial
class of the seaports was absent in Newark, and the artisan class was equal
to and aligned with the small commercial class of shopkeepers and professionals. In the colonial era, the only "aristocracy" in the town had been
comprised of the ministers and a few gentlemen, but even then the artisans
had dominated the town government.[44] The lower class in Newark, and in
other towns, was composed predominantly of unskilled wage laborers, servants, and seamen.

THE ARTISAN IN PREINDUSTRIAL NEWARK   11

Local celebrations revealed the status of artisans in the community. In 1826 the township of Newark decided to commemorate the fiftieth anniversary of American independence with a day-long celebration—a church service, a parade, the dedication of a statue to Washington, a dinner, and speeches.[45] In honor of the occasion the town assessor took a census to show how beneficial national independence had been, a judgment based on the numerical increase of the population and the variety of crafts and businesses carried on in the township. The major part of the parade consisted of groups of craftsmen: The Ladies' Shoe and Men's Pumpmakers Benevolent Society ("a very numerous company"); the curriers carrying their standards; and the saddletree makers, saddlers, and harness and trunk makers. The carpenters had also made arrangements to march on the Fourth, and only the hatters and jewelers were not numerous enough to march *en masse*. Mechanics dominated the proceedings and were the leaders of local society.

This ceremony exemplified community values, which were those of the mechanics. The pride artisans had in their community was a pride in themselves, and this was not new in the 1820s. The first celebration of American independence in Newark in 1788 had followed the same scenario. The order of procession had been an industrial one, the various crafts represented by masters and their journeymen and joined by a group of farmers. Such industrial processions to celebrate American independence were also held in Newark in 1818, 1821, and 1829. The 1821 parade included floats—wagons on which each trade displayed its tools and its wares.[46]

The artisan class and its ideology dominated many towns like Newark in early nineteenth-century America. Even in the large port cities, mechanics' deference to the merchant elite had waned by the Revolution, as they sought political power for themselves.[47] In tones heard in many other towns, a Newarker declared in 1829 that crafts were "the life blood, bone and sinew of the land—may pursuits *so* honorable and useful, result in individual prosperity and happiness."[48] Master craftsmen valued their own activities, and local society agreed. The economic ethic guiding towns like Newark identified the "useful" with the "good."[49] By their useful endeavors, mechanics glorified God as they helped themselves and their neighbors to prosper. The honest "callings" were those demanding skill and pursued with diligence but without greed. Newarkers still believed that commerce was not exempt from morality rooted in religious teaching, and those who violated the economic ethic were chastized just as violators of the social code were. A citizen accusing bakers of short weights and unfair practices suggested that "although you may fancy yourself under no *legal obligations* or restrictions to impart *equal justice* and conform to long established and wholesome rules—nevertheless, there are certain moral obligations by which every man, or set of men, are bound."[50] In a society in which work was not separated from "life," there was one code of morality for all occasions.

The mechanic's economic ethic was often fused with a political one. During the 1760s, American artisans had seen their work, home manufactures, as vital to American freedom and had supported the nonimportation agreements; by the end of the Revolution, some were advocating protective tariffs on this ground.[51] In the 1790s Newark became a stronghold of Jeffersonianism in New Jersey, a mechanic's Jeffersonianism that supported all sorts of internal improvement companies to bolster manufactures. William Pennington, a hatter who studied law in middle age and later became governor of the state, was Newark's leading Jeffersonian.[52] Many a Fourth of July celebration in the 1820s reiterated the connection between American democracy and freedom and the mechanic's economic ethic, crediting the Revolution with providing the opportunity for the individual to do both God's work and man's. Under English tyranny, human faculties had been cramped, and the mechanical arts had advanced but slowly. The craftsmen of Newark knew that their work, God's order, and American independence were intertwined, and they interpreted their labor as the bulwark of freedom. William Halsey, a lawyer and future mayor of Newark, delivered a discourse on liberty on 4 July 1826 that recalled the Revolutionary rhetoric of home manufactures. He praised not only the Revolutionary heroes but also Robert Fulton for his development of the steamboat and De Witt Clinton for his sponsorship of the Erie Canal. Such improvements in transportation stimulated manufacturing, and Halsey insisted that "we boast in vain of our Independence whilst we are tributary to other nations for an indispensable supply from their manufactories."[53] The "American System" of government aid to internal improvements and tariff protection for industry thus found sanction in the world view of the artisan class. Newark mechanics acted to further their economic ethic in the political arena: John Quincy Adams, not Andrew Jackson, carried Essex County in 1824, and by 1830, Henry Clay was becoming a local favorite.[54]

Although they dominated local society, Newark's mechanics were not totally satisfied with the world as they knew it. Many issues agitated craftsmen throughout America in the 1820s, and these were discussed in Newark's newspaper, *The Sentinel of Freedom.* Imprisonment for debt and the excessive fees of the judicial system were major concerns, attacked for putting the "little man" at a disadvantage.[55] There was still a debtor's prison in Newark in the 1820s, although many described imprisonment for debt as "a relic of barbarism."[56] Men opposed imprisonment for debt on two grounds. One was that of natural rights and the Constitution—personal liberty was an unalienable right and "every contract for *liberty* or *life* is void."[57] But artisans also criticized imprisonment for debt on the basis of the labor theory of value. Mechanics believed that labor alone created wealth; this was their economic rationale for according the farmer and the craftsman a higher status than the merchant, the banker, the speculator, or the lawyer. Mechanics thought imprisoning a debtor was unfair because:

Credit is essential to commerce... But there can be no creditor without a debtor—and hence the debtor is essential to this interest and as meritorious as the creditor, and more so—for the debtor is the active and efficient man in business—he furnishes labour against capital.... The same motive has influenced both that of *gain,* and in this both have failed.[58]

Master craftsmen had a large stake in this issue because they were enmeshed in credit relationships. They bought materials on credit and had to grant it to their customers; they could easily become overextended.

Other groups in society supported the mechanics' positions on judicial fees, imprisonment for debt, and other issues. The "farmers, mechanics, and workingmen" of 1830 who were organizing for the upcoming elections wanted the same reforms.[59] They complained in particular that too many lawyers and speculators were in the government. The concept current in Jacksonian America—that all producers were united in opposition to a small group of parasites such as lawyers and speculators—was expressed in many letters to the local newspaper by mechanics, farmers, and other citizens. In arguing for juror compensation, for instance, one mechanic asked, "Have not the farmer and the mechanic fought their way to equality and justice? If so, why pay every person in the community for services rendered, and except the intelligent industrious juror?"[60] Jury duty imposed a financial loss on all active "producers" but not on the "parasites" or the indolent rich.

During the 1820s the culture of the artisan class of preindustrial Newark reached its fullest development. The town functioned comfortably with the traditional forms of production and of town and family governance and with the old values of the artisan class and the Protestant churches. Certainly none of the rhetoric of the day reflected great unease over the permanence of this system, although craftsmen did seek to right what they perceived to be inequities in government and law. Master craftsmen continued to follow the dictates of their consciences to work hard and well. Little did they realize that within a decade their efforts to improve production techniques and expand markets would overthrow the society artisans had fashioned.

CHAPTER 2

The Process
of Industrialization

Industrialization was a motive force in the physical growth of Newark, producing a large city from a town, but it also created an industrial city, the home of a new working class and the graveyard of the artisan class. The economic strengths of the mechanics' town—the skilled labor force, the entrepreneurship of local masters and merchants—along with innovations in transportation and access to the marketing facilities and capital supplies in New York City fostered the expansion of production. Industrialization then further spurred growth and created a new social milieu as well.

In its most narrow terms, industrialization consisted of innovations in the methods of production: task breakdown and mechanization. Such innovation was related to the development of markets; manufacturers producing for wholesale rather than retail markets were the first to introduce new techniques. But wholesale production did not sweep all before it in the first half of the nineteenth century. A luxury market of middle and upper-class urbanites who desired quality products developed as the cities grew and allowed some skilled workers to continue using the old hand methods. Neither did early industrialization end the old seasonality and irregularity of production, since manufacturers had had little practice in calculating and controlling demand for their goods.

Industrialization was more than a technological process, however; it was also a social process because of its effects on workers. As manual skills became obsolete, apprenticeship waned, and a worker no longer spent his boyhood in a master's home. Mechanization removed work from the household to the factory, and household production became less prevalent. One aspect of mechanization, the introduction of sewing machines, also specifically undercut family labor by decreasing the number of females working in those crafts in which women had done sewing. Industrialization thus

15

made new demands on the families and households of craftsmen; at the same time, it changed the concept of work. Working was more dangerous around machines, so workers' lives were less secure. The pace of the machines and the institution of the wage system led workers to conceive of their jobs in terms of time spent, not tasks accomplished, and thus to demand a limitation of their hours.

Ultimately, industrialization destroyed the artisan class. Workers lost control over their wages when they had fewer skills, and competition caused employers to cut wages whenever possible. The old unity of masters and journeymen disappeared, and workers often formed unions to oppose their employers. Wage levels in various crafts frequently differed more because of the profitability of the individual trades, however, than because of the extent of technological innovation. Industrialization as a social process transformed work and its meaning, modified household and family functions, and created a new class structure in Newark.

Newark's Economic Development

Industrialization began to revolutionize Newark's crafts in the 1830s, and by 1860 a tremendous spurt of economic and physical growth had made Newark America's major industrial city. Craft workshops had become large factories, and the population had increased more than six-fold. Expansion in Newark was grounded in manufacturing rather than in finance or commerce, and it commenced when other crafts followed the path shoemaking had begun earlier and moved toward the modern factory form of production.

Economic development began in the early 1830s in the increased demand for Newark's specialties and the creation of wholesale markets. Newark's goods had a reputation for high quality, a reputation publicized throughout the East at Mechanics' Fairs, where Newark products won many prizes. To meet this demand, masters in several crafts—shoemaking, hatting, saddle making, and carriage making—expanded their workshops to factory scale. These were rarely mechanized mills; most work was still done by hand, and in many mills the differentiation of tasks was just beginning. But even those "factories" that were simply large accumulations of craftsmen and raw materials under one roof created a new efficiency in production and marketing and thus greater profits.[1] Although there were many large factories in Newark, many small traditional shops remained in those crafts producing for the local market. The average firm in Newark employed only about twenty people in 1836.[2]

The expansion of the early 1830s created hundreds of jobs every year, and Newark's population expanded rapidly. The demand for hands was so great that even a hundred workmen left unemployed by a fire that destroyed their work place were assumed to be able to find work quickly.[3]

TABLE 1
Population of Newark[a]

	1820	1830	1840	1850	1860
Newark	6,507	10,953	17,290	38,894	71,941
Mean city size Northeast	12,779	15,439	17,650	19,047	22,396

[a]Jeffrey G. Williamson and Joseph A. Swanson, "The Growth of Cities in the American Northeast, 1820-1870," *Explorations in Entrepreneurial History*, 2nd series, vol. 4, no. 1, Supplement (1966), p. 11 and U.S. Census Office, *Compendium of the Eleventh Census: 1890* (Washington, D.C., 1897), Part I, p. 434. Northeast means New England, New York, New Jersey, and Pennsylvania. Cities are defined as places with at least 2,500 people.

People flocked to Newark to take advantage of the new opportunities, and the population soared. Prior to the 1830s, Newark had been smaller than the average city in the Northeast (Table 1). By 1836, with a population of 19,732, it was of average size.[4]

Newark's export statistics reflect the impressive economic development resulting from production for the wholesale market in the early 1830s. In 1835 Dr. Jabez Goble, a local physician and town booster, estimated that the annual exports of Newark to the South, South America, and the West Indies exceeded $8 million—a total composed of such items as saddles, carriages, shoes, hats, springs, lamps, plated ware, cabinet ware, patent leather, and malleable iron.[5] Shoe manufacture still played a large part in the export economy. In 1836 the largest shoe company, Shipman, Crane, and Co., sold shoes worth between $400,000 and $500,000 to Southern customers.[6]

To develop as a manufacturing center, a city needed both markets and raw materials, access to which varied in the early nineteenth century because of the immature canal and railroad networks. Newark was one of the towns that enhanced its transportation facilities and thereby created a stimulus to production. In 1832 the Morris Canal opened, connecting Newark with the Delaware Valley. This new, easy access to natural resources stimulated the range of iron-dependent and leather-dependent industries, since coal, ore, hides, and wood bark could now reach Newark in large quantities.[7] Improvements in transportation connecting Newark to New York also aided industrial expansion. The opening of the railroad to Jersey City in 1834 reduced the travel time between Newark and New York to approximately one hour.[8]

Even prior to this increase in accessibility, Newark had become a satellite of New York, relying on the capital supply, labor force, and customers there to facilitate production.[9] The jewelry industry of Newark depended on its proximity to New York, where wholesalers from all over the United States and Canada met. By 1835, Newark's businessmen needed capital from New York, since the three local banks could not supply enough to the burgeoning

TABLE 2
Increase in Urbanization[a]

ΔU/P	1820–30	1830–40	1840–50	1850–60	1860–70
New Jersey	3.03	4.88	7.01	15.10	10.10
Eastern New York	6.76	5.56	7.87	4.19	1.05

[a]Jeffrey G. Williamson, "Antebellum Urbanization in the American North East," *Journal of Economic History* 25 (1965): 599–600.

ΔU/P is the change in the percentage of the total population who lived in urban (≥2500) areas.

TABLE 3
Population Growth[a]

%Growth	1820–30	1830–40	1840–50	1850–60	1860–70
Newark	68	58	125	85	46
New York	59	59	65	56	17

[a]Derived from Table 4a, *Compendium of the Eleventh Census: 1890,* Part I, p. 434.

industries. The labor pool for Newark's businesses also crossed state lines. As early as 1825, New York firms were advertising for workmen in Newark newspapers, and Newark firms advertised in New York papers. When trade unions were formed in many crafts in 1835 and 1836, Newark, New York, and Brooklyn workers enforced common lists of piecework rates.

Newark's growth rate, like its economy, was more closely connected to New York's than to that of the rest of New Jersey. The incremental increase in urbanization in eastern New York (including New York City) peaked in the 1840s, whereas that of New Jersey peaked in the 1850s (Table 2). But the growth of Newark fluctuated with that of New York City, and its greatest increase in population occurred in the 1840s (Table 3).

Although the New York area possessed a common labor pool and adequate transportation, and businesses could choose to locate within it at many sites, many found Newark especially attractive. Both employers and employees moved to Newark because rents and the cost of living were cheaper there than in New York City.[10] This advantage may have been especially important in an age when employers were often but a year or two or a few hundred dollars removed from employee status. Newarkers were aware of the possible advantages of their city, and they did their best to enhance them: the government kept taxes low to attract businessmen, Newarkers promoted and invested in the improvements in transportation, and local speculators invested both in factory buildings and in new industries.

Newark's prosperity continued throughout the mid-1830s despite credit problems that local initiative could not control. During the contraction after Jackson's Bank War in 1834, manufacturers had difficulty paying wages, and unemployment reached a point where beggars and vagrants became a common sight. The credit situation eased some in 1835, but the next year the whole system of domestic exchange through local banks was virtually suspended. Manufacturers sold the drafts they received from their Southern customers at enormous discounts, and mechanics complained of interest rates as high as 48 percent to 60 percent per annum.[11] The city continued to grow through 1837, however, although other signs of weakness were appearing. In the mid-1830s, Newark's shoemakers began to lose the Southern market to New England manufacturers who produced a cheaper product. The sharp panic of 1837 stopped business in its tracks, and the wholesale shoe firms collapsed.[12] The depression that followed destroyed firms, large and small, in every field. The factories were empty, and people began to leave the city to find subsistence elsewhere. By 1840 the population had declined to 17,290—a loss of 2,500 from the recorded peak in 1836. The depression that began in 1837 lasted for six long years; Newark's economy stagnated, and no further strides toward industrialization were made.

When the national economy revived, in the 1840s, Newark grew once more as industrialization accelerated the evolution of crafts toward modern production methods. In response to further economic growth Newark broke through the ranks of the national urban hierarchy in the 1840s to become twice as large as the average city and one of the larger cities in the country (Table 1). Newark's population increased by 125 percent between 1840 and 1850, so that it stood at 38,894 at mid-century. By 1860, Newark was a thriving industrial center of 71,941 with 74 percent of its labor force employed in manufacturing, and the value of its manufactured products ranked sixth in the nation.

Economic recovery did not appear in the city until 1844, but Newark's integration into New York's metropolitan economy increased quickly thereafter. The commercial ties between Newark and New York strengthened as Newark's manufacturers continued to rely on the credit and transportation facilities of New York. Wealthy businessmen still left New York to locate in Newark, seeking cheaper prices and lower taxes. The area around Newark began to respond to its economic potential too, and soon even the rural areas of Essex County were alive with industry. Almost every foot of available water power on small streams in the vicinity was in use. Newark began to develop its own satellites as its commercial and financial facilities expanded to serve its citizens and those of the surrounding area. Workers even began to move out to Elizabeth, where rents were cheaper, and commute back to work in Newark.[13]

Newark's strong commitment to manufacturing was the foundation for the economic recovery on which population growth and urban development rested; in 1840, 80 percent of Newark's labor force worked in the manufacturing sector.[14] The diverse industries, which had produced the boom of the 1830s and cushioned the shock of the loss of the shoe market, formed a base for recovery. New markets for some of Newark's specialties— patent leather, coach springs, prefabricated steps—appeared, even in the Far East, and army contracts during the Mexican War, especially for harness and wagons, underwrote industrial expansion.[15]

Not only the demand for Newark's products, but also a greater productivity made possible by industrialization stimulated economic recovery. The earlier existence of factory organization, however primitive, and Newark's initial commitment to manufacturing made the introduction of the new technology possible. The use of steam power to drive machinery was the most important innovation. By 1846 more than one hundred factories used steam power; in 1840 none had. Seth Boyden, a prolific local inventor, specialized in perfecting small steam engines for industrial use, and his work gave Newark an edge over other cities in attracting firms. Other machine makers in Newark also furthered industrialization by designing machines that "ordinary workmen"—rather than skilled workers—could operate.[16]

As in the 1830s, more intangible factors, like entrepreneurship, spurred economic development. For instance, when the California gold rush began, many Newarkers went along—not to search for gold but to make their fortunes by selling supplies to miners.[17] This thirst for commercial venture and industrial activity pushed Newark ahead of other cities. Those who did not participate directly in production also helped: in the 1840s private speculators began to devote parts of tenements to shop space and also to build large structures specifically for industrial use. This undifferentiated industrial space was available on lease to the many small firms that could not afford large initial investments for their own buildings. One such venture in Newark was the Phoenix Buildings; in 1847 these two brick workshops housed ten companies employing about two hundred workmen. At the same time, about three hundred people worked in various firms in the Clinton Works. A central steam engine in the basement drove all sorts of small machines, such as grind stones, printing presses, lathes, and saws. Twenty different firms, ranging from one-man shops to small factories of thirty hands, occupied the Hamilton Works.[18] Speculation and technological change worked hand-in-hand to foster economic development.

Newark's evolution into a major industrial city, however, meant it could no more resist national economic trends in the 1840s and 1850s than it had in the 1830s. If anything, with more and more firms and workers producing for regional and national rather than local markets, Newark was increasingly vulnerable. In Newark, as in the nation at large, the prosperity of the late 1840s did not continue through the 1850s.[19] There was periodic unemployment throughout the mid-1850s, and in the winter of 1854–55 soup kitchens had to be established. The panic of 1857 hurt many of Newark's industries, and by October perhaps half of all manufacturing workers were unemployed. While production resumed in some lines within three months, a year later overall production had yet to reach the heights attained in 1856. Industrialization had obliterated the self-sufficiency of the mechanics' town.

Industrialization as a Social Process

Industrialization was the mainspring of economic development and population growth in Newark, but it functioned as a social process because of its effects on mechanics—a complex social process, since its impact varied from craft to craft. Many trades industrialized between 1830 and 1860, but others like carpentry and blacksmithing remained in their traditional forms throughout the mid-nineteenth century. The pace of technological change was faster in some crafts than others. Two extreme examples in Newark were shoemaking and trunk making. Shoemakers failed to use even simple machines before the late 1850s, although they had begun to break down the tasks of their trade by the early nineteenth century. Trunk making, on the other hand, evolved in less than twenty years from a traditional craft into a factory-based industry using steam-powered machinery. Because industrialization did not affect all crafts equally, at any one time the work experience and the prospects of mechanics differed considerably from one trade to another. There was, however, a regular sequence to the process of industrialization as it affected craftsmen, a sequence revealed by viewing industrialization as the transition between two ideal states. At one end of a continuum lies the traditional craft; at the other lies the modern factory-based industry making the same product.

The traditional craft had two basic characteristics:

1. Every workman made the product in its entirety and learned all production techniques in a long apprenticeship;
2. Only hand tools were used.

These characteristics determined the large amount of independence each worker had since:

3. Workmen owned their tools, and master craftsmen owned the materials and the product as well;
4. By owning their tools and monopolizing knowledge of the techniques of production, journeymen controlled their remuneration;
5. Journeymen had realizable expectations of becoming masters, i.e., self-employed, themselves.

At the other end of the spectrum lies the modern factory-based industry. In it the work characteristics have completely changed, at least for the major phases of production. In many industries, one or two minor processes may have escaped great changes, but this does not affect most workers or the overall organization of the industry if the structure is "modern." The factory-based industry has these basic characteristics:

1. The process of making a product has been broken down into myriad tasks. Each worker knows but one task and needs little or no training to master it;
2. Mechanized production using nonhuman energy sources predominates.

The worker in the modern factory lacks independence because:

3. The workers do not own the tools or materials used nor the product;
4. Possessing neither tools nor skills that are not generally available, the workmen cannot directly control their remuneration;
5. There is little likelihood that workers can rise to ownership or even managerial positions in the field.

When a craft industrialized, changes took place in both the modes of production and the attributes and experiences of the labor force. Although alterations in production techniques and in the nature of the labor force were related, they can be examined separately for the sake of clarity. Changes in the former included decreasing the complexity of the task assigned to any one worker and employing new types of tools and new power sources. Changes in the labor force occurred in the types of skills required, in the workers' control over the tools and materials used and over the disposition of the product, and in the method of recruiting and training new workers. In the transition from the traditional craft to the modern industry, alterations took place in these areas at different times and to various degrees.

Three broad stages can be defined in the transition from craft to modern industry. The first stage began with task differentiation—breaking down the craft into a series of simpler jobs. In Newark this occurred first in the early nineteenth century in shoemaking with its three-person teams. As a result of such differentiation, part of the total work force had fewer skills than all had formerly. Those who already possessed skills were not always superseded, however; owners or foremen still had to know the entire process in order to teach others the separate tasks, and some apprentices continued to be trained to take their places. Often, however, the boys hired were apprentices in name only, exploited as cheap labor and not taught all the tasks of the trade. In the first stage of industrialization workers often still owned their tools but usually did not own the materials used nor the finished product. The wage system, typically in the form of piece rates, was established. Without as much skill, the workers' control over their remuneration lessened, and unions often arose because of wage disputes. Those who were already skilled could still become self-employed by exploiting the semi-skilled labor of others, although the new recruits had less chance for such advancement. The aim of task differentiation was to increase the volume of production per worker, and the technique led to an increase in the size of shops or the establishment of the putting-out system.

The second stage of industrialization arrived with the introduction of simple machines for some tasks. These were mainly human powered, although a few used a nonhuman power source. Work places became incipient factories, larger on the average than those of the earlier stage because of the centralizing effect of machinery. Putting-out was used for certain tasks that were still done by hand. Because of mechanization, the skill level of the labor force as a whole decreased further, and few if any apprentices were trained. More importantly, the workers ceased to own the tools of production, and their wages declined further. In 1860, for instance, hatters working with simple machines earned an average of $34.48 per month, while those who used only hand tools earned $41.50.[20] Although those with skills might still become supervisors or foremen, the increasing capital requirements of mechanization decreased the chance for self-employment. The capital invested in 1860 in the average hatting firm owning simple machines was over $1,000 greater than that invested in firms without machines.[21]

The third stage in the process of industrialization began when machines using nonhuman power sources were introduced for some important phases of production. Skill was gone from all but a few tasks. At this point apprenticeship was dead, and wages in the industry were near those for other unskilled occupations. In 1860 hatters who worked with steam-driven machines made even less than those who worked with simple ones; they averaged only $29.23 per month.[22] Putting-out, if used at all, was confined to a few minor tasks. Factories at this stage were large (several hundred workers), and the high capital requirements of power-driven machinery made rising to self-employment unlikely for any worker. The average capital invested in 1860 in hat firms using steam-powered machinery was ten times that invested in those using only simple machines.[23] The transition to the ideal industrialized state relied on a continuation of these trends: an end to putting-out and the mechanization of all major processes.

Industrialization was not completed for any craft in Newark prior to 1860. Even in the most advanced firms, human labor entered the picture at almost every stage of production. As yet machines did not run each other nor work in concert, and all were far from the constant-flow, mechanized pattern of twentieth-century factories. Even within a craft, the impact of industrialization was not uniform. As long as a retail or custom-order market existed, some local craftsmen could ply their trade in the old manner.

Most of Newark's industries included not only large factories using the latest techniques to produce goods for the wholesale market, but also small shops using traditional methods to meet a local or luxury market. Skilled hatters using traditional methods continued to exist twenty-five years after mechanized factories dominated the hat making industry in Newark. Prior to 1860, then, craftsmen in Newark labored under a great variety of conditions and experienced industrialization in different ways, and the complexity of this process was central to the development of the distinctive character of Newark's working class.

The Industrialization of Eight Crafts

The stages of industrialization progress neatly in the abstract, but the variations on the theme were many in reality. In general the factory with a large and varied work force replaced the household in which the craftsman, his family, and his apprentices had labored. Skill levels declined, apprenticeship disappeared, and wages decreased. Unskilled men, but rarely women, appropriated the new jobs; women were confined to their traditional tasks—sewing and textile production. Craftsmen formed unions in an attempt to assert control over their work, raise wages, and restrict their hours. The casual work day of old became obsolete as mechanization increased the pace of labor, but because of the primitive state of production planning, employment continued to be sporadic or seasonal in nature.

But few crafts fit this mold exactly. Some resisted change, and technological advance occurred mainly in those that engaged in production for wholesale rather than retail markets. When a local retail market continued to flourish, skilled craftsmen used their customary techniques and maintained high wages without unionizing. The new unskilled workers in the modern factories often had not personally experienced a downward trend of wages or skills and therefore might also be slow to unionize. Furthermore, wage levels in crafts at the same stage of industrialization differed considerably because the crafts had varied in profitability while in their traditional states and wage cutting had begun from different bases.

Carpentry and blacksmithing both relied on local markets, and these trades did not industrialize throughout the mid-nineteenth century. Population growth produced the demand for housing, and the number of carpenters fluctuated with the population (Table 4). Between 1836 and 1845, for instance, there were many years of depression and little population growth in Newark; with only a minimal demand for housing then, the number of carpenters remained stationary. As the population soared in the late 1840s and 1850s, however, so did the number of carpenters.

Since they produced for a local market, carpenters had no competition from craftsmen elsewhere, and so they had little incentive for making

TABLE 4
Total Workers Employed, Male and Female[a]

Craft	1826	1836	1845	1850	1860
Carpentry	89	433	400	515	794
Blacksmithing	19	294	44[b]	301	425
Shoemaking	685	734	689	1,135	1,198
Saddle making	57	527	494	488	1,044
Jewelry making	22	100	234	547	777
Trunk making	7	35	107	308	740
Leather making	81	169	319	568	957
Hatting	70	610	894	1,324	1,677
Population of Newark	8,017	19,732	25,433	38,894	71,941

[a]See Appendix A for an explanation of the construction of this table and the sources used.
[b]This figure seems totally unreliable, but no other information is available.

TABLE 5
Average Number of Workers Per Firm[a]

Craft	1845	1850	1860
Carpentry	8.9	9.4	6.6
Blacksmithing	2.4	2.8	7.7
Shoemaking	23.8	23.1	14.2
Saddle making	54.9	48.8	52.2
Jewelry making	12.3	39.1	35.9
Trunk making	17.8	77.0	82.2
Leather making	13.9	23.7	36.8
Hatting	38.9	63.0	76.2
All industries in Newark	—	—	28.3[b]

[a]Averages compiled from sources described in Appendix A.
[b]Compiled from statistics for Essex County in U.S. Census Office, *Manufactures in the United States in 1860* (Washington, D.C., 1865).

changes in their techniques to reduce costs. Through 1860 carpenters went about their work much as earlier generations had; the carpenter's skills were unchanged, and apprenticeship remained necessary for entry into the craft. Carpenters worked in small groups, usually in shops that had fewer than ten employees (Table 5). They owned their tools, and, consequently, they retained control over their wages and kept them high in comparison to other workers (Table 6).[24] No major technological innovations were made in carpentry, perhaps because carpenters resisted all attempts to implement them. Factories for mass-producing sashes and blinds were established in Newark in the 1830s, but as late as 1853 some carpenters were refusing to install the factory-made variety, insisting on making their own at the construction site.[25]

TABLE 6
Average Monthly Wages, Male and Female[a]

Craft and type of technology	Males		Females	
	1850	1860	1850	1860
Carpentry	$31.20	$40.97	–	–
Blacksmithing	26.91	29.51	–	–
Shoemaking:				
sewing machines—no steam	–	25.47	–	$15.83
hand	22.10	28.26	$ 9.52	12.96
average	22.10	26.86	9.52	13.91
Saddle making:				
sewing machines—no steam	–	35.69	–	22.24
hand	27.40	28.56	13.50	–
average	27.40	33.75	13.50	22.24
Jewelry making:				
using steam	31.58	49.32	14.35	21.25
hand or tools—no steam	33.81	49.36	18.95	22.67
average	32.75	49.33	16.43	21.33
Trunk making:				
using steam	19.23	25.54	–	16.47
sewing machines—no steam	–	28.15	–	–
hand	21.28	29.05	16.67	12.00
average	21.17	26.70	16.67	16.00
Leather making:				
using steam	29.55	30.00	–	–
hand or tools—no steam	28.40	32.39	12.50	18.00
average	28.83	30.51	12.50	18.00
Hatting:				
using steam	21.38	29.23	9.39	13.90
sewing machines—no steam	–	34.48	–	16.54
hand	30.65	41.50	12.28	26.64
average	24.73	31.92	10.20	17.79

[a]Compiled from the manuscripts of the U.S. Censuses of Manufactures, 1850 and 1860.

Blacksmithing also retained a traditional structure before 1860, but a shrinking of the scope of the craft created real differences between the experiences of blacksmiths and carpenters. Quite early, forges and machine shops began to take over the heavier tasks once done by the neighborhood blacksmith, and consequently the number of blacksmiths in the United States decreased by 37 percent between 1850 and 1860.[26] In Newark, factories producing articles like hardware for wholesale distribution usurped part of the traditional blacksmith's role, and less and less remained of what the craft of blacksmithing once had encompassed. Because of the decreasing scope of the trade and its local orientation, the number of blacksmiths rose very slowly (Table 4). Blacksmiths did the remaining work, primarily horse shoeing and repairs, in the traditional ways in small shops (Table 5).[27] But unlike carpenters, the blacksmiths received low wages (Table 6); only shoemakers, trunk makers, and hatters in the most mechanized factories made less. Apprentices and journeymen in blacksmithing did not form unions to protest their relatively low wages, however. This suggests that the traditional character of the craft, including the personal relationship between master and apprentice and the real chance for self-employment for the journeyman, operated to counter discontent.

Despite their resistence to technological innovation, carpenters, unlike blacksmiths, found it necessary to unionize; industrialization was not the only change craftsmen faced. In the 1830s the contractor emerged as the middleman in construction. Customers began to use contractors rather than hire labor themselves, and wage disputes arose since the contractors paid journeymen day wages, and any increase in wages after a building contract was made came out of the contractor's profit margin. The journeymen carpenters formed a union to fight for wage increases; it was active and generally successful from the 1830s on. Carpenters were earning the high wage of $1.50 per day in 1836, and although their wages declined during depressions, whenever they demanded increases in good times they were successful.[28] But unionization in a craft that had not begun to industrialize was atypical, and other crafts that maintained their traditional methods in the 1830s—such as blacksmithing, jewelry making, and trunk making—saw no such developments. The existence of the contractor was unique to the construction trades and was the reason for this early unionization.

Crafts that had begun task breakdown did not necessarily mechanize quickly. Newark's shoemakers had introduced task differentiation—the three-person teams—early in the century, but shoemaking did not follow the pattern of increasing industrialization between 1830 and 1860. Shoemaking was in the first stage of industrialization in the mid-1830s. There were fourteen large shoe factories in Newark with an average of fifty-two employees each; skill was needed for the making of high quality goods, and some apprentices were still being trained.[29] But Newark's shoe manufacturers experienced severe competition in the wholesale market from the products of New England factories. In 1837 manufacturers from Lynn, Massachusetts, sold one pair of shoes for every 2.5 white females in the country.[30] After Newark shoe manufacturers lost the Southern market, they produced mainly for the local market. As wholesale markets evaporated, the size of the average shop in shoemaking decreased (Table 5). In the new smaller units of the 1840s and 1850s the three-task system, payment by piece rates, and the putting-out system remained unchanged.[31] Some apprentices were still being trained in shoemaking in the 1840s, but no signs of true apprenticeship could be found during the next decade.

The stagnant quality of the industry continued in the 1850s, and there was, consequently, little growth in the labor force (Table 4). In the late 1850s, however, mechanization began as some manufacturers bought sewing machines for their plants. This led to a decrease in the proportion of women

TABLE 7
Percentage of Employees Who Were Female[a]

Craft	1850 (number)	1860 (number)
Carpentry	0	0
Blacksmithing	0	0
Shoemaking	34 (275)	14 (109)
Saddle making	8 (40)	3 (33)
Jewelry making	8 (42)	10 (54)
Trunk making	19 (60)	13 (95)
Leather making	1 (6)	1 (6)
Hatting	49 (643)	28 (462)
All industries Essex County		27
All industries New Jersey		23

[a]Compiled from the manuscripts of the U.S. Censuses of Manufactures, 1850 and 1860 and the *Manufactures of the United States in 1860*.

employed (Table 7) because the machines were used, at first, only for binding uppers—women's work. By 1860, however, less than 50 percent of all shoemakers worked in establishments using sewing machines, and no other machines were introduced in this period (Table 8). Even the largest shoe firm, which employed 400 people, still maintained the putting-out system and used no machines except for sewing machines.[32] Only after the Civil War did shoemaking in Newark leave the very first stage of industrialization.

Even in the first stage of industrialization—with task breakdown—workers lost control over wages. What had once been prices agreed on by both master and journeyman became piece rates dictated by the manufacturer. Inflation made these piece rates ever more inadequate, but manufacturers refused increases in order to maintain their competitive positions in the wholesale market. In 1833 the average yearly wage of shoemakers in Newark's factories was $163. This average is based on the wages of both male and female workers, but it is not indicative of men's wages because the women were paid much less. In 1835, male shoemakers claimed that at the current piece rate of $0.45 to $0.50 a pair they could make no more than $5.50 to $6 per week.[33] A carpenter could make $275 in seven months, but a male shoemaker could earn that only if he worked for fifty weeks, an unlikely possibility since production was irregular and lay-offs were frequent. Besides, most businesses suspended operations for many weeks every summer to settle accounts and rest.[34] To combat low piece rates, workers typically took joint action. In Newark five unions of male journeymen shoemakers and one of women binders and fitters formed between 1834 and 1836. They were the Ladies' Shoe and Men's Pumpmakers Union, The Journeymen Bootfitters Society, the Second Rate Bootmakers Society, the Men's Fudged Boot and Shoemakers Society, the Union Benevolent Society of Journeymen Cordwainers, and the Ladies' Shoe Fitters and Binders

TABLE 8
Percentage of All Employees by Technology Used[a]

Craft	1850	1860
Shoemaking:		
sewing machines, no steam	0.0	47.7
some steam-powered machinery	0.0	0.0
Saddle making:		
sewing machines, no steam	0.0	55.7
some steam-powered machinery	0.0	17.9
Jewelry making:		
some steam-powered machinery	48.1	79.2
Trunk making:		
sewing machines, no steam	0.0	8.8
some steam-powered machinery	4.2	67.6
Leather making:		
some steam-powered machinery	36.8	78.3
Hatting:		
sewing machines, no steam	0.0	15.0
some steam-powered machinery	67.5	66.2

[a]Compiled from the manuscripts of the U.S. Censuses of Manufactures for 1850 and 1860.

Union.[35] The formation of these unions signaled the arrival of the cleavage between worker and manufacturer that occurred with even the first steps of industrialization. The existence of a separate union for women also suggests that the days of domestic manufacture were long gone in shoemaking. The women binders and fitters hired out as individuals and were not wives and daughters helping craftsmen who worked within households.[36]

Although shoemakers' wages remained low in comparison to those of other crafts throughout the pre–Civil War period (Table 6), the shoemakers' unions were not impotent. Journeymen Shoemakers' Unions continued to exist in the 1840s and 1850s, and they managed to keep wage levels in Newark higher than those in other areas.[37] Newark's manufacturers were never able to counter the competition from New England with new techniques or lower wage levels, and the continued existence of journeymen's unions throughout this twenty-year period explains at least some of the resistance to change.

When manufacturers maintained wholesale markets, however, and unions were weak, industrialization was more rapid. Like shoemaking, saddle and harness making was a leather-working trade that had entered the first stage of industrialization prior to 1840. There were eleven factories in Newark by the mid-1830s, but the domestic system continued to some extent in saddle making as craftsmen took work home for female relatives to sew. As in shoemaking a few apprentices were still in training, but in 1835 the male craftsmen formed a union, the Journeymen Saddlers, Harness Makers and Trimmers, because of wage disputes with their employers. In 1833 the average yearly wage of a saddler was $257, slightly more than a shoemaker earned, but much less than a carpenter. In saddle making as in shoemaking, the techniques of production remained much the same throughout the 1840s. But in response to a growing national market for their products, saddle makers continued to work in large groups (Table 5). The Journeymen Saddlers and Harness Makers Union disappeared after 1837, however, and the saddle manufacturers more easily introduced mechanization in the 1850s than the shoe manufacturers did. Sewing machines, among others, were used by the companies employing most of the workers, and the largest firm was using some steam-powered machinery by 1860 (Table 8). Some skilled craftsmen were still working, however, because custom order work was done even in the large plants. As skill levels decreased in the 1850s, no further calls for apprentices were made, and if apprenticeship continued it was on a small scale. Thus after two decades in the first stage of transition, saddle making inched into the second stage.[38]

In these four crafts, lack of technological innovation, some worker resistance, or subdivision of the industry meant that many craftsmen experienced little or no change in their work over long periods of time. But in other crafts in Newark, like leather making, new inventions were made and adopted swiftly, and workers had to adapt quickly to mechanization. Leather making had always been odious, dirty work, even if it was a skilled craft. Industrialization only compounded the situation.[39] Throughout the first half of the nineteenth century the leather industry was centralized in Newark in a swamp along Market Street, and the factories constantly polluted the city. By the 1830s leather making had entered the first stage of industrialization. While large factories did not develop prior to the 1840s, new processes such as patent leather making and the great demand for leather by shoe and saddle makers led to task differentiation. Firms often specialized in tanning, currying, morocco dressing, or japanning, and men specialized in less complicated operations within these subdivisions.[40]

Leather manufacturers introduced new processes continually in the 1840s and 1850s. By the mid-1840s, they had divided the making of a piece of leather into six or eight separate steps.[41] Because of the new processes the leather was ready in approximately six weeks rather than the year or two necessary with the traditional technology. Machines were available for such processes as splitting leather, and by 1850 one-third of all workers were employed in plants that had some steam-powered machinery (Table 8). The shift to a new technology was quickest in the manufacture of patent leather, while the techniques used in making other types of leather changed more slowly. Leather making had entered the second stage of transition to a modern form in the late 1840s, and it had progressed to the third stage by 1860. Manufacturers simplified tasks further so that they advertised for shavers

TABLE 9
Percentage of All Employees by Size of Shop[a]

Craft	Year	1–24	25–49	50–99	100+
Shoemaking	1850	25.5	23.4	35.0	16.1
	1860	36.7	11.7	25.5	26.1
Saddle making	1850	7.2	24.2	25.6	43.0
	1860	10.2	6.3	23.5	60.0
Jewelry making	1850	18.3	17.7	39.3	24.7
	1860	21.7	20.8	13.9	43.6
Trunk making	1850	4.2	9.7	0.0	86.0
	1860	1.4	16.2	14.9	67.6
Leather making	1850	17.1	27.8	37.5	17.6
	1860	12.6	10.9	12.5	64.0
Hatting	1850	10.3	8.9	8.3	72.4
	1860	3.9	17.9	19.1	59.0

[a]Compiled from the manuscripts of the U.S. Censuses of Manufactures for 1850 and 1860.

and buffers, not for curriers or tanners. By 1860 two-thirds of the leather makers worked in factories with more than one hundred employees, and 78 percent worked in factories that had steam-powered machinery (Tables 8 and 9). Two groups of leather makers, the curriers and the morocco dressers, formed unions in the mid-1830s in response to wage disputes accompanying the first stage of industrialization; the curriers union reappeared briefly in the 1840s. Leather makers did not oppose mechanization itself, however, and the leather manufacturers used their freedom to change the methods of production drastically.[42]

Although leather making industrialized faster than shoemaking, leather makers' wages remained higher than shoemakers (Table 6). Industrialization tended to lower wages, but crafts had not been equally remunerative in their traditional stages, so wage differentials between crafts often persisted. Tanners and curriers were usually "middle class" if not wealthy in colonial times, while shoemakers were typically rather poor.[43] In 1836 the Curriers Union claimed the men were making a maximum of $8 per week, with three-fifths of them making less; they demanded $10 per week.[44] Yet at the same time, the best paid curriers earned one-third more than the best paid shoemakers. The differential between leather makers' and shoemakers' wages had narrowed by 1860 because leather making had industrialized so much more quickly, although the leather makers still received higher pay (Table 6).

Jewelry making was another remunerative craft that continued to pay well even as it industrialized. Newark's jewelers were not numerous in the 1830s, and they began to introduce task differentiation only in the mid-1840s (Table 4). In 1849 manufacturers introduced the first steam-powered machinery, but mechanization was confined to a few operations, such as gold chain making and watchcase making.[45] The best jewelry was made by artists who executed the complete process. Manufacturers hired girls to do polishing (Table 7), but men held most of the jobs. Skill levels were high, and while most apprentices no longer boarded with their masters, the term of apprenticeship remained at least five years.[46] Jewelry manufacturers paid much higher wages than any other manufacturers, and no unions arose to point to conflicts between journeymen and their employers (Table 6). In a luxury trade like jewelry making, costs were more easily passed on to the consumer, so wages could remain high.

Even in such a trade, however, industrialization created adverse working conditions. In the 1850s jewelry making moved from the first to the second stage of industrialization with the introduction of small machines such as circular saws, lathes, and the like. Manufacturers hired more female workers (Table 7) and differentiated more tasks: diamond mounters, diamond cutters, and ring makers joined chain makers, watchcase makers, and engravers. Steam-powered machinery was still used for only a few tasks, but industrial accidents became much more common; in 1856, for example, a jewelry apprentice mangled his arm in a circular saw.[47]

Factories of one hundred to three hundred workers were not rare in the late 1850s, but many medium-sized firms also arose in response to the growing demand for luxury goods by the new urban wealthy class. Many of these firms did custom-order work, such as the $1,800 diamond-studded watchcase made for a customer by Baldwin and Company in 1855. This gave employment to jewelers who possessed the old skill and encouraged boys to apprentice themselves for five years to them. Despite these vestiges of the old ways, however, industrialization destroyed the traditional relationship between employer and journeyman jeweler. About one-third of all Newark jewelry companies had their showrooms and offices in New York City or Philadelphia by the late 1850s. With the increase in mechanization and the separation of showroom from factory, the division between manufacturers and journeymen became more pronounced, and in 1859 the first union of journeymen jewelers was formed.[48] Journeymen felt the conflict with their employers, although the exceptionally high wage rates remained not only for men but for women too (Table 6).

As the craft of trunk making industrialized, skilled and unskilled workers existed simultaneously as they did in jewelry making, but more rapid technological advance in the former shifted the balance drastically toward the unskilled. In the 1830s Newark's few trunk makers, like its jewelers, used traditional methods to produce goods for the local market (Table 4). No conflicts arose between journeymen and masters, and the trade union movement of 1835–36 did not touch trunk makers. Beginning in the mid-1840s, however, trunk manufacturers overturned the old methods of production. By 1846 some trunk making companies had begun to produce a wholesale line of trunks of lower quality, simplified design, and cheaper price, in addition to filling custom orders for ornate baggage. While the latter employed the skilled workers, the cheaper products were made by less skilled personnel, each doing one task. As task differentiation increased, some of the larger employers instituted the putting-out system and hired women to make carpet bags (Table 7). Through 1850, however, almost all work, whether skilled or not, was done by hand (Table 8). As skill became less necessary for employment, the system of apprenticeship broke down. Boys would remain apprentices only a few years and then leave to get journeymen's wages. Most workers were employed in two large firms where wages were lower than those in any of the other crafts (Tables 6 and 9).[49] No unions arose among the trunk makers though, perhaps because the few older skilled workers could still do custom work in the big factories or produce luxury goods for the growing urban wealthy class. Trunk makers, like jewelers, opened new small firms in the 1850s to meet this demand for quality products. Those with something to lose were forced neither out of the field nor down to task work.

In the 1850s such great changes were made in the production of trunks that trunk making moved from the first into the third stage of industrialization in a decade. The large companies, employing two-thirds of all workers in the field, introduced steam-powered machinery for many tasks (Tables 8 and 9). Although smaller establishments did not use steam-powered machinery, they did follow the larger ones in using sewing machines, which lowered the percentage of women employed (Tables 7 and 8). Apprenticeship disappeared as skill levels declined, and wages remained low in comparison to other trades. Wages were lower for men in the large "modern" factories than for those using older techniques of production (Table 6) because unskilled workers had less leverage with their employers. Most companies had offices in New York City or Philadelphia for their wholesaling and retailing operations, and Newark retained only the production facilities.[50]

Industrialization in trunk making, as in other fields, led to deteriorating working conditions and, in response, workers' demands for more leisure. Mechanization eliminated the casual work day of old, where masters and journeymen labored sporadically throughout the day. Trunk makers were packed in "close workshops amid the din of machinery and manufacture," and employers gave them occasional picnics and outings in the summer for relief.[51] It was also necessary to limit hours when mechanization and lower piecework rates speeded up the pace of work. The ten-hour day became standard for men in most crafts in Newark by the 1840s. The sixty-hour week was so firmly established in trunk making that in the summer one large trunk making firm operated on a weekly schedule of five eleven-hour days and one five-hour morning in order to give workers Saturday afternoons off. Even day laborers worked only ten hours, although some workers, like steam engineers, might put in a thirteen-hour day, and some pieceworkers may well have had to work more than ten hours to make a living wage. By the 1850s, in fact, it seemed that all Newarkers had ceased to think of work as a task to be accomplished in conjunction with rest and sociability. Because of the influence of industrial values, they saw work as time taken away from "life." Even dry goods merchants, for instance, tried several times to agree to shorten their hours. In 1856 they were still trying to decrease hours from fourteen per day to twelve, so that they could open at 7 A.M. and close at 7 P.M.[52] Merchants had begun to see long hours at their businesses as a burden.

In the most completely mechanized crafts like hatting all the major effects of industrialization appeared by 1860. Hatting in Newark had reached the second stage of industrialization by 1836 with the existence of eight hat factories averaging seventy-six employees each; task differentiation was well advanced, and the putting-out system was prevalent. Many small machines were used in the larger factories, such as those for ironing and finishing hats and for stiffening hat bodies. One man using a machine for stiffening hat bodies could do the work five had done by hand. Because of these innovations, apprenticeship had broken down and become a cloak for exploitation. Manufacturers hired men over twenty-one years of age as "apprentices" to hide their employment of unskilled labor. Boys found no future in the trade, and, although innovations were rapid, neither did women. Manufacturers employed large numbers of women in trimming and binding hats, but in no other tasks. Community values kept men's jobs from women and confined the latter to needle work. To protest inadequate wages and the competition of adult "apprentices," the journeymen hatters formed a union in the mid-1830s and conducted strikes.[53] In the 1830s only a few crafts had changed to this extent, but these were the industries that were the basis for Newark's economic growth.

The industrialization of the hatting trade was well underway in the 1830's, and technological changes continued in the 1840s, so that by the end of the decade, hatting had entered the third stage of transition. A silk hat could be made from a rough hat body in two hours and five minutes in 1850.[54] At mid-century, two-thirds of all hat makers worked in factories using steam-powered machinery, and 72 percent worked in factories with more than one hundred employees each (Tables 8 and 9). A small local retail market for hats continued to exist, however, and a few skilled craftsmen still made hats by hand. The tremendous difference in wages paid the vast majority who worked in the mechanized plants and the few who continued to use the old manual technology reveals the magnitude of the skill loss caused by mechanization (Table 6). While wages were low for the ma-

FIGURE 1   Stages of Industrialization

	1826–30	1836–40	1846–50	1856–60
TRANSITION STAGE THREE			hatting	hatting leather making trunk making
TRANSITION STAGE TWO		hatting	leather making	jewelry making saddle making
TRANSITION STAGE ONE	shoemaking	leather making saddle making shoemaking	trunk making jewelry making saddle making shoemaking	shoemaking
TRADITIONAL	hatting leather making saddle making trunk making jewelry making blacksmithing carpentry	trunk making jewelry making blacksmithing carpentry	blacksmithing carpentry	blacksmithing carpentry

jority, unemployment was also common. Ten months per year was considered steady employment in hat factories. In the large factories, moreover, working conditions were often dangerous, as hatters sometimes suffered from mercury poisoning, although this hazard predated industrialization. On the other hand, the large modern factories with steam heat and gas lighting had some comforts the older cramped workshops lacked.[55]

Technological changes in hatting continued in the 1850s with the invention of the hat wire brim and the inflexible hat. The introduction of sewing machines displaced many of the women who had been trimmers or binders (Table 7), and, as in the other trades in which women had done needle work, they faced a narrowly constricted job market, for few new tasks were open to them. But the modern factory form was not reached in hatting at that time. Some tasks were still done by hand, and some machines had yet to be steam-driven. Much labor was involved, and some skill was needed in hat finishing. In the mid-1850s the finishers formed an association that demanded a closed shop to limit the number of apprentices.[56] They were successful in some shops, even some large ones, but not in others. By mid-century few, if any, industries were more advanced than Newark's hat making industry, but none had reached the modern stage of constant-flow processes and homogenized work force.

The history of these eight crafts, despite the similarities of general development, reveals the diversity of mechanics' experiences with industrialization. Charting the course of industrialization in the crafts emphasizes the progress from homogeneity to heterogeneity (Figure 1). The variety of work settings and technologies experienced by craftsmen forms a striking contrast with the uniformity of other aspects of their lives, notably their family structures and social forms.

CHAPTER 3

Industrialization and the Labor Force

Task breakdown and mechanization rendered craftsmen's skills obsolete, lessened their control over their work, and changed the content of their jobs, but industrialization also altered the character of the work force itself. As manufacturers introduced new methods to increase the volume of production, they needed cheaper labor to keep their prices competitive. When, as in Newark, journeymen struck for wage increases, manufacturers often sought a totally new, cheaper, and more tractable labor force to replace them. Newark's native population provided three possible sources of cheap labor: blacks, women, and children. Teenage apprentices had provided cheap labor in the preindustrial workshop; in the early stages of industrialization, the values of the community, the force of united journeymen, and the nature of mechanization combined to prevent manufacturers from using other sources of cheap labor. But as apprenticeship declined and mechanization ensued, even teenage boys lost their place in production. The adult male immigrants from Europe who swelled Newark's population in the 1840s and 1850s provided manufacturers with a cheaper, less skilled labor force—one that was acceptable to the community. Men from Ireland and Germany were absorbed into the economy relatively rapidly, but the diversity they brought divided the working class along ethnic and religious lines.

Community prejudice and the small number of blacks in Newark prevented manufacturers from using blacks as cheap labor. Few blacks were attracted to the town because of the negative effects of white racism on their job opportunities, social life, and civil rights. The black people of Newark comprised less than 6 percent of the total population between 1830 and 1860, and they formed a continually segregated group within the city. Prejudice against them was so strong that they were forced to have all their own institutions: schools, churches, lodges, and the like. When a black person attended a public facility like the theater or the library, there was an immediate outcry by insulted whites. White fears of black equality caused Newark's first riot in July 1834 when enraged whites sought to disrupt an abolitionist lecture. Blacks, themselves, continued to demand their rights in the 1840s and 1850s by staging celebrations of West Indian emancipation and holding mass meetings for emancipation in the South. Although no further race riots occurred, blacks were often insulted or attacked by gangs of young white toughs who inhabited the street corners. The police did not interfere.[1]

This community prejudice helped to close jobs to blacks, and their proportion in the eight crafts was always less than their proportion of the population. The underrepresentation of blacks in the eight crafts in their traditional form might be expected from the inferior caste position blacks held in American society, but no amount of change in the eight crafts opened them to black workers; the craftsmen, however else they may have differed, were virtually all white (99 percent). Indeed, the absolute number of blacks working in these industries was minute (nineteen in all eight crafts in 1860).[2]

While there were few blacks for manufacturers to hire, there were many women, both the daughters and the wives of journeymen and laborers. In the American textile industry the cheap labor of women was vital to the success of the new enterprises.[3] But opportunities for Newark's women to participate in craft production actually shrank during industrialization as the tasks they had done were mechanized in the new factories.[4] Before industrialization, women often had helped in the crafts—shoemaking, hat making, and saddle and harness making—that required some sewing on the product. Needlework had always been woman's work, but women had labored in the home under the direction of men. Craftsmen in these trades, whether they worked at home or brought work home from the shop or factory, gave such sewing to their female relatives. During the putting-out stage, women were still involved in manufacturing as whole families were hired for task production.[5] Since women labored for their male relatives in the home, no estimates of the amount of female labor usually employed can be made. In shoemaking, however, where the minimal production team included three people, one of these, the binder, was usually a woman.

Prior to 1860 women found no opportunities in the crafts, regardless of level of industrialization, other than this sewing. As production moved out of the home and into the factory, women, be they relatives of male workers or not, still did the sewing tasks.[6] According to the U.S. Censuses of Manufactures for 1850 and 1860 in toto hundreds of women worked in the crafts, mainly as hat trimmers, shoe binders and fitters, and carpetbag makers (Table 7). The only nonsewing tasks assigned to women were in jewelry making, where women polished silver and made gold chains. No women worked in carpentry or blacksmithing, and only a handful were employed in the making of leather. Women never formed a majority in any craft, although they approached equality of numbers with men in the hatting trade in 1850. But when manufacturers introduced the sewing machine women lost their jobs, and from 1850 to 1860 the percentage of women in most of the crafts declined.

American society had always designated work as male or female; craftsmen kept their jobs designated as "masculine" throughout industrialization, but men increasingly encroached on "feminine" work. A person trying to find new occupations for needy women in Newark complained of men doing shopkeeping, clerking, and the lighter tasks in any trade that women were "strong enough" to perform.[7] Furthermore, men tended to monopolize any new positions arising during industrialization. While needlework was "female," for instance, men as well as women ran sewing machines. In the nineteenth century, American women on balance lost industrial jobs to men.[8]

If the employers' only criterion had been profit, male preponderance in the labor force would have been surprising since women were a source of cheap labor. Men talked often of chivalry, but required more work from women for lower pay. The wages of women in the eight crafts ranged from two-fifths to two-thirds that of men in the same craft (Table 6). Women and men in these crafts, of course, did not generally perform the same tasks; in those lines of employment where men and women did the same jobs, however, inequality of wages was common at the time. In the 1830s, for instance, those proposing public schools for Newark claimed that taxes could be held down by hiring women as teachers, for they would gladly work for one-third of what men got. In the 1850s the school board paid female teachers exactly half the salary of male teachers.[9] Probably women would have taken more jobs in the crafts because women were better paid in the eight trades than in many other fields, especially garment making; even when the comparison is restricted to the same type of work—sewing—a strong differential in wages appears. Women who sewed in the hat industry averaged $17.79 per month in 1860 while those who sewed in the shoe industry averaged $13.91 per month (Table 6). But those who sewed in the Essex County shirtmaking industry, which was 93 percent female and employed 445 women, averaged only $10.90 per month.[10] Wages for women in the crafts were one-third to two-thirds higher than those in other fields.

Manufacturers did not open new jobs to women even though they worked for less, for women had many deficiencies as a work force. Above all, their employment violated the values of Newarkers, who, like Americans in general, viewed woman's domestic function as paramount.[11] Victorian tradition dictated that mothers belonged at home, and that young girls should learn domestic skills, not factory jobs. Newark's manufacturers believed in the Victorian ideal too; these values pervaded the publications they dominated. As the editor of the *Newark Daily Advertiser* said on viewing two German immigrant women shoveling coal: "What would the American woman say to such an employment? In nothing else does the superiority of our social condition to the great mass in Europe appear more manifest, than in the different estimates of the character of the sex."[12] Manufacturers also had little interest in married women because, from their point of view, married women were unreliable workers—prone to pregnancy. According to the 1860 population census, only 2 percent of the women in the crafts were married and living with their spouses.[13] Manufacturers did not hire many widows or deserted wives either; only 7 percent of the women workers had children.

Manufacturers preferred unmarried girls for the few jobs open to women. According to the 1860 population census, the average female worker in the crafts was an unmarried girl in her late teens who lived with her parents; there was a 50 percent chance she worked in the same industry as someone else with whom she lived. The Census tells us what society wanted to believe: that wives and mothers did not labor, and that women's work was generally connected to their homes and families. This profile of the "average" female worker may be a figment of nineteenth-century values, however, because the population census recorded only 42 percent of the women said to be working in the crafts by the Census of Manufactures. Many men and women may have been ashamed to admit they were violating Victorian standards.

The typical woman working in the crafts was an unmarried girl who contributed to the support of her family but was not its chief breadwinner. The average woman who admitted being employed in the crafts was much younger than the average male craftsman: she was twenty-two, while he was thirty-three. Most of the women workers were minors: 61 percent were under 21. More than half of the women workers listed in the census, 58 percent, lived with one or both of their parents. Another 30 percent were not members of a nuclear family but lived with others, usually as boarders. In contrast, 61 percent of the male craftsmen were heads of households. Manufacturers justified paying women less than men because most women workers did not have to support families by themselves.

Unlike male craftsmen, women tended to work in the same industry as other members of the households in which they lived. Only 17 percent of the male craftsmen had a possible relationship between work and home, while 48 percent of the female workers did. This may reflect a holdover of the practice of giving sewing to female relatives, although most of the women worked in the same industry as siblings, often sisters. It may also mean that women's occupations were most likely to be reported if they worked with or for someone else in the household. It does show that a woman's entry into the working world was a far less independent move than that of a man.

Women also failed to capture new jobs because of their lack of skills.

Women who knew only sewing could not easily adjust to machine production in the crafts if the jobs required any skill; men monopolized the job of hat finishing, which required skilled workers to operate machines. Similarly, when linotype machines were introduced in printing, women printers who had never been trained in the finer points of the trade could not run the machines and thus lost their jobs to skilled male printers.[14]

The last major native source of cheap labor was children, but true child labor—by those under fifteen—seems not to have been a product of industrialization in crafts. The extent of child labor cannot be known with accuracy because the best source for studying the labor force, the Censuses of Population, listed occupations for those over fourteen years of age only. But for most crafts the number of male workers found in the Census of Population equalled or excelled the number given by the Census of Manufactures (see Appendix A), and we might conjecture, therefore, that child labor could not have been very prevalent in these trades.[15] It may not have been unknown, however. For instance, a jeweler who wanted an apprentice advertised for a fifteen or sixteen-year-old boy but demanded prior experience; and a sixteen-year-old advertised for an apprenticeship in harness making citing good references from his last employer.[16] Perhaps the best evidence against the widespread use of child labor is that, although many of the craftsmen protested the employment of unskilled teenagers, none complained about competition from child labor.

The most likely native source of cheap labor was teenage boys, who, as apprentices, had a recognized and important place in production. They worked for lower wages than men, and because of the paucity of educational facilities, they were available. But teenagers, too, failed to gain—and in the long run actually lost—jobs in industrializing crafts. Apprenticeship disappeared, and adult male immigrants monopolized jobs in the mechanized factories because boys, like women and children, were not as desirable a labor force as they seemed at first glance. It was acceptable for a boy to labor outside his home, but teenagers lacked skills and stability. Journeymen organized to exclude them from jobs, and manufacturers found their best source of labor to be the immigrants coming to Newark in ever greater numbers in the late 1840s and 1850s.

In the traditional crafts in Newark prior to the 1830s, the worker's age largely defined his economic position. If a worker was under twenty-one, he was an apprentice; generally journeymen were in their twenties and thirties. By the time a man was forty, he had probably achieved his independence as a master craftsman. Industrialization destroyed this pattern by ending the probability that age would lead to increased knowledge or skill and therefore to increased wealth and status. In the modern factory a worker attains his maximum earning capacity within the few weeks or months it takes him to reach the level of peak efficiency; age can only slow his reflexes and de-

TABLE 10
Age Distribution of White Males of Working Age[a]

		15–19	20–29	30–39	40+
1830	Newark	23.2	39.6	19.0	18.2
	New Jersey	19.8	31.1	20.0	29.1
1840	Newark	18.0	31.7	26.7	23.7
	New Jersey	18.8	30.3	21.0	29.9
1850	eight crafts	17.6	38.7	21.9	21.8
	Newark	16.6	34.0	23.6	25.8
	New Jersey	17.1	29.8	21.3	31.8
1860	eight crafts	11.5	33.9	27.9	26.7
	Newark	15.0	28.5	26.9	29.6
	New Jersey	16.3	28.3	22.7	32.7

[a]Figures for New Jersey and for Newark, 1830, 1840, and 1850 come from published federal censuses. Figures for Newark, 1860 are derived from a systematic sample taken of Newark white males aged fifteen and over in the manuscript of the population census. The percentages for this sample have a confidence interval of ±5 percent at the 90 percent level. Figures for the eight crafts are derived from the manuscripts of the U.S. Censuses of Population, 1850 and 1860.

crease his rate of production. The changing age distribution of male workers in nineteenth-century crafts reflects these new circumstances. Relatively few old men worked in the crafts as they industrialized. At the same time teenage labor decreased in importance, so that these industries became the preserve of those in their twenties and thirties, who would have had the highest incomes when working for piece rates.

There is no specific information on the age distribution of each craft prior to 1850, but general population trends suggest the changes taking place. In 1830, when industrialization barely had begun, Newark had proportionately more white men aged fifteen to twenty-nine, the prime ages for apprentices and young journeymen, than did the predominantly rural state of New Jersey (Table 10). Young men from all over the country thronged into the city to take advantage of the demand for apprentices and journeymen, and the natural balance between the sexes was lost. In 1830 the sex ratio of white males aged fifteen to nineteen (the prime age for apprentices) to white females of the same age was 1.34; the sex ratio for these groups in the state of New Jersey as a whole was 1.02.[17] Most of the young men remained in Newark for only a few years and had little interest in anything but business. They were encouraged to work and learn by the promise of handsome profits. Mechanics' Fairs like the one at Castle Garden, New York, where a Newark apprentice won a prize for his work, were a constant source of inspiration for the young craftsmen in search of success in the expanding economy.[18]

In 1840, when industry was at a standstill due to the depression, the age distribution of Newark's white males over fourteen was similar to that of the state as a whole: the young had moved elsewhere in search of work. In the following twenty years the age distribution of the white male popu-

TABLE 11
Age of Male Workers by Craft[a]

Craft	1850					1860				
	15–20	21–30	31–40	41+	Mean	15–20	21–30	31–40	41+	Mean
Carpenters	18.3	39.6	20.4	21.7	31.6	9.0	42.8	25.5	22.7	33.4
Blacksmiths	16.9	41.5	23.9	17.6	30.9	14.5	37.8	25.7	22.1	32.8
Shoemakers	10.2	36.5	23.6	29.6	34.5	5.3	25.1	34.8	34.8	38.2
Saddlers	30.7	36.2	18.5	14.6	28.2	26.9	36.0	22.5	14.5	29.1
Jewelers	36.1	39.3	17.0	7.7	25.6	22.1	43.9	20.4	13.6	28.6
Trunk makers	43.7	40.3	6.3	9.8	25.0	17.0	41.0	25.4	16.6	30.7
Leather makers	16.6	41.5	20.8	21.0	31.0	11.0	41.9	27.5	19.5	32.6
Hatters	25.5	36.4	20.7	17.4	29.6	17.2	35.9	22.5	24.7	32.8
Average of crafts	21.8	38.5	20.3	19.4	30.4	14.7	37.2	26.0	22.3	32.8
Newark	22.3	31.2	22.7	23.8	32.3	15.8	34.2	23.8	26.2	33.3
Traditional	17.8	40.3	21.7	20.2		10.9	41.0	25.6	22.5	
Stage one except shoes	34.8	38.1	16.2	10.8						
Stage two	16.6	41.5	20.8	21.0		24.5	39.9	21.5	14.0	
Stage three	25.5	36.4	20.7	17.4		14.7	39.0	24.9	21.4	

[a]Data for all male workers in the eight crafts are compiled from manuscripts of the U.S. Censuses of Population of 1850 and 1860. The data on craftsmen in all succeeding tables, not otherwise labeled, is also from the manuscript censuses. Statistics for "Newark," 1850 and 1860, are from systematic samples of white males aged fifteen and over in the manuscripts of the censuses of population. The percentages for these samples have confidence intervals of ±5 percent at the 90 percent level.

lation of both the city and the state changed very slightly in the direction of increased age. There were fewer teenagers and more of the middle-aged and old, proportionately, in 1860 than there had been in 1830 or 1840, presumably because of the family limitation that New Jersey residents, like other Americans, were practicing. But teenagers in Newark also found fewer job opportunities in the crafts, and by 1860 proportionately fewer teenagers were employed in the eight crafts than lived in Newark.

Teenage labor expanded only during the first stage of industrialization, that of task differentiation. As mechanization proceeded, semiskilled and unskilled adults replaced the teenagers. The two crafts that were organized along the lines of the traditional model, carpentry and blacksmithing, had age profiles like the town itself (Table 11). The average carpenter or blacksmith was among the older craftsmen and equal in age to the average Newarker. Less than one in every five was of apprenticeship age. Because of their dependence on local markets, carpentry and blacksmithing were not expanding quickly, and so apprenticeship was limited. Since unskilled boys could not replace the adult workers because of the high skill requirements, the number of teenagers in the work force was small.

Boy labor increased dramatically during the first stage of industrialization, and those crafts with many teenage workers were jewelry making, trunk making, and saddle making, all of which were changing rapidly by 1850. Over 30 percent of the saddlers, jewelers, and trunk makers were minors. The very small percentage of men in these trades who were over the age of forty also indicates the relative lack of older master craftsmen. Tremendous numbers of apprentices and journeymen were working for a very few manufacturers in these trades during the first stage of industrialization. The teenagers were taken on as apprentices, but used as cheap labor in task breakdown. Between 1850 and 1860, however, as mechanization proceeded in these fields, the proportion of teenagers was reduced, especially in jewelry making and trunk making. The most mechanized trades, hatting and leather making, had age profiles similar to the most traditional crafts. They did not include large numbers of teenagers.

The only exception to this pattern of a young work force during the first stage of industrialization occurred in shoemaking, a dying trade in Newark. In both 1850 and 1860 the average shoemaker was much older than the average man in the other crafts or in the city as a whole. Shoemakers were training few apprentices; only 10 percent of the shoemakers in 1850 and 5 percent in 1860 were teenagers, while a third of all shoemakers were over forty. Certainly the stagnation of the craft in this period, which distinguishes it from the others, would seem a likely reason for this situation. Shoemaking was simply unable to absorb many new members; only replacement was possible, and young men undoubtedly looked elsewhere for opportunity. This situation sets shoemaking apart from the other crafts at a similar level of industrialization and reveals the success of the shoemakers' unions in protecting members' jobs.

In the course of industrialization the traditional apprentice disappeared, and a young wage worker of the same age as the former apprentice, a free capitalist worker, took his place. But such workers were most prevalent in crafts in the first stage of industrialization, in the first flush of accelerated growth in response to market demand. In the long run there were proportionately many fewer of them. In 1850, 65 percent of Newark's white males aged fifteen to twenty worked in skilled crafts compared to 66 percent of all white men over fourteen years of age (Table 12). But in 1860 only 41 percent of this teenage group were employed in the skilled crafts while 54 percent of all men over fourteen were. The expulsion of the young from the crafts was a city-wide phenomenon. And youths were not finding other jobs easily. In 1860, 22 percent of the boys aged fifteen to twenty had no steady occupation, not even unskilled labor, and another 5 percent were students. In comparison, only 7 percent of the youth in 1850 were either students or unemployed. This was part of a long-term trend toward teenage unemployment in the United States: by 1890 only 50 percent of American boys aged fourteen to nineteen were employed.[19]

The decline of apprenticeship had begun by the mid-1830s. Continuing

TABLE 12
Occupations of White Males in Newark[a]

Type of Occupation	1850		1860	
	15–20	over 14	15–20	over 14
None or student	6.7	4.8	26.9	9.2
Unskilled, service	6.7	10.1	7.2	15.0
Semiskilled	3.4	5.2	7.3	8.6
Skilled[b]	65.2	65.9	41.2	54.0
Proprietors, managers, professionals	1.7	9.0	0.0	9.0
Clerical, sales	16.7	5.2	14.6	4.6
Armed Forces	0.0	0.0	2.4	0.4

[a]See Appendix B for the definition of these occupational classifications.
[b]Many of these trades, including the eight studied in detail, were no longer truly or completely skilled due to industrialization. But sufficient information is not available to classify all of them in a more precise manner.

the eighteenth-century custom of binding out the poor, the authorities indentured pauper children. However, many other children were apprenticed not by written contract but on the verbal promises of the child and his parents. A newspaper editorial of 1839 thus complained that the system of apprenticeship seemed dead in Newark. Boys often did not serve their whole time, and employers did not bother to use legal measures against them. In order to raise production levels, the masters had had to turn to piece or task rates. Many shops had no regular apprentices, and some boys went from one employer to another, sometimes changing crafts two or three times before coming of age.[20]

The decline of apprenticeship was caused mainly by changes in the organization of production. While some Newarkers felt that American youths were not interested in apprenticeship because they wanted "short cuts and sudden results," the new methods of organization that together constituted early industrialization were far more important in limiting apprenticeship. Even before total mechanization eliminated the need for skill, true apprenticeship became less necessary.[21] The primary criterion of the employer was profitability, and apprenticeship began to violate that standard. When there were many tasks to be learned the apprentice had to be shifted to a new one just as he had attained peak efficiency at another. Once task differentiation had begun in a craft, true apprenticeship, in which the boy learned all the tasks, lessened efficiency and profits. Manufacturers consequently exploited boys in task production through false apprenticeships. One young man who ran away from his master said that he had come to Newark from South Carolina to learn to be a carpenter, but had been taught nothing but sashes and blinds. So he left and took his tools with him to find a true apprenticeship.[22] In addition, as firms underwent rapid expansion they began to steal apprentices from each other. Apprenticeship became less profitable to the individual employer who trained boys, since the apprentice produced little in the first years of his term and only paid his way toward the end. The employer invested in the apprentice and had no guarantee of getting a return on that investment if the boy could run off and get a job elsewhere.

Between 1840 and 1860 the nature of apprenticeship changed radically, even for those few apprentices who still were indentured. The personal ties between master and apprentice were replaced by a purely economic relationship, and the responsibilities of the master for the morals and education of his apprentice lessened. By 1844 a standard printed indenture in jewelry making provided for a cash payment if the apprentice would not be boarding with the master, but had no provison for any education beyond the industrial. Another indenture in jewelry making, from 1853, not only failed to mention schooling but also assumed the apprentice would not be boarding with the master and set an increasing rate of board money to be paid to the apprentice. Although the traditional apprenticeship was gone, however, the system was not dead entirely. In 1859 four indentured apprentices were tried for not conforming to their indentures and given sentences of one to three months in jail.[23]

On the one hand, the elimination of teenagers from the crafts is understandable as a product of the decline of apprenticeship. But on the other, the exclusion of unskilled boys from the factories in favor of unskilled adults must be explained, since boys would, presumably, have worked for less than men. They were expelled for some of the same reasons that women were not hired. Some manufacturers thought that boys were unreliable, lacking in discipline and subject to wandering. Manufacturers complained, for instance, that when the fire alarm sounded whole shops were upset as boys ran out to follow the engines and got drunk and brawled along with the fire companies.[24] To the extent that reliability and permanence were important to a manufacturer, he might have to pay for adult labor.

The type of mechanization that occurred also was important. A novice could not easily operate every machine. The hat finishers had a union that regulated apprenticeship in their craft, since their work, though mechanized, required too much skill for their employers to hire unskilled boys in their stead. Many boys, just like women, lost their foothold in the printing trades when mechanization began.[25] In the early nineteenth century, printers employed hordes of boys who were called apprentices but who were not taught most aspects of the business. Set to work on "straight composition," they could perform with fair speed after a very short period of training. With the introduction of typesetting machines in the 1880s, most boys were ousted, and skilled adult printers, who trained a few apprentices, ran the linotypes. While the printers' union desired this end, its force was not decisive. Experiments revealed that while the machines increased volume tre-

TABLE 13
Birthplace of Male Workers by Craft

Craft	1850				1860			
	U.S.	Ireland	Germany	Other	U.S.	Ireland	Germany	Other
Carpenters	79.2	7.2	8.2	5.5	64.7	7.6	18.1	9.5
Blacksmiths	55.5	20.3	16.6	7.6	39.3	20.3	30.4	10.0
Shoemakers	54.2	15.5	18.0	12.2	36.2	19.0	32.2	12.5
Saddlers	59.2	8.8	23.6	8.4	39.9	15.8	35.2	9.1
Jewelers	58.5	3.3	25.5	12.7	60.5	2.1	25.9	11.5
Trunk makers	62.5	12.5	20.1	4.9	40.1	15.2	40.8	3.9
Leather makers	36.0	38.7	10.1	15.1	28.0	42.6	19.2	10.2
Hatters	51.4	25.3	5.6	17.7	38.2	27.8	16.0	18.0
Average craft	56.1	17.0	15.4	11.5	42.9	19.9	25.6	11.5
Newark	53.5	20.1	14.1	12.3	44.6	21.2	26.2	8.1

mendously, operators had to be skilled to use them properly. Because a linotype was expensive to buy and had high fixed operating costs, the employer was willing to pay for a skilled workman to avoid damaging the machine and thus to make the investment worthwhile.

To these factors—the unreliability of boy labor and the need for skilled operators for some machines—was added the existence of a relatively abundant labor market in Newark because of immigration. Reaching massive proportions by the mid-1840s, the migration of adult foreigners to the city supplied labor to Newark firms at a price employers wanted to pay. At least some of this labor was already skilled, and in this way adult male dominance of the crafts was maintained.

The city census of 1836 revealed that only 18 percent of Newark's population were foreign-born, chiefly Irish.[26] By 1850 the proportion of the population who were foreign-born had risen to 32 percent, with the Irish and Germans predominating (14 percent and 10 percent respectively). As in most large nineteenth-century cities, the size of the foreign-born population sharply distinguished Newark from the more rural areas of the state. In 1850 the foreign-born represented only 12 percent of the population of the state as a whole, less than they had in Newark fourteen years earlier. Between 1850 and 1860 the foreign-born population of both the city and the state increased so that 18 percent of the state's population and 37 percent of Newark's were foreign-born. At the state level the Irish were still more prevalent than the Germans, 9 percent and 5 percent of the population respectively, while in Newark the groups were then about equal (16 percent and 15 percent respectively).[27]

In the aggregate the birthplaces of members of the eight crafts were the same as those of the white male population of the city (Table 13). In 1850,

44 percent of the craftsmen were foreign-born and in 1860, 57 percent were, while 46 percent and 55 percent respectively of the comparable Newark population were foreign-born. In this way the crafts were a microcosm of the city: immigrants found the same range of opportunities in these industries that they did in the city as a whole, for many of the immigrants were at least semiskilled.

The labor force in the crafts was as diverse in ethnic background as it was in age. In 1850 between 37 and 49 percent of the workers in most crafts were foreign-born, much as Newark's men in general. Two crafts were exceptional. Four-fifths of the carpenters were native-born, while only one-third of the leather makers were. Most of the foreign-born leather makers were Irish (39 percent). The relationship of the ethnic structure of each craft to its age distribution shows how immigration and industrialization proceeded together.

All age groups of the carpenters were predominantly native-born in 1850 (Table 14); there had been no appreciable influx of foreigners into this trade. Almost one-third of the carpenters were Americans in their twenties. The maintenance of the traditional apprenticeship meant the foreign-born were excluded. In 1850, blacksmithing, the other craft that remained traditional in technique, included more foreign-born adults, both Irish and German, than did carpentry. But these were journeymen of the ages twenty-one to thirty. Those blacksmiths of apprenticeship age and those over forty (probably masters) were primarily native-born. This use of foreign-born journeymen, who may or may not have been skilled, might account for the much lower average wages of blacksmiths. But the apprenticeship system was still strong in both crafts, and each attracted native-born youth.

The labor force in shoemaking, which was in the first stage of industrialization in 1850 but stagnating, was rather like that of blacksmithing. Most of the older shoemakers were native-born, and there had been an influx of foreign-born journeymen aged twenty-one to thirty. Proportionately fewer of the apprentices in shoemaking, however, were native-born. The stagnation of this craft must have made it relatively unattractive to native-born youth, who presumably had more choice in a career.

The labor forces in the other crafts in the first stage of industrialization—saddle making, jewelry making, and trunk making—were distinctive. The majority were native-born, in their teens or their twenties. Most of the older workers were native-born too, but some Germans, generally under forty years of age, also worked in these crafts. The jewelry companies sent to Europe expressly for skilled German and French workers. With only the beginnings of task breakdown and the great expansion of markets, native-born youth saw opportunities for themselves in these crafts.

The industries that were most industrialized in 1850—hatting and leather making—contained the largest proportions of young Irishmen and the larg-

TABLE 14
Birthplace and Age of Male Workers by Craft

Craft and Age	1850				1860			
	U.S.	Ireland	Germany	Other	U.S.	Ireland	Germany	Other
Carpenters								
15–20	16.4	1.0	0.4	0.6	6.4	0.6	1.0	0.6
21–30	32.4	2.5	2.9	1.6	30.6	4.0	5.0	3.2
31–40	15.4	1.6	2.7	0.8	14.4	1.5	6.5	3.2
41+	15.0	2.1	2.1	2.5	13.1	1.5	5.6	2.6
Blacksmiths								
15–20	12.6	3.3	0.7	0.3	9.4	2.2	1.9	0.7
21–30	17.9	10.6	9.6	3.3	13.0	8.7	13.0	3.4
31–40	11.3	4.7	5.0	3.0	7.0	6.5	9.2	2.9
41+	13.6	1.7	1.3	1.0	10.1	2.9	5.8	3.1
Shoemakers								
15–20	5.2	1.4	1.9	1.6	2.9	1.1	0.7	0.5
21–30	15.9	9.0	7.8	3.8	6.3	6.7	8.8	3.1
31–40	13.5	2.7	5.1	2.3	9.8	6.9	14.0	4.4
41+	19.6	2.4	3.3	4.4	17.3	4.3	8.8	4.5
Saddlers								
15–20	20.1	2.4	6.0	2.2	11.3	4.4	9.1	1.9
21–30	19.2	3.8	10.6	2.6	13.3	7.1	13.3	2.7
31–40	10.8	1.5	5.1	1.1	8.3	2.5	9.5	2.3
41+	9.1	1.1	2.0	2.4	7.2	1.6	3.2	2.3
Jewelers								
15–20	29.0	1.7	2.7	2.7	14.6	1.1	4.1	2.1
21–30	19.3	1.0	14.3	4.6	31.7	0.6	7.9	3.8
31–40	7.3	0.6	6.2	2.9	8.4	0.3	9.3	2.7
41+	2.9	0.0	2.3	2.5	6.0	0.1	4.8	2.7
Trunk makers								
15–20	25.0	9.0	6.9	2.7	8.7	4.2	4.2	0.0
21–30	25.7	3.5	10.4	0.7	18.4	7.4	14.2	1.3
31–40	4.2	0.0	1.4	0.7	7.8	2.9	12.6	1.6
41+	7.6	0.0	1.4	0.7	5.2	0.6	9.7	1.0
Leather makers								
15–20	5.2	9.8	0.7	0.9	3.8	5.4	0.9	0.8
21–30	13.5	16.6	5.5	5.9	10.9	20.7	7.5	2.9
31–40	7.2	6.8	2.6	4.2	6.5	11.3	5.9	3.9
41+	10.1	5.5	1.3	4.1	6.8	5.2	5.1	2.6
Hatters								
15–20	15.5	7.4	1.1	1.4	8.0	3.4	4.0	1.8
21–30	16.2	10.1	2.9	7.2	13.1	12.7	6.3	3.8
31–40	9.7	4.9	0.9	5.2	7.6	6.5	3.1	5.3
41+	9.9	2.9	0.7	3.8	9.7	5.3	2.5	7.2

est percentages of the foreign-born in that year. Most of the oldest hatters, those likely to be employers, were native-born, while half of the oldest leather makers were. The younger workers tended to be foreign-born. Oscar Handlin has shown that the Irish in Boston formed a cheap labor pool that made industrialization possible, and the Irish in Newark may have had the same role.[28] The native-born young were not nearly as attracted to these trades, and manufacturers hired the most easily exploited foreigners, the unskilled Irish.

By 1860 all crafts except jewelry making had many more foreign members than they did in 1850. Most of the increase consisted of German workmen; the percentage of Irish employed stayed relatively stable, but the percentage of Germans increased. Germans entered the crafts at all levels since theirs was a heterogeneous migration of skilled and unskilled. The replacement of native teenagers by foreign-born adults continued in all crafts, regardless of the stage of industrialization. As the proportion of native-born apprentices in the traditional crafts—carpentry and blacksmithing—decreased, the proportion of immigrant journeymen, especially Germans, increased. The vast majority of those of apprenticeship age in carpentry and blacksmithing remained native-born, however, and, at least in carpentry, the foreign-born adults had probably been apprenticed in Europe.

In the 1850s crafts in the first stage of industrialization absorbed immigrants when less skilled labor was needed. As saddle making industrialized slowly in the 1850s and the proportion of native-born teenagers decreased, it absorbed many Germans under forty and also a few Irishmen aged fifteen to thirty. Trunk making, in keeping with its very rapid rate of change, experienced a wholesale reshuffling of the composition of its work force. The proportion of older workers increased, and by 1860 the vast majority of those over thirty years of age were German. With the drastic reduction in the percentage of the labor force under twenty, trunk making approximated the pattern of the other most industrialized crafts, hatting and leather making.

Though jewelry making, like saddle making, progressed to the second stage of industrialization in the 1850s, it did not absorb many immigrants. Jewelers remained skilled, and a five-year apprenticeship continued to exist in the craft in the late 1850s. The high wages paid made the craft attractive to natives. In the decade from 1850 to 1860 the majority of the new journeymen were the native-born apprentices who had been trained in the late 1840s. Though the age structure of the craft changed, the native-born journeymen remained, and the overall percentage of the native-born in the craft did not vary from 1850 to 1860. Shoemaking, on the other hand, which failed to industrialize further and continued to stagnate, absorbed only adult Germans; natives of all ages avoided the craft.

In hatting and leather making, which were both extensively mechanized, the Irish continued to be a major force, although Germans of all ages joined

them. Hatting and leather making still employed the largest number of foreign-born workers in 1860. Foreign-born journeymen entered all the crafts,
but the availability of adult foreigners, especially the Irish, who worked for
less and were semiskilled, allowed mechanization to proceed without the
substitution of child for adult labor. While the adult craftsmen desired to
protect their jobs from competition, their force alone would never have prevented the influx of teenagers into the crafts. The unreliability of boy labor,
the need for skill in many tasks and machine operations, and above all the
availability of other adults—immigrants—to compete with boy labor kept
the overall age distribution of the crafts from shifting in favor of youth. In
fact it shifted in favor of age.

Industrialization, interacting with community values, significantly altered
the composition of the labor force in the crafts. Newark did not resemble
the textile towns where men relied on the labor of women and children to
make ends meet. Adult men managed to protect their jobs because of their
own actions, the widespread animosity to female employment outside the
home, the nature of mechanization, and the immigration of masses of adult
male foreigners. The role of women and teenagers in production contracted,
and the effects of this change in the labor force for the family and society
were great. Within the family both women and teenage boys became more
dependent on their husbands and fathers for support. As the controls of
apprenticeship broke down, the community perceived an increase in juvenile delinquency and misbehavior. And, as more immigrants found jobs in
Newark, extreme ethnic and religious antagonisms developed that split local society and the working class.

CHAPTER 4

Family Life
Among Craftsmen

In preindustrial Newark, membership in the artisan class provided a definite status and a secure role in the polity. But new technologies destroyed the coherent social and economic ethic of the artisan class and turned employer and employee into antagonists. In the growing city, high residential mobility limited the effectiveness of the neighborhood as a source of identity and culture. The slow formation of new group networks on class, ethnic, or religious lines meant workers increasingly relied on their families for a sense of security or belonging. In preindustrial Newark, the family had played a central role in ordering and governing society through its supervision of the young, and it had been vital to the economy through its role in organizing labor and production. Although the family lost its role in production as industrialization spurred factory development, it remained the single institution on which the worker could rely for economic and emotional support. For this reason if for no other Newark's craftsmen sought to strengthen their families and to shield them from any disruptive forces in the industrial order.

Focusing on the British textile industry, historians have described industrialization as a cataclysm for workers' families: the paternal order destroyed as women and children became the chief breadwinners and families crumbling under the combined weight of impoverishment and violated traditions.[1] For Newark's craftsmen, however, the effects of industrialization on family life were not nearly so disastrous. The household lost its centrality in production, but most craftsmen retained the ability to support their families. Certain aspects of patriarchal control even intensified as wives and teenagers relied more heavily on their husbands and fathers for financial support. The father's role ceased to be that of the leader of a household enterprise and became that of the breadwinner and authority in a unit of consumption.

The persistence of preindustrial family values and concepts of male and female roles limited the changes in family life that were caused by industrialization. The institution of the family has changed greatly since 1800, but at a pace separate from that of industrialization.[2] Between 1800 and 1860, the continuities in the family style of craftsmen were great, and the changes that occurred were part of long-term trends that eventuated in the small companionate family. The very uniformity of family life among craftsmen forms a striking contrast with the variety of their work experiences and attests to their desire for permanence in a time of change.

Nineteenth-century Americans, rich and poor, shared many values. Between 1800 and 1860 Newark's craftsmen maintained some older patterns of family life and altered others, but they generally followed the same fashions as other Newarkers. While the Victorian family ideal found its most perfect embodiment in bourgeois homes, craftsmen patterned their households on the same lines as their employers. By excluding women and boys from their crafts, they could be the breadwinners for home-centered families and preserve patriarchal dominance.[3] Through adherence to a well-defined cycle of family formation, function, and dissolution, Newark's craftsmen created a stable, if malleable, institution to meet their needs. Craftsmen married late by present standards in order to accumulate some property or savings before taking on the support of a wife and children. They became fathers early in their marriages; by mid-century, however, craftsmen and their wives sought to limit the number of their children and to space them relatively close together. Craftsmen's households often included people besides their wives and children, primarily servants and employees if they were wealthy, boarders if not. As homes ceased to be centers of production and the apprenticeship system declined, however, the craftsman's household increasingly became limited to the nuclear family, and teenage boys—who as apprentices had lived out—began to stay home in large numbers.

The average young craftsman, in his mid-twenties, married a woman of similar age and ethnic background and had fathered one or two children in quick succession. Edward Knox, a Newark hatter, was in most ways the typical young family man. In 1860 Knox was thirty and his wife, Bridget, was thirty-two. They were both Irish-born, but their two children, Margaret, aged six, and John, aged four, had been born in New Jersey. Knox had accumulated $150 in personal property, probably before he had married. No others lived with the Knoxes, and Knox supported the family while Margaret went to school.[4]

For most craftsmen the cycle of family life began rather late, since they, like earlier generations of Americans, tried to accumulate some property before marrying. In colonial New England the average age at first marriage for men had ranged between twenty-five and twenty-seven years, and in

TABLE 15
Position in Household and Marital Status of Male Craftsmen by Age

Age	1850				1860			
	Head	Other[a]	Child	Married	Head	Other	Child	Married
21–25	28.5	50.8	20.7	34.3	31.4	39.4	29.2	33.1
26–30	62.4	32.4	5.2	66.9	68.6	22.9	8.5	73.0
31–35	77.6	19.5	2.8	80.7	82.3	15.1	2.6	85.8
36+	87.3	11.9	0.8	86.0	88.5	10.9	0.6	87.2

[a]"Other" means all those outside a nuclear family relationship. Most of these were boarders.

1890 the median age of American husbands at first marriage was still 26.1 years. Only in the twentieth century did men begin to marry earlier, so that by 1950 the median age at first marriage was 22.8 years.[5] In 1850 only one-third of Newark's craftsmen aged twenty-one through twenty-five were married and had established their own homes (Table 15). Another third married when they reached their late twenties; the most common age at first marriage for craftsmen was somewhere between twenty-six and thirty. A plateau of family formation was reached at age thirty-five, with just under 90 percent of the craftsmen married and heads of households. Almost every marriage led to the establishment of a separate household, since young workers did not marry until they could set up their own homes. There was no tradition in America of three-generation households, and the neolocal family clearly dominated. Industrialization did not so impoverish young workers that they had either to unduly delay marriage or to move in with parents. Indeed, by 1860 more of the craftsmen were marrying and setting up households while in their late twenties and early thirties. That is, marriage and headship came slightly earlier for the craftsmen in 1860, a movement toward the modern practice.

This pattern of family formation applied throughout American society; it was the norm for almost every group. Especially immovable was the average age at first marriage. For instance, in 1850 craftsmen as a group were slightly younger than the typical Newarker over fourteen and, as a consequence, slightly fewer craftsmen were married (52 percent vs. 59 percent). Also, variation in the age structures of the crafts accounted for the differences between them in percentage of married craftsmen. In 1850 the coefficient of correlation between the percentage of the workers in each craft over twenty-five years of age and the percentage married was .997; in 1860 the correlation coefficient was .976. Once adulthood was reached, occupation did not affect the timing of forming families and households.

The vast immigration of diverse cultural groups to Newark in this period might well have brought a new variety to local customs of marriage and

TABLE 16
Percentage of Male Craftsmen Who Were Married and Heads of Households
by Birthplace and Age

Age and Birthplace	1850		1860	
	% Head	% Married	% Head	% Married
21–25				
native-born	28.4	36.8	25.8	28.6
foreign-born	28.7	31.3	36.7	37.5
26–30				
native-born	69.5	77.8	59.6	70.1
foreign-born	57.1	58.9	74.4	74.9
31–35				
native-born	80.4	85.5	73.6	83.1
foreign-born	74.8	75.7	86.8	87.4
36+				
native-born	91.1	91.2	88.7	89.2
foreign-born	81.6	80.7	88.4	85.9

family life. It also might have disrupted family formation, since the sex ratio of male to female immigrants in the United States between 1820 and 1860 was 1.54, and most craftsmen, like Edward Knox, married women born in the same country as themselves (73 percent did so in 1850).[6] The immigration to Newark, however, was not as unbalanced; in 1860 there were as many foreign-born women as men in Essex County (35 percent of the men were foreign-born and 34 percent of the women). On the surface at least, the opportunities for the foreign-born to pursue a normal family life were greater in Newark than elsewhere.

Slight differences in the pattern of family formation did exist, however, between the native-born and the foreign-born craftsmen, especially in 1850 (Table 16). The percentages of native-born and foreign-born craftsmen under twenty-six years of age who were married or heads of households differed little in 1850. But among those over twenty-five, more of the natives were married and heads of household than were the foreign-born. Different cultural styles among the foreign-born and the recency of their migration caused the diversity between natives and foreigners in the rate of marriage. In 1850 the Irish formed the largest group of foreign-born craftsmen, and only 75 percent of the Irish craftsmen who were over thirty-five years of age were married and living with their spouses. Edward Knox was a typical craftsman but not as typical an Irishman. Other foreigners showed a greater propensity to marry; 81 percent of the Germans and other foreigners of that age group were married. Even more, 90 percent, of the natives were married, however. The large number of bachelors among the foreign-born

TABLE 17
Age of Oldest Child by Age of Father

Age group	1850					1860				
	0–5	6–10	11–15	16–20	21+	0–5	6–10	11–15	16–20	21+
21–25	98.7	1.3	—	—	—	94.2	5.8	—	—	—
26–30	77.9	21.1	0.9	—	—	68.8	28.4	2.4	0.4	—
31–35	39.5	43.1	16.7	0.7	—	41.4	42.4	15.3	0.8	—
36–40	12.5	29.5	43.1	14.6	0.4	22.0	32.8	32.2	12.0	1.0
41–50	4.5	10.4	25.5	41.8	17.8	7.5	12.4	23.8	36.3	20.0
51+	3.1	3.6	8.3	27.5	57.5	2.4	4.8	10.1	27.3	55.4
Average of										
8 crafts	35.0	20.0	17.8	16.1	11.2	35.7	23.8	15.6	13.4	11.5
Newark	33.6	17.6	19.2	19.2	10.4	33.8	26.6	13.7	17.3	8.6
			$\gamma = .8588$					$\gamma = .7980$		

craftsmen might have been a function of the recency or unsettling conditions of migration. By 1860, the foreign-born in general no longer lagged
much behind the natives in propensity to marry. Of craftsmen aged twenty-
one to twenty-five in 1860, more foreign-born than natives were married.
There were no appreciable differences between older craftsmen, but the foreign-born aged twenty-one to thirty-five were more often the heads of their
own households than were the native-born of the same ages, perhaps because they had left parents and relatives behind in migrating. There was
one vestige of cultural variance remaining, however. In 1860 only 82 percent of the Irish craftsmen over thirty-five years of age were married, while
90 percent of the Germans were, the same as the proportion of the native-
born who were married. In both 1850 and 1860 the Germans were married
more frequently than the Irish, and as more Germans settled in Newark
and the Irish ceased to predominate among the foreign-born, the marriage
customs of native and immigrant converged. The prevalence of bachelorhood among the Irish has often been noted and has continued well into the
twentieth century.[7] Even so, the differences in 1850 were not great enough
to separate the majority of the immigrant craftsmen from the dominant cultural tradition of the natives.

Craftsmen and their wives expected to have children, and, as in eighteenth-century American families, the first child typically was born a year
or two after the marriage took place.[8] When a craftsman in mid-nineteenth-
century Newark first became a father can be approximated by the age of his
oldest child. The age of the oldest child was strongly related to the age of
the father both among craftsmen and among the population as a whole
(Table 17).[9] If a craftsman in his twenties had children, they were usually
five years of age or younger. The average age of the oldest child increased
steadily thereafter as the age of the father increased. This relationship suggests that the craftsmen began to have children early in their marriages just

as preceding generations had, and, indeed, with earlier marriage and headship in 1860 came earlier fatherhood. In 1860 more of the craftsmen who were married in their twenties had at least one child before they reached age thirty than had been the case in 1850 (76 percent vs. 65 percent). And they had more children while they were in their twenties than the craftsmen of 1850 had had. In 1860, 23 percent of those aged twenty-six to thirty had more than two children, while in 1850 only 14 percent had that many. The first child continued to be born soon after the marriage, since in 1860 the age of the oldest child also increased for those who were in their twenties.

Although they had children early in their marriages, by mid-century Newark's craftsmen had joined with other Americans in having many fewer children than had been customary. Between the colonial period when large families were common and the mid-twentieth century when there were 2.3 children per family, a drastic change in American attitudes toward childbearing took place. This change occurred primarily in the nineteenth century, and in the cities, at least, it seems to have occurred before 1850. Although there was a fearful rise in infant mortality in nineteenth-century cities, the birthrate was also declining. At mid-century the average Newarker had 2.1 children, and the average craftsman had 2.2. Ten years later the statistics had barely varied. The average number of children in craftsmen's families remained at 2.2, and the average Newarker had 2.3 children. In this Newarkers and craftsmen differed little from Americans in other cities, such as Detroit, where the average family had 2.5 children. Only rural families remained larger, although not nearly as large as colonial ones had been. The average rural family in southern Michigan, for instance, had 3.1 children in 1850.[10]

John Logus, a Newark carpenter born in Hanover (Germany), typified the settled family man with a "modern" smaller family. In 1860 Logus, forty-one, lived with his wife, Caroline, aged forty-two, and three sons aged nine to sixteen. Mrs. Logus had been born in Hanover, too, and they had married and had their first two boys there before migrating to New Jersey where the third was born.[11]

Newarkers, like Logus, not only had fewer children than had been customary, but they spaced them closer together, limiting the years a wife spent in childbearing. In the late eighteenth century the median length of childbearing for women had been 17.4 years, but for those women born in the 1880s the duration of childbearing was shorter—it had dropped to 11.3 years.[12] There were only seven years between the Loguses' children. The range between the ages of the youngest and the oldest child in completed families of craftsmen provides a statistic comparable to the duration of childbearing. This range increased as the father aged for all craftsmen under fifty (Table 18); it decreased for those craftsmen over fifty as the older children left home. The group aged forty-one to fifty can be used, therefore, as a surrogate for completed families, those who have had all the children

TABLE 18
Range Between Ages of Oldest and Youngest Child by Age of Father

Age of Father	1850				1860			
	0–5	6–10	11–15	16+	0–5	6–10	11–15	16+
21–25	97.2	2.8	—	—	93.8	6.2	—	—
26–30	82.0	18.0	—	—	79.6	19.2	1.2	—
31–35	51.4	40.9	7.7	—	58.8	35.2	5.9	—
36–40	29.7	39.0	25.8	5.5	37.8	37.8	21.4	3.0
41–50	18.3	25.7	33.9	22.1	25.0	28.2	30.8	16.0
50+	25.9	28.6	25.2	20.4	28.6	32.2	24.7	14.5
Average of 8 crafts	39.9	29.6	20.1	10.4	47.6	29.8	16.4	6.3
Newark	31.8	37.5	21.6	9.1	43.8	31.3	17.9	7.2

they will have, but whose children have yet to leave home. In 1850 craftsmen aged forty-one to fifty had, on the average, only 3.5 children, and 44 percent had a range in the ages of their children of ten years or less, having moved toward the childbearing style of the early twentieth century. The average craftsman was more likely to have a range of five years or less between the ages of his oldest and youngest child than the average Newarker, suggesting that craftsmen were leading the way in spacing children closer together. The relatively small number of children in completed families, combined with the pattern of having them early in the marriage, is evidence that Newarkers were consciously limiting the number of children they had.

By 1860 real change toward the modern pattern had occurred. Not only were craftsmen having children earlier in 1860, but they were having even fewer of them and spacing them even closer together in the modern style. The average number of children living with craftsmen aged forty-one to fifty had declined to only 3.0. Also the range between the ages of these children was smaller; in 1860, 53 percent of these craftsmen had a range of ten years or less between their oldest and their youngest child.

Coming as it did so early, this change in childbearing cannot be attributed to industrialization. The urban pattern of small families was followed by craftsmen regardless of the level of industrialization they experienced. In 1850, the average number of children living with craftsmen aged forty-one to fifty ranged from 3.3 for those in traditional crafts to 3.5 for those in crafts in the first stage of industrialization and 3.6 for those in the second and third stages. This range is not sufficiently large to be statistically significant. In 1860, all had smaller families, the average ranging from 2.8 children living with those in crafts in the first and second stages of industrialization to 3.0 for those in traditional crafts and 3.2 for those in the third stage.

The declining birthrate was not a simple function of impoverishment either. The self-employed craftsmen did not have appreciably more children than the journeymen. In 1850 the average number of children living with those who were self-employed and aged forty-one to fifty was 3.7; in 1860 it was 3.1. Family limitation was a practice the whole urban society was adopting. This cultural unity reflected the continued economic dominance of adult males in the crafts. Industrialization did not strip from them the ability to follow widely held, if changing, family patterns.

The families of the middle-aged, such as that of John Logus, also reveal the extent to which the household had ceased to be a center of production. Logus' youngest son was in school, but his eldest son, John, had a steady position as a saddler's apprentice. Like most of Newark's craftsmen, Logus did not teach his own trade, carpentry, to his son, and his home was not a center of production nor a training ground for it.[13] In only a few short decades, industrialization had destroyed apprenticeship and moved production into factories. The ideal Victorian household shielded the family from the economic world, and produced only children and demand for goods. By mid-century the households of almost all craftsmen, regardless of trade, approximated this ideal. This further differentiated urban from rural households, as the latter still combined family and economic life. Even in those homes in Newark where three generations lived together, the day of the household enterprise had passed. Isaac Mills, a fifty-nine-year-old shoemaker, lived with his wife, their four unmarried children, their married son, Isaac S., and his wife and two children. Mills owned a combination shoe store and grocery, but no sons followed his trade; Isaac S. was a blacksmith and a younger son, Elias, was a carpenter.[14]

The overwhelming majority of craftsmen over thirty-five did not live with anyone who worked in the same industry (Table 19). Seventy-five percent had no such relationship in 1850, and 86 percent had none in 1860. Boys were not following in their fathers' footsteps, and boarders might be engaged in any business. In general what change took place from 1850 to 1860 was in the direction of a smaller proportion of craftsmen working in the same industry as others in their households. Deviations between crafts in the number working with others who lived with them were not related systematically to the stage of industrialization that the craft was experiencing.

In past centuries, many, if not most, households had contained members who did not belong to the nuclear family, since the concept of a traditional apprenticeship necessitated a wider "family." Even after the family lost its production function, however, rapid urbanization kept a type of "extended" household alive. Migrants from both America and Europe looked for a home environment when they left their natural families to seek work in the cities. Early American society saw the family setting as the proper one for the unattached person, and during a housing shortage in 1836 the local newspaper even asked Newarkers to help out by taking in boarders.[15] If a man had neither wife nor children, he was unlikely to live alone; less than 1

TABLE 19
Percentage of Males Over 35 With a Possible Work–Home Relationship by Craft

Craft	1850	1860
Carpentry	16.1	10.7
Blacksmithing	11.8	6.9
Shoemaking	27.9	13.9
Saddle making	28.3	16.9
Jewelry making	36.4	14.7
Trunk making	11.8	8.3
Leather making	23.3	12.0
Hatting	29.3	20.9
Average of 8 crafts	24.7	14.1

percent of the craftsmen did. A man with no family of his own either took in boarders, became a boarder himself, or lived with relatives. Not until the late nineteenth century did Americans begin to believe parental influence on the child was healthy while the influence of others—boarders and servants—was corrupting. In nineteenth-century America, many households contained boarders and servants; until at least 1920, 15 to 20 percent of all American families included boarders or lodgers. The decline to the present level of fewer than 5 percent of all households containing boarders began in the 1930s.[16]

Nineteenth-century households tended, therefore, to be larger than modern ones. There were 5.2 people in the household headed by the average craftsman in 1850. The households of the craftsmen were comparable in size to the households of the average Newarker and the average American, which contained 5.3 and 5.6 people respectively. Though a majority of the craftsmen lived with only their wives and children, 45 percent lived in households that included other people besides the nuclear family. This was characteristic of Newark households in general, 48 percent of which contained people who were not members of the nuclear family of the head. Such others in a nineteenth-century household could be grandparents or other relatives, employees, or boarders. While the censuses of 1850 and 1860 sporadically identified certain of these non-nuclear members as boarders, usually their relationship to the head of the household was not noted. But the isolated nuclear family was not the overwhelming norm in stark contrast to twentieth-century practice.

Men in all the crafts followed this pattern of taking others into their homes; the proportion varied from 39 to 49 percent. The only deviation from the norm was in jewelry making, where more of the craftsmen, 60 percent, had others living with them. Because boarding and living with relatives was so common, the decline of apprenticeship did not cause those in the industrialized crafts to abandon the "extended" household for the nuclear family in any greater numbers than those in traditional crafts. The nativity of the craftsmen did affect the prevalence of the nuclear family, however. A few more of the native-born craftsmen took others into their households than did the foreign-born, reflecting, perhaps, the number of relatives and friends the migrant had left behind. Forty-nine percent of the native-born craftsmen had others living with them; only 39 percent of the foreign-born did.

While craftsmen were moving toward modern family patterns in marriage and childbearing, they were also moving toward the modern norm of the isolated nuclear family. By 1860 only 29 percent of the craftsmen who were heads of households lived with people who were not members of their nuclear family. This new lower level was characteristic both of all groups within the population and of the city as a whole, as only 34 percent of Newarkers had others living with their nuclear family. Between 20 and 32 percent of the craftsmen lived in "extended" households, except for jewelers, 41 percent of whom took in others; in all crafts these figures represent a decline from the practice of a decade earlier. Much of this drop reflects the increase in the immigrant population, since only 21 percent of the foreign-born craftsmen, but 42 percent of the natives, took others into their homes. The slower growth rate of the city in the 1850s may have influenced this trend; proportionately fewer migrants needed homes in 1860 than during the tremendous expansion of the 1840s.

Because of this increase in the prevalence of the isolated nuclear family, the average craftsman's household decreased in size from 5.2 in 1850 to 4.8 in 1860, even though the average number of children remained the same. Similarly, the average household in Newark contained only 4.9 persons in 1860, although it had contained 5.3 a decade previously.

While the households of all craftsmen approached the Victorian ideal in form, those of the master craftsmen and the manufacturers most perfectly fit the stereotype. The household of David C. Keep exemplified the Victorian ideal. Keep was a partner in Field and Keep, jewelry manufacturers, a firm employing thirty-four hands in 1860 and using some steam-powered machinery. According to the census, he owned real property worth $4,000 and personal property worth $20,000 (his firm had a capital investment of $40,000). Keep was forty-eight and had been born in Massachusetts. His wife, Mary, was the same age and had been born in Rhode Island, as had their three children. The eldest child, Frederick, was twenty-one and employed as a clerk, probably for his father; two younger daughters were in school. As a manufacturer, rather than a master craftsman, Keep did not have apprentices living with him, but, like others in the bourgeoisie, he had a live-in servant, an Irishwoman named Mary Smith.[17]

Most masters and manufacturers, like Keep, had larger and more varied

TABLE 20
Percentage of Male Household Heads With Others in
Household by Value of Property

Value of property	1850	1860
None	40.3	28.2
$1–500	35.8	24.5
$501–1,500	47.2	19.0
$1,501–5,000	61.5	40.2
$5,001+	86.3	64.1

households than did their employees. In 1840 the average self-employed craftsman had 6.5 people in his household; in 1850 and 1860 he had 6.6 and 5.9. Journeymen always had smaller households: in 1840 and 1850 the average journeyman's household contained 5.1 members; in 1860 it had 4.7. The self-employed had larger households because they more often had people living with them who did not belong to their nuclear families: boarders, employees, relatives. In 1850, 72 percent of those who were self-employed had such others in their households, and 62 percent did in 1860. The majority of their employees did not; in 1850 only 41 percent of the journeymen had "extended" households, and in 1860 only 26 percent had. The reduction of household size among both the self-employed craftsmen and the journeymen was caused by the same trend toward expelling non-nuclear members from the household, but large households including people not in the nuclear family remained more characteristic of the self-employed than of their employees. The largest households of all belonged to the wealthiest manufacturers. While 62 percent of those craftsmen owning property worth over $1,500 but less than $5,000 had others in their households, in 1850, 86 percent of those owning property worth more than $5,000 did (Table 20). Many of these wealthier craftsmen had more servants or relatives living with them. Few had apprentices in their homes, however, and, like the journeymen, the self-employed rarely worked in the same industry as someone else in their household. In 1850, 73 percent of the journeymen and 70 percent of the self-employed craftsmen had no such relationship; in 1860, the figure was 83 percent in both categories.

As the craftsman's children grew older, they left home to establish their own families or board elsewhere, and the craftsman's household began to contract. Nathaniel Green, a fifty-three-year-old shoemaker, was typical of these older craftsmen. In 1860 Green lived with his wife Ann, aged fifty-two, and two teenage children, Maria and John. The Greens may well have had older children, but, if so, they had left their parents' home. Green, a New Yorker, had lived in Newark long enough to win the trust of his neighbors, who elected him ward constable in 1857. Green's daugher Maria, who was eighteen, worked as a tailoress to help with the family's support, while fourteen-year-old John was neither at work nor at school.[18]

Despite the decrease in the length of childbearing in the nineteenth century, most of the years of every marriage were taken up with childrearing. Given the relatively late age at marriage and the range between the ages of the oldest and the youngest child, the average craftsman, like Nathaniel Green, had dependent children to take care of for most of his adult years. In 1850 only 19 percent of the craftsmen fifty-one years of age and older had no children living with them. This was the common pattern of marriage in the eighteenth and nineteenth centuries. The age of companionship in marriage, when both spouses live beyond the period when their children are minors, did not arrive until the 1920s.[19]

This cycle of family formation, function, and dissolution was the norm for the vast majority of craftsmen. Their desires for family life went beyond issues of change at the work place and lent a uniformity to their lives that was missing otherwise. Fewer than 15 percent did not follow this pattern. Ten to fifteen percent of the craftsmen over thirty-five years of age were not living with a spouse; the exact proportions of bachelors, widowers, or divorcees are unknown. At least some were in the latter category; while still comparatively rare, the number of divorces granted was increasing.[20] Workers conformed to trends in bachelorhood, however. Few statistics are available for the colonial period, but in the late eighteenth century between 12 and 15 percent of Quakers who lived to age fifty never married; in 1950 the proportion of the total population who never married was 7 to 8 percent.[21] Men of the mid-nineteenth century probably fell within these limits for bachelorhood, although whether they more closely approximated the eighteenth or the twentieth-century pattern is not clear.

Within his smaller family, isolated from the production process, the craftsman retained dominance, although his role shifted from that of leader of the household enterprise to breadwinner. Craftsmen accepted this new role and sought to perpetuate it. Newark shoemakers, for instance, demanded an increase in wages in order to support their families.[22] Consumption became an important family activity, and the craftsman who was paid well and on time had secured not only economic justice but authority in his family. The *Newark Daily Eagle* described the "happiest mechanic" as one who came home with his pay on Saturday night, ready to indulge his wife's requests:

While supper is preparing the happy wife is busily interrogating him about this and that little requisite to be purchased, so that a mutual disposition is made of the funds according to the best rules of economy. Tea over, they wend their way to the market,... and the purchases are made. The dry goods stores are thronged to excess, shoe shops literally crammed, and ready made clothing houses beseiged, and so on, every place of merchandize receiving its patronage and support from the earnings of the hard working mechanic. The fair sex also mingle in the throng, moving leisurely along with an air of gaity toward the milliners' shops, to make some little purchase similar to what Miss So and So wore at such and such a place. These little articles are of course requisite, and without them, existence would be miserable.[23]

Although many workers, especially the unskilled, could not support their families unaided, most craftsmen could. Rather than maximize family income by having all work, they preferred to be the breadwinners, with the authority that role conferred, and to keep their wives and small children out of the labor force. They shared this preference with the Victorian bourgeoisie, although workers thus limited their families to a modest level of consumption. In some ways the craftsman's role as breadwinner was not new: wives and small children had rarely engaged in paid labor. Child labor had never been respectable except in the case of teenage apprentices; only pauper children were indentured at very young ages. Child labor did not figure prominently in the industrialization of crafts in Newark, and even the pro-manufacturer *Newark Daily Advertiser* decried the labor of children under twelve.[24] Although many craftsmen had worked at home before industrialization, there is no evidence that wives had helped them with production beyond doing any necessary sewing. Women usually retired from the paid labor force at marriage, and most wives, regardless of class, did not labor for wages either inside or outside the home. In Newark in 1860 only one out of five women over the age of fourteen was gainfully employed in manufacturing.[25]

The U.S. Censuses of Population do not provide information on the occupations of children under fifteen and their coverage of women's employment is incomplete, but inferences from census data suggest strongly that most craftsmen were the sole breadwinners in their families until their sons were teenagers. According to the census, in 1850 only 14 percent of the craftsmen who were not self-employed had wives or children who worked; in 1860 only 15 percent had. In this, journeymen conformed to the habits of their wealthier employers. Since self-employed craftsmen were older on the average than journeymen, they had more older children, and thus slightly more of them had dependents who worked (18 percent in 1850 and 24 percent in 1860).

It is unlikely that many craftsmen had wives or small children who worked, because if they had needed help in supporting their families they probably would have turned to their teenagers first. Fathers would have most needed help when they had the most children, in middle age, but only one-third of those in their forties and half of those over fifty had dependents who worked, even though almost 60 percent of fathers in their forties and 85 percent of fathers over fifty had children sixteen years of age or older living with them.[26] Neither industrialization nor wage level forced craftsmen to rely on their dependents to make ends meet; there were no systematic deviations between men in different crafts as to the number who had dependents who worked (Table 21).

TABLE 21
Percentage of Males With Dependents
Working by Craft and Age

Craft	1850		1860	
	41–50	51+	41–50	51+
Carpenters	34.0	47.8	34.7	50.0
Blacksmiths	22.9	38.9	43.6	60.6
Shoemakers	35.3	46.4	37.3	50.3
Saddlers	24.3	47.8	34.8	57.1
Jewelers	52.0	66.7	19.1	40.9
Trunk makers	33.3	57.1	50.0	52.4
Leather makers	37.5	52.2	36.8	49.3
Hatters	30.4	45.2	41.5	49.5
Average of 8 crafts	33.9	47.5	36.6	50.8

Craftsmen fought hard and successfully to close most paying jobs to women and children, and they did so in part to protect them from exploitation in the factories. During the strike of female and child operatives in Paterson textile factories in 1835, all the major crafts in Newark banded together to lend their support to the strikers. Whether their own crafts were being industrialized or not, the men rejected the exploitation of women and children through long hours, abuse, and cruelty.[27] They kept their own dependents out of such situations whenever possible.

Nor were craftsmen likely to take in boarders solely to help pay the rent. In 1840, on the average, 83 percent of the craftsmen who headed their households were the sole workers in them; in 1850 and 1860 the proportions were 68 percent and 69 percent. (The figure for 1840 may well represent the devastating effect of the depression on local employment, or it could be a gross inaccuracy in reporting.) In this case as in others, the households of the craftsmen were not unique. In the average Newarker's household, only one person, the father who was the head of the household, worked (67 percent of male-headed households had only one worker in 1850 and 1860). Comparison of the number working in each household and the number of households containing non-nuclear members provides further evidence for the economic dominance of the craftsman in his family. Since 45 percent of the craftsmen had non-nuclear members in their households in 1850, but 68 percent of them were the sole workers in their households, 13 percent of them were apparently supporting people besides those in their own nuclear families.

But how were craftsmen able to support their families unaided? Since the wages in Newark's most industrialized plants were generally lower than those in more traditional establishments, one would expect that by 1860 many workers might have found it impossible to be the sole support of their families. Despite the trend toward lower wages with industrialization, however, male craftsmen were advantaged compared with other workers. In 1848 laborers in Newark made only $1 per day, and the laborer who worked twenty days a month was lucky. But the average wage in each craft was more than $20 per month in 1850 (Table 6). In 1860, too, the average craftsman in any of the eight trades received as much or more than the average worker in manufacturing in Essex County ($23.40 per month).[28]

Significant differences in wage levels existed, however, within this group of eight crafts. In 1850 the wage hierarchy, from best to worst, was: jewelers, carpenters, hatters who used hand methods, leather makers, saddlers, blacksmiths, shoemakers, hatters working with machines, and trunk makers. The jewelers' wages were almost 50 percent higher than the trunk makers'. In 1860 the hierarchy by average wage was practically the same, but the range between the crafts' average wages had grown in the decade, so that the jewelers' average wage was twice that of the trunk makers.[29] These differences in wage levels were not a function of the age structure of the craft; those crafts with proportionately more young members did not necessarily pay the lowest average wages, even though boys might have been paid less than adults.

Because of the range in wage rates it is probable that craftsmen had widely differing standards of living, but the translation of wages into living standards is difficult. The knowledge of retail prices in other cities or estimates of the buying power of the dollar in general are not helpful, because of the importance of local variations. For instance, although close together and part of the same regional economy, Newark and New York City had different wage rates and different retail price levels; both wages and prices seem to have been lower in Newark than New York.

In 1846 the organizers of the local poor relief estimated the average cost of living in Newark for a family of five at $8 per week. Almost two years later their budget calculation yielded the same result.[30] These were spare budgets, with no allowance for savings or recreation; they included money spent for meals, fuel, clothing, furniture, rent, doctors, newspapers, church, and school. A much reprinted budget from Horace Greeley's *Daily Tribune* of 7 May 1851 set the weekly need of a Philadelphia worker's family of five at $10.37.[31] This budget and the two for Newark allow similar amounts for food ($4.20 for Newark, $4.26 for Philadelphia); fuel (40¢ each); and clothing and furniture ($2.45 for Philadelphia, $2 for Newark). Miscellaneous expenses were higher in Newark: 40¢ versus 26¢. The big difference was rent. In Philadelphia $3 per week was allotted for rent ($156 per year), while in Newark, supposedly, rent was $1 per week ($52 per year). Periodic reports that rents were substantially lower in Newark than in New York City suggest that this differential might have been accurate.

On this income, obviously, workers did not live at the level of their employers even though they were able to follow the same norms of family structure. The Philadelphia budget included two pounds of meat per day, staples, and coffee, tea, and sugar—adequate, but hardly sumptuous fare. The allotment for rent in Newark also presented severe constraints. Single-family dwellings, for instance, were preferred by those who could afford them. Seventy-three percent of the self-employed craftsmen lived in single-family dwellings in 1850, as did 74 percent of them in 1860. Only 52 percent of the journeymen in 1850 and 50 percent in 1860 could afford such dwellings. And those the workers lived in were doubtless inferior. Housing was a constant problem in Newark because of rapid population growth and sloppy construction; the poorer homes were built on half-reclaimed marshes that were a health hazard. Overcrowding has a habit, and in 1860 the newly appointed Health Commissioners reported that Newark's tenements were inhabited from cellar to garret. One or more families lived on each floor, making an average of eight families per building and two persons per room. The "eight families" often shared their building with a grocery or a small workshop.[32]

The budgets publicized by the charity workers suggest that $416 per year was the minimum needed to support a family of two adults and three children in Newark in the late 1840s at a near-subsistence level with no savings. At that rate only the jewelers, according to the average wage rate, could support a family of five at the minimal level, and they would have needed twelve months' work to do so (Table 6). Wages, however, may not have been as inadequate as they seem at first glance.

First, since the average married craftsman, as well as the average New-arker, had two children and not the three for which the budget allowed, he needed, perhaps, only $360 rather than $416 per year to support his family at the budget's level.[33] Also, if there was a correlation between age and wage level, the craftsmen with families might have been able to support them at the minimal level. To the extent that boy labor was cheap labor, the average wage paid in an industry with many teenage workers would not be the wage which the older workers in the craft were paid. If one could assume that the older men (those most likely to be married) made the higher wages, a very different picture of the adequacy of wages would result. This assumption is not unreasonable given the reluctance of craftsmen to be undercut by cheap "apprentice" labor.

For instance, in 1850 the jewelers were paid the highest average monthly wage, which yielded $393 a year.[34] But only about one-third of the jewelers were married.[35] If the married men, who were among the oldest workers, were paid the highest wages, all of them probably would have received the average of $393 per year or more. Since the married jewelers had an average of only 1.7 children, the typical married jeweler would have had more income than was required to meet minimum living expenses.

TABLE 22
Value of Property of Males by Craft

Craft	1850		1860		
	None	Some	None	$1-500	$501+
Carpenters	71.4	28.6	46.6	27.8	25.6
Blacksmiths	84.4	15.6	57.9	27.5	14.6
Shoemakers	85.0	15.0	43.3	37.4	19.2
Saddlers	89.4	10.6	58.7	27.5	13.8
Jewelers	87.9	12.1	57.7	24.8	17.4
Trunk makers	96.5	3.5	52.6	30.8	16.7
Leather makers	84.9	15.1	53.7	29.3	17.1
Hatters	88.2	11.8	62.6	25.7	11.8
Average craft	84.9	15.1	53.7	29.1	17.1
Newark	81.8	18.2	52.5	23.8	23.8

By the same logic (assuming the older craftsmen were paid the highest wages and that wages paid in a craft were distributed normally over its population), the carpenters, the hatters using traditional methods, the saddlers, and the leather makers would have had enough income to support their wives and children at the minimum level. Most of the blacksmiths with families could have supported them at the typical budget's level, but some could not have. Many, or perhaps all, of the trunk makers and the hatters in the mechanized plants would not have earned enough to support families at this minimal level. But the shoemakers fared worst. Two-thirds of the shoemakers were married, and they had an average of 2.3 children, but the average annual wage in shoemaking was $265, which was barely sufficient for three people. Even the married shoemakers who made more than the average wage might not have had enough for the minimal standard, and many were probably making less than the average. It was only among the shoemakers, the trunk makers, and the hatters in mechanized factories, therefore, that the father's role as breadwinner was clearly threatened. This suggests that the shoemakers and others who received low wages and had no "extra" dependents working lived at a level below that of the other workers or went into debt.[36]

The incomes of many craftsmen were adequate to support their families, and many also amassed some property. It was suggested in 1847, for instance, that a large number of the depositors at the Newark Savings Institution were mechanics and workingmen.[37] If their wages had been very deficient, even massive underconsumption would not have enabled craftsmen to save, since so few had dependents working. Although they may have had savings, however, few of the craftsmen owned real property in 1850 (Table 22). Carpenters, who could build their own houses and were comparatively well-paid, were more likely to own property (29 percent)

TABLE 23
Value of Property of Male Craftsmen by Age

| Age group | 1850 | | | | | 1860 | | | | |
	None	$1–500	$501–1,500	$1,501–5,000	$5,001+	None	$1–500	$501–1,500	$1,501–5,000	$5,001+
15–20	99.6	0.1	0.1	0.1	–	98.3	1.4	0.1	0.1	0.1
21–25	94.8	1.7	2.8	0.7	–	77.1	19.0	1.5	1.8	0.8
26–30	87.5	2.8	6.0	3.5	0.2	51.5	34.6	6.7	5.3	1.8
31–35	80.2	3.1	7.5	6.7	2.6	36.8	40.4	9.1	10.5	3.4
36–40	68.2	3.1	10.8	13.9	3.9	35.8	41.5	8.3	9.6	4.8
41–50	66.0	3.5	11.5	13.4	5.6	29.1	40.1	9.1	14.4	7.3
51+	65.0	1.5	10.8	14.6	8.0	26.4	32.6	9.1	17.9	14.0
		$\gamma = .6112$					$\gamma = .5523$			

than were the other craftsmen (less than 16 percent). Home ownership was valued for the respectability it conferred, but also for the security it brought; those who owned homes often had gardens, which gave them greater self-sufficiency.[38] But few craftsmen could save enough to invest in real estate. In 1860, when information on personal as well as real property is available, almost half of the craftsmen owned some, primarily personal property worth less than $500. In fact the proportion of those with no real property in 1850 is approximately equal to the proportion of those with property worth $500 or less in 1860, suggesting that many workers in 1850 did indeed have some savings. These eight crafts formed a representative cross section of the economy, and in the aggregate, craftsmen were no less wealthy than Newarkers in general; the extent of property ownership and the value of the property were similar.

There was no correlation between a craft's stage of industrialization and the proportion of its members owning property, or between wage level and property ownership, in part because the ownership of property was a function of age both for the craftsmen and for the population as a whole (Table 23).[39] Accumulating wealth, like forming a family, was part of a life cycle. In 1850, one-third of the craftsmen owned real property by the time they were over thirty-five. In 1860, when personal property was included, 74 percent had managed to accumulate property by the time they were over fifty, although almost none of those under twenty-one owned property. Half had managed to accumulate some property by the time they had reached thirty, before most of them would have had more than one small child to support. In middle age, when a man's family was largest, his wages might not have left anything extra for saving. But the average craftman's wealth did not decrease then, suggesting he was at last managing to break even.

Some of the personal property that craftsmen owned in 1860 may have come from advances in real wages during the 1850s that made saving easier. Precise calculation of such advances is not easy, however. Statistics on food prices in other New Jersey cities reveal that prices increased from 1851 to 1860, and the commodity index of wholesale prices was also higher in 1860 than in 1850. Indices of the cost of living in general indicate a 9 to 12 percent increase between 1850 and 1860.[40] If this kind of rise took place, the wages of blacksmiths barely kept up with inflation, while those of leather makers fell behind (Table 6). The other craftsmen, however, would have made gains in real wages between 1850 and 1860, and their standard of living or their ability to save would have risen.

While the structure of families and households was changing slowly across all levels of society, and craftsmen were perpetuating their role as head of the household, industrialization did directly affect the craftsmen's families. The most obvious alterations involved the role and position of their teenage sons. In the nineteenth century few teenagers were married or were independent heads of households. Less than 5 percent of Newarkers aged fifteen to twenty were heads of households or married in 1850 and 1860. Teenagers lived with their parents, in boarding houses and hotels, or as boarders in other people's households until they reached their majority. As traditional apprentices, they had lived with their masters; when masters began to take on many apprentices they often had boarded elsewhere. But when industrialization destroyed apprenticeship and increasingly eliminated teenagers from the work force, boys were forced to stay with their parents. The family style of the entire population was altered as male teenagers were pushed back into their natural families.[41] Between 1850 and 1860 alone there was a tremendous increase in the percentage of Newark's male teenagers who lived at home. Seventy-one percent of the young men aged fifteen to twenty lived with their parents in 1860, while only 40 percent had in 1850 (Table 24).

This shift toward the home was directly correlated with the extent of industrialization. In 1850, teenage workers in the most traditional crafts—carpentry, blacksmithing, and shoemaking—were most likely to live with people other than their parents, since apprenticeship was still the norm for the young in these trades. Between 1850 and 1860 the proportion of teenage workers living with their parents rather than with others increased in all the crafts, as the new style was affecting the whole society. In 1860, however, those teenagers in the most traditional crafts were still most likely to be living away from their parents (between 45 and 50 percent). Most teenagers working in the highly industrialized crafts, hatting and trunk making, lived with their parents (85 percent and 77 percent respectively). With time, the independence of the apprentice from his own family circle was lessened, and teenagers increasingly found employment only in unskilled jobs close to home.

Because of the move to factory labor, most teenagers did not work in the same industry as others in their households. In 1850 only one-fourth to one-half of the teenage members of most crafts were living with others who

TABLE 24
Position in Household of Male Craftsmen
Aged 15 to 20[a]

Craft	1850		1860	
	Child	Other	Child	Other
Carpenters	25.5	74.4	50.7	45.1
Blacksmiths	37.3	60.7	49.2	47.5
Shoemakers	46.6	52.2	50.0	50.0
Saddlers	66.9	32.4	68.0	29.5
Jewelers	55.2	44.2	66.7	32.1
Trunk makers	61.9	38.1	84.9	15.1
Leather makers	51.1	46.6	57.7	41.3
Hatters	65.2	34.7	77.0	22.4
Average of 8 crafts	53.6	45.7	65.5	32.9
Newark	40.0	58.3	70.7	29.3
Traditional	29.7	69.7	50.0	46.2
Stage one	58.0	41.4	50.0	50.0
Stage two	51.1	46.6	67.4	30.7
Stage three	65.2	34.7	72.5	26.9

[a]Rows do not add to 100 percent because teenage heads of households are not shown.

TABLE 25
Percentage Male Craftsmen Aged 15 to 20 Living With Others
Who Worked in the Same Industry

Craft	1850	1860
Carpenters	42.6	25.4
Blacksmiths	25.5	18.0
Shoemakers	76.1	70.7
Saddlers	25.2	21.2
Jewelers	39.1	31.4
Trunk makers	12.7	32.1
Leather makers	43.3	36.1
Hatters	39.7	39.7

worked in the same industry (Table 25). The only exceptions were in trunk making and shoemaking. Only 13 percent of the teenage trunk makers lived with fellow trunk makers, but three-fourths of the teenage shoemakers lived with other shoemakers. Few young men worked in shoemaking, and these needed familial or household ties to gain entry into the craft. In 1860 only one-fifth to two-fifths of the teenagers lived with fellow craftsmen. The teenage shoemakers remained exceptional: almost three-fourths lived with other shoemakers.

TABLE 26
Relationship Between Young Male Craftsmen and Those Who Worked
in the Same Industry

Age and Stage	1850				1860			
	Head or parent	Other	Child	Sibling	Head or parent	Other	Child	Sibling
15–20								
Traditional	—	75.5	22.6	1.9	—	44.8	41.4	13.8
Stage one	—	49.2	29.4	21.5	—	36.6	63.4	—
Stage two	—	56.4	30.8	12.8	—	26.4	34.1	39.6
Stage three	—	30.4	39.3	30.4	—	14.0	37.2	48.8
21–25								
Traditional	24.4	58.5	9.8	7.3	12.1	42.4	33.3	12.1
Stage one	13.3	55.8	18.3	12.5	13.5	64.9	21.6	—
Stage two	9.3	55.8	20.9	14.0	15.4	16.9	16.9	50.8
Stage three	4.2	62.5	16.7	16.7	12.8	17.0	31.9	38.3

Industrialization also altered the relationship between those few who still lived with someone working in the same craft. In 1850 teenagers in the traditional crafts tended to live with their masters rather than their fathers, learning their trade under the old form of discipline. Teenagers in the industrialized crafts more frequently lived with parents or siblings who worked in the same industry (Table 26); these were less frequently teachers, and, in the case of siblings, they were not disciplinarians either. By 1860 even fewer teenagers lived with masters, and those who lived and worked together tended to be relatives. The most traditional crafts, however, still had the highest proportion of teenagers living with their masters rather than their parents; in the most industrialized crafts, the prevalence of siblings working together increased. The typical relationship between work and home for those in their early twenties reinforces this picture of change with industrialization. In the traditional crafts many fewer workers who were in their twenties had siblings similarly employed. Family ties may have helped young men get jobs in the large factories, but in this situation the relationship between family and employment was much changed from the traditional one.

Industrialization destroyed production relationships within the household by abolishing apprenticeship and forcing teenagers to live with parents who could neither use their labor nor teach them skills. There were, however, exceptions to these patterns. In 1850 and 1860 leather makers failed to follow the norms. Fewer young leather makers lived at home and fewer of their parents or siblings worked in the leather industry than would be expected of a craft in that stage of development (only 13 percent had siblings in the same industry in 1850, and only 37 percent in 1860). Compared to other crafts, a much higher proportion of the young leather makers were foreign-born in both 1850 and 1860, and thus fewer of them may have had siblings or parents in this country. In 1850 the four crafts in the first stage of industrialization had a wide range in the percentage of teenagers living at home and working with parents or siblings. More young saddle makers (66 percent) than jewelers or shoemakers (47 percent and 42 percent) worked with relatives. The small number of teenagers in shoemaking sets it apart and accounts for the more traditional figures, while in jewelry making indentured apprenticeship lasted even after mechanization began.

Not only individual families, but all of local society felt the effect of industrialization on teenage employment. The community faced the ramifications of the disruption of apprenticeship and the system of discipline it enforced, almost immediately, as citizens perceived an increase in juvenile misbehavior in the 1830s. Juvenile delinquency or rowdyism produced much debate about the system of apprenticeship, since the apprentices were thought to be the perpetrators of these excesses. Idling on the street corners and verbally assaulting passers-by was the least of their sins, for on the streets they formed associations with those "more mature in vice." In places such as ten-pin alleys or in the fire houses, youths from sixteen to twenty years of age congregated at night to gamble, drink, and brawl. Now that apprentices received wages, they spent their money on "frivolous amusements and vicious habits" like shows, tobacco, and liquor, rather than living modestly and saving as they had been forced to do by the master in the old regime.[42]

At first, the public blamed the master craftsmen for the widespread juvenile misbehavior.[43] The law gave the master the power to protect the morals of his apprentice, since the typical indenture forbade actions such as gambling and fornication. But masters protested that "the spirit of the age is so democratic, that public sentiment recognizes little beyond the law of the family circle, and if a master attempts to control the movements of his apprentices after the usual hours of labor the sympathies of friends and the public are disastrously exerted to deflect the good results."[44] In the industrial world, the sanctions of a preindustrial era were losing their legitimacy.

Many masters were not, however, legally responsible for the actions of their apprentices, for there were often no written contracts. And the new realities often made it impossible for the master to control his apprentices even when contracts existed. In a firm that was in the first stages of industrialization the number of apprentices was often so large that all of them could not possibly live with the manufacturer and his family. The indentures suggest that most apprentices lived elsewhere, usually in boarding houses, outside the master's supervision after work. In the 1830s, Newark was flooded with transient young men who were not subject to family governance and had no stake in the social order of the community. One concerned citizen summed up the situation as follows:

Here lies the ground of complaint: *Masters* do not look after their *Servants* any further than to see that a certain amount of labor is performed by them in their shops. Their apprentices are scarcely known by the Boss: he sees them as he passes through his factory; he boards them in places where neither himself nor others have control—and is it to be wondered at that they should be led astray? Few would be willing in the country to send their sons to learn trades in this town, did they know that *big* boys and *little*, from 11 to 30 years of age, and upwards, are permitted to meet in gangs, and nightly parade our streets. Besides, gaming and other infamous houses, and grog shops, are suffered to exist in the place and are so many receptacles of iniquity, and schools of vice.[45]

In order to combat juvenile immorality, the community prescribed libraries, lectures, and evening classes for the apprentices' spare time. But none of these activities seemed to take root; every few years they became defunct and had to be reconstructed anew. In 1838 some thirty or forty apprentices started an Apprentices Lyceum for reading and debates. But their attempt to set up a Circulating Library was not as successful, since the trustees of the old Apprentices Library refused to let the young men use the volumes entrusted to them. The next year an Apprentices Association began giving night classes in reading, geography, and grammer for about two hundred young men. The classes continued through 1840, but then lapsed. In 1846 moralists complained again that nothing was being done for apprentices' education or enlightenment, and evening classes commenced once more, only to disappear by the next year. Some continued to hope that employers would help, and as late as 1856 the few large firms that paid for library privileges for their teenage workers were held up as an example to the majority who did not. These activities never busied more than a small percentage of the apprentices, however, and moralists continued to criticize the pursuits of the majority. Some Newarkers realized that education and libraries were not the whole answer to moral leisure-time pursuits, and they recommended other wholesome activities such as coffee houses, club or conversation rooms, or chess clubs. But in 1859 the Library remained the only place young workers could go at night that was free of liquor, gambling, or prostitutes.[46]

Although older Newarkers usually blamed the new crime and disorder in the city on apprentices, vagrant children rather than apprentices caused much of the crime problem. Even boys under twelve years of age committed robberies, and boys aged fourteen to sixteen formed gangs that were tied into networks of older, more vicious criminals. In keeping with their preferences for low taxes, however, Newarkers dealt with the delinquents in the most "inexpensive" way: children were put in jail with adults, where they were schooled to be hardened criminals.[47]

By the 1850s, critics began to shift the blame for juvenile misbehavior from masters to parents, who were not responding well to their new-found responsibilities for their teenage sons.[48] The family and its roles could not be adjusted overnight to such rapid change. Many an editorial bemoaned the state of families that lacked unity: "broken into as many fragments, as there are persons in them."[49] Noting the decline of the household as a production unit, the moralists complained that the home was becoming a hotel, in which each of the family members went his own way. The family did not gather together, when supervision of the young might occur, except at dinner and possibly tea. In the evening, especially, all the male members, except for small children, deserted the home for their favorite pleasures: theater, ballroom, or taproom. While the rights of parents were recognized, some Newarkers began to call for state intervention, even in the form of reform schools, to assume the duties parents could not or would not perform.[50] The parents of sixteen-year-old John Brady acknowledged their failure when they had him committed for vagrancy; he and his friends were in the habit of "wandering around the streets in the day time, begging and stealing their food, and sleeping in sheds and outhouses at night."[51] As families tried to control their own teenagers, perhaps for the first time, they had difficulty isolating them from the "vice" that was becoming more prevalent among adults in this growing city and from the ill effects of unemployment.

Industrialization may be credited with laying the material basis for adolescence as we know it and creating new responsibilities for parents by lessening opportunities for teenage employment. It also fostered the isolation of women in the home by moving the locale of production to factories but not opening jobs to women. In this way working-class men were able to approximate the ideals of the Victorian family. Although their standard of living was much lower than that of their employers, most craftsmen supported their nuclear families and kept them isolated from the world of work. The family became a specialized institution for childbearing and consumption when it lost its production function. Its social function also changed as new leisure activities separated men from women and the young from the old. In the family, craftsmen retained a measure of control over their lives and a source of their own self-respect as the old class structure was overturned, and they lost the status that mechanics had once had.

CHAPTER 5

Class and Status
in the Industrial City

Newark's craftsmen created stability in their family lives in this era of change, but industrialization revolutionized their relations with each other and with others in the community in only a few decades. Preindustrial Newark was predominantly Protestant and native-born, and was dominated by the artisan class. From their craft experiences and their American Protestant heritage, Newarkers had developed a world view that prized the skill, independence, and useful work of the mechanic. The institutions of the artisan class bound craftsmen together and cemented social networks in the community. As industrialization divided the self-employed craftsmen from their employees and caused changes in some trades but not others, the craftsmen ceased to have a common source of identification in their work, and the institutions proceeding from that identification withered. The large-scale immigration that accompanied industrialization destroyed the ethnic and religious homogeneity of the city.

From a variety of work experiences and a plethora of cultural and religious values, men forged new group identifications only with difficulty. By 1860, Newark's craftsmen had divided into two new classes, the working class and the bourgeoisie, each with a tangible existence in separate institutions and a sense of mutual opposition over the work situation and the virtue of business practices. At the same time, craftsmen, regardless of class, were drawn to coreligionists and those of similar ethnic background and warred with others when diverse values made a uniform social policy coercive. Until the middle of the twentieth century, when large-scale immigration ceased, American workers were caught between two identities: they were members of the working class but also members of ethnic or religious subcultures. Only in exceptional, usually transient, circumstances were they, like Newark's preindustrial artisans, able to give full allegiance to their class and their religious or ethnic group at the same time. To make sense of a complex world, they tended to delimit two separate spheres: work and "life." At work, members of the various ethnic and religious groups often surmounted their differences; they banded together in opposition to their employers, formed unions, and tried to better their working conditions. Outside the work place, however, they tended to go separate ways to distinct neighborhoods and segregated social groups, and to fight each other in the political arena over social policies that would conform to their differing values.[1]

Industrialization transformed Newark's class structure by destroying the foundations of accord between master and journeyman. With the advent of wholesale production, journeymen lost control over their wages, and with mechanization they lost control over their tools. The destruction of the artisan class was complete once journeymen could no longer expect to become self-employed. Many fewer craftsmen, proportionately, were self-employed in the 1840s and 1850s than had been previously; the chances of achieving this independence were slim when large capital outlays were necessary for machinery. In the new class structure of the nineteenth-century industrial cities, those who produced the same product were no longer automatically in the same class, as possession of capital rather than occupation became the basis for the division between men. Not only could few journeymen become manufacturers within their own craft, but few also found self-employment or better jobs in other fields. By the 1850s, only a handful crossed the line between employer and employee, and the relatively small number of employers in Newark's crafts had joined with other capitalists—both manufacturers and merchants—in opposition to those who worked for them. For their part, the employees in the crafts more and more realized their common interests with other wage earners as the membership of the classes became fixed.

The new self-employment opportunities created by industrialization did not equal those lost because of the changing scale of production. In the replacement of most retail production by wholesale manufacturing, a few manufacturers succeeded a multitude of master craftsmen. In 1840, 17.3 percent of the heads of household who worked in the eight crafts were self-employed. In 1850 only 11.5 percent were, and by 1860 there had been a further decline to 8.7 percent self-employed. Regardless of the opportunities for some individuals, under the impact of industrialization the percentage of self-employed had been halved among older men with families to support. The proportion of all craftsmen who were self-employed was even lower. In 1850 and 1860, when information on all male members of crafts is available, only 6.9 percent and 6.1 percent of the male craftsmen were self-employed. This low rate of self-employment was characteristic of Newark's male population in general; in 1850 only 6.2 percent of the white

TABLE 27
Percentage of Male Household Heads Who Were Self-Employed by Craft

Craft	1840[a]	1850	1860
Carpenters	19.4	4.9	3.7
Blacksmiths	5.1	7.8	7.4
Shoemakers	13.3	10.6	12.7
Saddlers	17.9	6.3	7.1
Jewelers	42.3	22.2	14.3
Trunk makers	38.5	19.0	7.2
Leather makers	32.4	14.6	7.4
Hatters	15.2	16.0	8.1
Average of eight crafts	17.3	11.5	8.7

[a]Includes all listed in 1840 census manuscript who were also listed in the city directory of that year as working in the crafts.

males over fourteen years of age in Newark were self-employed, while 8.8 percent were in 1860.

Industrialization adversely affected self-employment in all the crafts, but estimating the extent of self-employment is difficult, since men often did not designate themselves as such at this time. A man calling himself a "saddler" might work in a large factory or own one. Advertisements in city and business directories help to identify owners and partners, but they never listed many small operations, especially those of carpenters or blacksmiths. The estimates for self-employment among carpenters or blacksmiths, therefore, are probably highly inaccurate. Only in the six crafts that were to some extent industrialized and had larger firms are the data on self-employment accurate enough to reveal the effects of industrialization.

In 1840 these six crafts fell into two groups in terms of the percentage of household heads who were self-employed (Table 27). A fairly large percentage of jewelers, trunk makers, and leather makers were self-employed; many fewer shoemakers, hatters, and saddlers were. Forty-two percent of the jewelers and 39 percent of the trunk makers who were heads of households were self-employed in 1840 when these crafts were practiced on a small scale using traditional methods. In the next two decades, as these crafts became industrialized, the percentage of household heads who were self-employed declined by two-thirds in jewelry making and four-fifths in trunk making. Leather making had entered the first stage of industrialization in the late 1830s, but one-third of its members who headed households were still self-employed. After twenty years of further industrialization, however, only one-fourth as many leather makers who were heads of households were self-employed. The other three crafts, which were more industrialized in 1840, had lower levels of self-employment: 13 percent of the shoemakers, 15 percent of the hatters, and 18 percent of the saddlers who headed households were self-employed then. Shoemaking and saddle making were in the first stage of industrialization; hatting was in the second. All were characterized by some large factories producing for regional and national markets, depressing the rate of self-employment. Since shoemaking stagnated in the coming years, the percentage of self-employed barely fluctuated. Hatting and saddle making each moved through one more stage of industrialization, and each experienced over a 50 percent decline in the percentage of household heads who were self-employed. By 1860 there was a uniformly low level of self-employment among the household heads in all the crafts.

Since the opportunities for self-employment in manufacturing were decreasing overall, upward mobility within a craft was fairly unusual. In any five-year period, few of Newark's craftsmen who stayed in town more than one year rose to self-employment within their fields, although one or two employers lost their businesses. There was more occupational mobility between 1836 and 1840 than in later years, but at that time barely 3 percent of the adult males in the crafts became self-employed (Table 28).[2] Even this minimal move to self-employment may have resulted primarily from the depression in this period: as large companies closed, their best workers tried to go into business on their own.

Few craftsmen were able to rise to jobs of higher status or reward in other fields. In any five-year period from 1836 to 1860 there was little movement into or out of the eight crafts studied; 6 percent or less of the craftsmen who stayed in Newark more than one year left their trades for other occupations, while 4 percent or less of the craftsmen came to their trades from other jobs.[3] Regardless of the extent of industrialization or economic conditions, the craftsmen stayed with their trades; in any five-year period, between 85 and 95 percent of the members of each craft neither left their trade for another job nor entered the trade after working at something else. The workers' ability to engage in job actions and form unions was built on this stability. Trunk making provided the only exception to this pattern: between 1836 and 1840, 30 percent of the trunk makers changed their occupation; between 1846 and 1850 the figure was 21 percent. There were, however, so few trunk makers in those decades that these figures may not be significant. In the 1850s, when the size of the work force in trunk making had increased, trunk makers were as stable occupationally as workers in other crafts.

Newark's economic development determined the types of occupational changes which craftsmen could have made, and most of the jobs available in Newark were in manufacturing, in industries that were or had been skilled trades (Table 12). In 1850, 66 percent of the men of Newark worked in "skilled" crafts, but the nature of those jobs was changing. From the analysis of eight crafts it is clear that industrialization had obliterated some of the necessity for skill in those trades. Presumably some of the other

TABLE 28
Movement to and from Self-Employed
Status for Male Craftsmen[a]

Period	None	Gained self-employed status	Lost self-employed status	Gained and lost again
1836–40	95.7	3.5	0.4	0.4
1846–50	97.7	1.6	0.6	0.1
1856–60	98.5	1.1	0.3	0.1

[a]Data derived from Newark city directories.

"skilled" occupations not studied here also included unskilled or semi-skilled workers because of industrialization. Only 14 percent of the men were in white collar jobs, and there may well have been relatively fewer jobs available in commerce in Newark than in other cities, because of the preponderance of manufacturing. Another 5 percent of Newark's white males had no occupation, and 15 percent were definitely in low-status jobs—10 percent in unskilled and 5 percent in semiskilled jobs.

But in only a decade further economic development had produced an important change in Newark's occupational structure. By 1860 only 54 percent of Newark's white men over fourteen worked at jobs categorized as skilled, and, considering the increased pace of industrialization in the eight crafts studied, it is probable that many of those listed as skilled were not. The proportion of white collar jobs remained stationary during the decade. The shift was from the skilled category to the unskilled, the semiskilled, and the unemployed; one-third of the men over fourteen were in these categories in 1860, while only 20 percent were in 1850. As fewer and fewer teenagers were hired in the crafts, more young people found no job opportunities, which boosted the unemployment rate. More men of all ages had jobs demanding no skill. With the declining size of the skilled category and the stability of the proportion of white collar jobs, competition for places "at the top" was increasing and opportunity was decreasing.

For the 6 percent of the craftsmen who left their trades, this decline in opportunities severely limited the possibilities for upward mobility, for moving to jobs of greater prestige and reward. In the period 1836 to 1840, 86 percent of those who left one of the eight crafts studied entered other skilled trades or white collar jobs.[4] Seven percent took up agricultural pursuits, and only 8 percent went to unskilled or semiskilled jobs. Few craftsmen experienced downward mobility even in this time of depression, but a decade later craftsmen did not fare quite as well. Between 1846 and 1850, only 32 percent left for other crafts; none took up agriculture; but 22 percent were seemingly downwardly mobile to unskilled or semiskilled occupations. Craftsmen were still rather advantaged, however, since a disproportionate number of them (45 percent) took the relatively scarce white collar jobs, which comprised only 14 percent of the jobs in Newark. In the period 1856 to 1860 even more of the craftsmen seemed to be downwardly mobile, however: 28 percent of those who left their crafts entered unskilled or semiskilled jobs, a change that paralleled the expansion of these categories of jobs in the city. Forty-one percent of the craftsmen who switched still went to white collar jobs. In each period, about one-fourth of those who left their crafts became proprietors of non-manufacturing enterprises, usually groceries or small stores. Although the majority of the craftsmen were still not downwardly mobile in the classical sense, the contraction of opportunity between 1840 and 1860 is clear.

Although a disproportionate number of craftsmen obtained white collar jobs, few experienced real upward mobility; they were more likely to switch to a job of comparable status. During each period, workers in those trades that maintained traditional technology and structure went primarily to other skilled crafts if they changed their occupations (Table 29). In contrast, those craftsmen in industrializing trades were more likely to take white collar jobs when they switched, and far fewer of them took up other crafts. This pattern suggests that changing from a blue collar to a white collar job may not have been "upward mobility." It would seem that much of the movement to white collar occupations, especially grocery-keeping and the like, by those whose crafts were in the first and second stages of industrialization, was the reaction of skilled workers who saw no future for themselves in their trades. Having managed to save a little money they struck out in new directions. They were in no sense becoming the equals of the large manufacturers, however. By the late 1850s, 43 percent of those leaving the most highly industrialized crafts—leather making, hatting, and trunk making—were going to unskilled or semiskilled jobs. Given the low skill level required in highly industrialized crafts, such a move can probably not be classified as downward mobility. Many shifts in occupation would seem to have been horizontal—to jobs of equal challenge and prestige—rather than vertical.

The comparative lack of movement toward either self-employment or more prestigious white collar work meant that the classes—capitalist and working—became clearly divided from each other. Demographic differences between the self-employed craftsmen and their employees deepened the gulf between the classes. The self-employed were older and more often native-born than the journeymen. In 1850 the average self-employed craftsman was thirty-eight years old, while the average journeyman was thirty.[5] In 1860 the differential remained, and the mean ages were forty-two and thirty-two respectively. Although ethnic variety cut across class lines, the self-employed were more likely to be native-born than the journeymen. Seventy-eight percent of the self-employed were native-born in 1850, and

TABLE 29
Status of New Occupation by Stage of Industrialization of Craft[a]

Stage of industrialization	Un- or semiskilled	Skilled	Nonmanufacturing proprietorship	Other white collar	Other
1836–1840					
Traditional	2.0	60.0	20.0	14.0	4.0
One & Two	13.0	22.2	33.4	22.2	9.3
1846–1850					
Traditional	27.8	47.3	11.1	13.9	—
One	21.6	30.8	24.6	23.1	—
Two & Three	17.3	17.3	34.5	31.0	—
1856–1860					
Traditional	22.4	44.8	15.5	17.3	—
One	—	38.1	42.9	19.0	—
Two	14.7	35.3	17.7	29.4	2.9
Three	43.0	17.4	25.6	12.8	1.2

[a]See Appendix C for classification of occupations.

TABLE 30
Employment Status by Value of Property
for Male Craftsmen

Status	None	$1–500	$501–1,500	$1,501–5,000	$5,001+
			1850		
Self-employed	47.3	2.3	9.0	23.8	17.6
Employees	87.6	2.0	5.4	4.2	0.8
			1860		
Self-employed	17.3	23.8	7.0	21.4	30.4
Employees	56.1	29.5	5.8	6.6	2.0

68 percent were in 1860. Far fewer of the journeymen were native-born in 1850, only 55 percent. In 1860 the majority of them, 59 percent, were foreign-born. Cultural variation thus reinforced the perception of class differences to some extent.

The greatest difference between the classes, however, was in their standard of living and their wealth. As is to be expected from their greater age, the self-employed were more likely to own property than the journeymen. But their property was also more valuable than that owned by journeymen (Table 30), so that their standard of living was much more luxurious. In 1850, 41 percent of the self-employed owned real property worth over $1,500, but only 5 percent of the journeymen owned such property. In 1860 over 50 percent of the self-employed owned property worth more than

$1,500, while 9 percent of the journeymen did. The journeymen owning property had small homes or savings; the employers owned the more valuable productive apparatus—machines and buildings. What is perhaps more surprising is that some of the self-employed owned no property; in 1850 only half of them owned real estate. This demonstrates the importance of rental properties in the establishment of small businesses and the limited capital base on which many were founded. In 1860, when personal property was included in the census, 17 percent of the self-employed still claimed no assets, although it is likely that some refused to provide such information to the census taker, deciding this was not a proper question. Although many craftsmen owned small amounts of property, especially personal property worth less than $500, only a few of them chose to use this property as capital. That only a few with small resources used them to achieve self-employment suggests the limited prospects of success for small producers in the industrial age.

As industrialization destroyed the unity of journeyman and master, the self-image of craftsmen began to change. Working-class consciousness did not arise full-blown in the 1830s, however, for the "mechanic" continued to be the exemplar of the Newark worker. Because of the diversity of workers' experiences with industrialization, many citizens failed to notice that the interests of journeymen and masters had diverged by the mid-1830s. When such tensions surfaced during political campaigns, citizens accused "artful politicians" of trying to divide and conquer the craftsmen by pitting employee against employer. A pro-Whig "mechanic," exemplifying the traditional meaning of the term, wrote that the tariff was good for journeymen as well as masters, since many "doubtless calculate to be employers, someday yourselves."[6]

But those most immediately involved with this drastic change in the methods of production no longer believed the interests of employers and employees to be the same, nor did they use the term "mechanic" to designate both. Journeymen began to appropriate the term "mechanic" for themselves and to express their realization of the gap between them and their employers. In a letter to the local newspaper, one unemployed "mechanic" wondered if the employers were suffering as much as the "mechanics," i.e., journeymen, from a recession.[7]

The result of this consciousness of the change in the effective relationship between employer and employee was that by 1834 Newark's journeymen in many crafts had formed trade unions that excluded the self-employed. Among the crafts that did not experience industrialization, the carpenters, masons, house painters, and building laborers formed unions, because of the role of the contractor as middleman in construction. All other unions formed were in crafts which were industrializing. Among the shoemakers there were five unions for men, based on type of work, and one for women.

There were two unions among leather makers, one of hatters, and one of saddle and harness makers. Unions also were formed by stone cutters, coach makers, and silver platers and metal workers.[8] In June 1834 most of Newark's journeymen's societies confederated in the Newark Trades Union, which joined with the General Trades Union of New York City and unions from other cities to form the National Trades Union. The Newark Trades Union, the city's first labor council, held regular meetings and, in the fall of 1834, set forth its principles publicly. Its objective was "to promote the general welfare of the mechanics of Newark and to sustain their pecuniary interests."[9] Although they used the term "mechanic," the unions were applying it only to journeymen, as they viewed the threats to mechanics' "pecuniary interests" as emanating from their employers.

The hostility between employer and employee, though new, was deeply felt. The newspaper *The National Trades Union,* responding to a diatribe against it by the *Newark Daily Advertiser,* expressed its view of employer-employee relations as follows:

The journeymen never have, nor never can meet their employers on fair and equal terms, unless they have some ostensible bond of union among themselves. The difference in the circumstances attending the situation of the two classes, precludes the possibility of the thing. The employers possess a great many advantages over the journeymen: and among the most important is wealth—and wealth is power; and we all know how prone any set of men are to exert whatever power they may possess to the advancement of their own private views, without regard to the injury they may occasion to others. The employers possess the power, and have, upon many occasions, exerted it to alter and settle, in an arbitrary manner, the price of labour, without reference to the relations of demand and supply, the scarcity or superabundance of money, and the circumstances, which alone should affect the rise or fall of wages.[10]

Journeymen did not reject the concept of private enterprise, but they realized that in the industrial world it led to their exploitation by employers. The individualism implied in traditional notions of private enterprise was an appropriate theory only for the preindustrial world in which the journeyman had exercised power through his monopoly of skill and tools and the master had faced no sharp competition to drive down prices. In the new industrial world journeymen could be equal only by combining.

This awareness of the altered power relations between employer and journeymen was coupled, however, with the journeymen's heritage from the artisan world view. The platforms of the National Trades Union were imbued with the labor theory of value, and Newark's journeymen criticized their employers for ignoring the old standards. In 1835, a committee of Newark saddlers and harness makers charged that one firm had "divided among *three* individuals the sum of $60,000, being the profits of last year's

business; whilst over *one hundred* hard working journeymen, the real producers in their employment, realized only $5000 over their necessary ex-
penses."[11] Journeymen viewed themselves as the producers of wealth and
manufacturers who did not engage in manual labor as the unjust ap-
propriators of that wealth.

The Trades Unions expressed the nascent class consciousness of journeymen, and the opposition to them revealed its analogue among employers.
Newark employers objected not so much to granting wage increases in prosperous times as to the Trades Union itself. They and their allies in the community saw anything that set the poor against the rich as "ruinous,"
insisting that there was no real basis for opposition between employer and
employee. From their artisan heritage, manufacturers saw themselves as
"producers" too, and considered their employees' interests as identical with
their own.[12]

The employers combined to destroy the Newark Trades Union, first by
trying to turn public opinion against it. They charged that the journeymen
were violating the mechanics' ideology by promoting monopolies in the
form of corporations. In Jacksonian America this was a potent criticism, for
artisans and small businessmen still imbued with the old world view considered corporations as unfair competition. Notices, apparently false ones, appeared in the local press stating that the Journeymen Cordwainers and the
Journeymen Saddle and Harness Makers Unions were applying to the state
legislature for corporate charters. This would have allowed them to form
producers' cooperatives, which were common in American cities in the
1820s and 1830s.[13] The earliest cooperatives were marketing warehouses established by small manufacturers to provide them access to the wholesale,
as well as the retail, trade. By the mid-1830s there was a fairly strong movement for cooperative warehouses organized through journeymen's unions;
many workmen could pool their meager savings and make themselves employers. Cooperatives usually arose after labor disputes so that the workers
could compete with their employers, and they expressed the widespread desire among journeymen for the independence that was their heritage. The
cooperatives would secure materials and give them on credit to journeymen
who could not secure credit through other means. As long as the journeymen owned their tools, a cooperative could enable them to be independent
producers. The Journeymen Cordwainers of Newark charged, however,
that they had not applied for a corporate charter and that:

We entirely disapprove of the incorporation of Companies, for carrying on manual
mechanical business, inasmuch as we believe their tendency is to eventuate in and
produce monopolies, thereby crippling the energies of individual enterprise, and
invading the rights of smaller capitalists.[14]

The journeymen accepted private enterprise as it had been practiced in preindustrial Newark, and rejected the new world of concentrated capital. Their employers, however, were not above making false accusations in their campaign to destroy the Trades Union.

But Newark's leather dealers made a more destructive assault on the Trades Union than the charge of monopoly. The journeymen curriers produced for employers who gave them the materials, paid them wages, and marketed the products. When the curriers struck for higher wages, the leather dealers of Newark combined with those of New York and Brooklyn to blacklist employees and to advertise throughout the country for strike breakers. The employers offered the piece rate the strikers were asking and more to those who would bolt the union. Even though the shoemakers of Newark engaged in a boycott of leather to help the striking curriers, the unions could not defeat the unified employers, and the leather dealers were successful in breaking the union. Following their lead, the hat manufacturers united in 1836 and fired all hatters who refused to desert the Trades Union.[15]

Although the objective reality of the class structure was changing and many journeymen recognized that fact, vestiges of the old cooperation between master and journeyman remained. An alternate response to inflation was to form consumers' cooperatives, which did not divide employers and employees the way unions and strikes did. One such cooperative formed in Newark in 1836 when all "mechanics" were requested to consider the "extravagant prices of Provisions, Rents, etc."[16] A Mechanics' Grocery was established, but nothing more is known of it. Employer and employee also joined together in other ways. In response to the growing insecurity caused by the reliance on wider markets, several more mutual benefit societies arose in the city in the 1830s: the Mutual Benefit Society of Mechanics, the Newark Mutual Aid Society, and the Newark Hibernian Provident Society. These were multi-class, multi-craft organizations that included employers and employees. Although many unions were also mutual benefit societies, other craft-based benefit societies existed, like the House Carpenters' and Masons' Benevolent Association, which included both employer and employee. In addition, some cultural life still flourished in the style of the mechanics' tradition. A Journeymen Mechanics Debating Society met, discussing such topics as "Is Conscience an innate or acquired principle?" The Newark Mechanics Association continued to sponsor lectures on such topics as natural philosophy, but it failed to grow and remained composed of an elite of the craftsmen.[17]

The concerted action of the craftsmen of Newark, both employers and employees, to aid other workers also reflected the continuation of some solidarity among "mechanics." In 1835, during the strike of the female and child operatives at the Paterson textile mills, each trade in Newark organized itself for the collection of funds for the strikers.[18] Men in traditional crafts like blacksmithing, which remained unchanged and without union organization before 1860, and jewelry making, in which no organized journeymen's group arose until the 1850s, joined with journeymen in industrializing crafts to protest the position of the Paterson manufacturers. All those who valued the preindustrial traditions, both journeymen and masters, viewed the harbingers of the new order, the manufacturers, with alarm.

The ceremonial culmination of the old era of employer-employee relations in the crafts and of the revered place of the mechanic in the community occurred in 1834 and 1835. The craftsmen had continued to dominate the city's status hierarchy in the early 1830s: in June 1833 the "different mechanical societies, and associations of mechanics" welcomed President Jackson to Newark. The dominance of the craftsmen at ceremonial occasions and the first flush of journeymen's class consciousness coincided in 1835, when the journeymen's unions in saddle and harness making, carpentry, shoemaking, and hatting marched in the Fourth of July parade just as their predecessors had in 1826. Moses Lee of the Cordwainers Society read the Declaration of Independence at the celebration, and S. B. Lyon led them in a toast to the National Trades' Union.[19]

But within months both the vestiges of mechanics' unity and the journeymen's unions were gone. The panic of 1837 produced a depression that destroyed firms, large and small, but which also exposed both the weakness of the new class allegiances and the bankruptcy of the old. This was the first modern industrial depression, but craftsmen responded to it as individuals; class consciousness was not strong enough to foster united action and the journeymen's societies collapsed. While some reported that "a hostile feeling, on the part of many of the poor and laboring classes, continues against those who are supposed to be a little better off," workers did not organize against the wealthy.[20] Some of the latter did hire private watchmen to guard their property, however. Other Newarkers left the city, lured away by newspaper advertisements for jobs in the West and the South or by the dream of starting over on the frontier. In 1838 a meeting of the "enterprising" was called to form an association for moving to the West, and some people did move to Illinois under the auspices of the association. Many of those who left the city were young men, and the usually popular fire companies became so understaffed they had to advertise for new members.

Those who stayed through the first difficult period faced further personal adjustments. Most unemployed workmen who stayed in the city worked out personal responses with the help of their families. Those who had some small savings could find alternatives to their customary employments. One man bought two cows and sold milk until he became re-employed. Others engaged in agriculture as some of the land that had been marked off as building lots during the speculative period went back into cultivation. While life was hard, it was not impossible, and only rare cases of suicide were reported to have been caused by impoverishment. Most survived somehow.[21]

During the depression, the idea of the unity of master and journeyman faded completely and with it went the institutions created by mechanics, like the Newark Mechanics Association. After the depression, there would be journeymen's unions, apprentices' groups, and employers' associations, but no longer would there be craft groups including men of all statuses within one trade, nor would "mechanics" engage in group action as they had in aid of the Paterson strikers. The mechanics as a group lost their status in the community in the late 1830s. In 1836 the employers and their allies in the community recaptured the celebration of American Independence from the journeymen; of the craftsmen, only the coach makers, saddle and harness makers, and tailors marched in the Independence Day parade. Other participants included the Hibernian Provident Society, the English Republican Society, and the Mutual Aid Society. No toasts were drunk to unions, much less the Trades Union, as had been done the previous year. In subsequent years no group composed solely of one craft, nor any union, was ever involved in the parade or the dinner, and the industrial processions disappeared. The Society of Cincinnati ran the celebration, and the new associations that came to dominate the city's social life, militia companies, benevolent societies, and various lodges, were the participants.[22]

The revival of business in the mid-1840s brought prosperity back to Newark, but the gulf in consciousness between employer and employee widened as their values diverged. Manufacturers saw labor as but one factor in production, to be bought at the lowest cost. When possible, they reduced wages. They interpreted their role in production as the accumulators and manipulators of capital as equally important to, if not more important than, that of manual labor. Hearkening to their artisan heritage, manufacturers saw themselves as producers who made money because God intended them to be useful to their community; their profits were the just reward of their hard work and thrift, but they were still enjoined to do good works, both as an example to others and as a benevolence.[23] Newarkers who disagreed with the new mores criticized the wealthy manufacturers for neglecting the moral and educational level of their young workers while donating large sums to local charities.[24]

The Newarkers who disagreed most consistently with the manufacturers' view of themselves were the journeymen in the crafts. Throughout the 1840s and 1850s they clung to their version of the labor theory of value as the standard for industrial relations, viewing manual labor as the source of wealth and justifying combination as the road to a fair division of the profits. Newark hatters accused some large manufacturers of "grinding the faces of the poor," because the owners had closed their plants during the panic of 1857 and had offered only one-third the old piece rates after reopening. The journeymen compared the manufacturers unfavorably to owners of smaller firms, who, more in the tradition of the old masters, had kept men employed on "short time" during the panic and had paid "fair wages" once business resumed. The journeymen concluded that the manufacturers "may give of their thousands to charitable and religious institutions—but all will avail nothing as long as they thus rob the laborers of their hire."[25] To implement their beliefs, journeymen in many crafts formed unions again, the carpenters and shoemakers as early as the mid-1840s. A few manufacturers tried to overcome the gulf between themselves and their workers by providing an occasional "treat" for workers, like a sleigh ride and dinner, "to create a better feeling between employers and employees."[26] But such sporadic social occasions did not remove real grievances nor change values.

These two divergent views of industrial relations did not find equal support in "public opinion." The employers' hostility to journeymen's unions dominated the local press as anti-union sentiment became part of the official community ideology. *The Newark Daily Advertiser,* ever the friend of the manufacturer, printed repeated admonitions to journeymen. During the depression of 1837, the newspaper proclaimed that journeymen had been ruined by joining unions, which had started them drinking and had destroyed the industries in which they worked. Another writer, after counseling frugality and self-education as the road to success for "mechanics," suggested that unions led not only to intemperance but to prostitution by the female relatives of strikers. Destroying men was bad enough, but an institution that led to the moral degeneracy of wives and daughters was surely a menace to society![27]

Moreover, in the 1840s and 1850s independence in the form of self-employment was still a prized possession, and "being your own boss" was an important component of status in Newark, as in the rest of America. The concentration of this attribute in a relatively few men in each city changed the status hierarchy rather drastically, to the detriment of journeymen. Americans believed that men achieved the success of self-employment and the wealth that accompanied it because of their superior capabilities. While self-employment continued to be a factor in status attribution in the late nineteenth century, the development of high-paying managerial positions destroyed the identification of self-employment with wealth; such nonentrepreneurial white collar jobs were created by the large corporations, of which there were few prior to the Civil War. Although the opportunities for self-employment were contracting, journeymen lost status for their lack of "independence." Manufacturers trying to bust a union always advertised for "independent men," feeding the beliefs of opinion makers that those in unions had abandoned the artisan heritage.[28]

Paradoxically, the growth of new companies during industrialization, the vast expansion of business, gave the impression that there were more opportunities than ever for the enterprising, and so men could still presume to judge each other as successes or failures on the basis of their "independence." Those who sought to rise in the world looked first to small business. The partnership was the most common form of business management, and it allowed a craftsman who had saved a few hundred dollars to become self-employed by joining with several others in the same position.[29] Many a factory or shop owner developed from a craftsman who invented a machine to simplify production in his own or an allied field. The patent laws of the time, which favored the inventor and not his employer, were favorable to journeymen seeking independence. Opportunities for self-employment arose in other ways, too: from the desire to use the by-products of production, from the need for auxiliary articles to incorporate into the manufacture of another item, and from industrialization itself. While in some fields all the tasks were performed within one factory, often separate enterprises would arise to make a "subproduct." This proliferation of types of businesses was a feature of industrialization; the fields of carpentry and blacksmithing, for instance, tended to subdivide. In the 1830s local carpenters began to set up factories of the semiskilled to produce stairs or sashes and blinds—prefabricated, standardized items for regular carpenters to install. In blacksmithing, the growth of the specialized industries of hardware and toolmaking left "all-purpose" blacksmiths with fewer and fewer jobs to perform.

In the early days, manufacturers usually processed any by-products in the shop; but as the volume of by-products increased, new industries formed to handle them. Jewelry making spurred metal refining to use metal sweepings, while leather makers sent trimmings to glue factories and hide shavings to chemical works.[30] Other industries produced enough demand for certain articles, which previously might have been made in the shop, to lead to the establishment of separate industries. Saddle making called for saddlery hardware and saddle trees; trunk making for rivets and frames; shoemaking for lasts; and hatting for hat blocks and japanned cloth. The partnership form allowed those familiar with the processes involved to take advantage of opportunities for self-employment in the subproduct or by-product field. All these opportunities served to bolster the belief that self-employment was possible for the capable, hard-working journeyman, even though in reality many fewer were self-employed than had been previously.

Journeymen who took the opportunities that were available, like Aaron Carter and William Scarlett, became exemplars who were cited by Newarkers seeking to prove the beneficent workings of the economy. In 1841 Aaron Carter, who had learned his trade with a local firm, formed the jewelry making firm of Carter, Pennington and Doremus; of the total capital investment of $924.79, Carter contributed $524.61 while Pennington provided $300.00 and Doremus $100.18. Despite such humble beginnings, the firm had a continuous existence in Newark at least through the 1890s and was well-known in the city. William Scarlett, a shoemaker employed by the

Newark India Rubber Company, had been a leader in the union movement of the mid-1830s, but a decade later he found a more profitable and respectable route to a better living. In 1847 Scarlett invented a machine for making suspender buckles, an item used by the Newark India Rubber Company in making one of its products. With merchants as partners he opened his own factory using steam-driven machinery and child labor and found his former employer to be a good customer.[31]

But a concomitant feature of the ease of entry into a partnership was the ease of departure from it. In its first twenty years the firm started by Carter, Pennington and Doremus either added or lost partners five times, beginning in 1844 when Pennington withdrew from the business. The unstable nature of partnerships provided opportunities for the rise of new men and new ideas, but this insecurity also adversely affected production and employment. In the industrial world, a journeyman had only a gambler's chance to succeed as an entrepreneur, although a few did make it. Most small manufacturers lived precariously. One businessman, who had started his firm with a few hundred dollars saved during his years as apprentice and journeyman, complained that Newark's banks refused credit to small manufacturers who were not "known," and that he and others like him were thinking of moving to areas where they would not be "obscure small producers."[32] The difficulties of becoming self-employed in the industrial world both confirmed the manufacturers' sense of their superiority and restricted mobility between the classes.

By the 1850s, craftsmen had divided into two new classes, each with roots in the old artisan class but attuned to the differing interests of employer and employee in the industrial economy. The class consciousness of journeymen was not strong enough, however, to weld them into a cohesive group outside their work places. In part the journeymen's rootlessness militated against cohesion. Community life based on home ownership and long-term residence in a neighborhood was not typical of the craftsmen or of most men in Newark or other cities; the common experiences of workers on the job were not bolstered by the shared culture and allegiance of long-time neighbors.

Residential and geographical mobility in the nineteenth century was caused mainly by the search of the poor and the propertyless for opportunity; the wealthier citizens were more rooted in the city and the neighborhood. To the extent that city directory listings reflect actual migration, the typical craftsman lived in Newark only 2.9 years in the late 1830s and 3.0 years in the late 1840s or 1850s.[33] The self-employed, however, were more firmly established in Newark than the journeymen. In 1840, 1850, and 1860, two-thirds of the self-employed craftsmen had lived in Newark at least five years. On the other hand, during this twenty-five year period no more than 29 percent of the journeymen stayed in Newark for five years, and that percentage occurred in the most prosperous period, from 1846 to 1850. The

TABLE 31
Value of Property by Number of Years in City for Male Craftsmen[a]

Value of property	1850					1860				
	1	2	3	4	5	1	2	3	4	5
None	25.0	15.4	10.8	12.1	33.6	26.1	17.6	16.0	14.9	25.4
$1–500	22.2	15.2	11.8	8.5	42.4	15.4	15.3	15.2	16.4	37.6
$501–1,500	8.1	7.6	9.2	17.3	57.8	9.9	9.5	13.4	16.2	51.0
$1,501–5,000	1.8	2.9	4.1	8.2	83.1	2.4	5.1	8.1	14.1	70.3
$5,001+	5.7	—	1.9	1.9	90.6	—	3.3	5.0	8.9	82.7
			$\gamma = .5603$					$\gamma = .4170$		

[a]Data derived from manuscripts of U.S. Censuses of 1850 and 1860 and Newark city directories.

self-employed were far less transient than the journeymen because they were much more resistant to economic pressure. They had found their opportunities in Newark, and their stake in the community was greater; the journeymen were mobile and still looking for opportunity.

A shared community life that bolstered class consciousness was more common for wealthy manufacturers than it was for journeymen. In 1850 only one-third of those craftsmen who owned no property lived in the city for five years (Table 31). The percentage persisting increased with wealth; 91 percent of those who owned over $5,000 worth of property had lived in Newark at least five years. In 1860 smaller percentages of all classes of craftsmen were long-term residents. Only one-fourth of those without real or personal property had persisted five years, while 83 percent of those worth over $5,000 had.

Moreover, during the few years the average journeyman spent in Newark, he moved frequently, further undercutting the possibilities for the creation of cohesive working-class neighborhoods. In 1850 only 28 percent of the craftsmen who were heads of households owned real estate; for male heads of households in Newark as a whole, the figure was 32 percent. Most urban dwellers in the nineteenth century were renters and many leases lasted but one year. Observers noted that thousands of Newarkers moved each April first, the traditional moving day. If he stayed more than two years in Newark, the average craftsman would change his residence at least once, and at least one-third of the craftsmen moved two or more times within five years (Table 32).[34] The craftsmen's average rate of residential mobility (the proportion who moved each year) was uniformly high across the decades. In the late 1830s it was 0.27; in the late 1840s and the late 1850s, it was 0.25. That is, one out of four craftsmen moved each year. This ratio seems to have been impervious to changing economic conditions and indicates the typicality of the mobile life. Between 1836 and 1840, only 6 percent of craftsmen who were not self-employed stayed in the city at least five years and never moved. In the late 1840s, 12 percent of the journeymen

TABLE 32
Number of Moves Per Number of Years Listed in Directory for Male Craftsmen

Number of years	Number of moves		
	0	1	2 or more
2 years			
1836–40	71.6	28.4	—
1846–50	43.9	56.1	—
1856–60	55.1	44.9	—
3 years			
1836–40	21.3	44.4	34.3
1846–50	30.3	38.2	31.5
1856–60	31.2	44.8	24.0
4 years			
1836–40	19.4	24.0	56.6
1846–50	25.7	30.9	43.5
1856–60	25.6	35.5	38.8
5 years			
1836–40	31.0	26.3	42.6
1846–50	42.3	28.7	29.0
1856–60	39.6	28.9	31.5

were similarly stable, and in the late 1850s the figure was only 9 percent. These were the few who could enjoy cohesive neighborhood life, but the movement of the others lessened the viability of neighboring since frequently men moved quite a distance. Approximately half of those who moved within the city crossed a ward boundary during one of their moves (56 percent from 1836 to 1840; 61 percent from 1846 to 1850; and 51 percent from 1856 to 1860).

The constant shifting from city to city and neighborhood to neighborhood undercut class cohesion among journeymen, but it reveals that they had come to accept many industrial values. By the 1850s men no longer sought fellow craftsmen for neighbors; neighborhoods were composed of those of equal status under the "new rules"—those of equal wealth. Money became a universally acknowledged symbol of superior status in America, and craftsmen, too, accepted its validity.[35] In the 1830s Newark still resembled a preindustrial city: artisans clustering together by trade, the wealthy at the center of the city, and the poor living at the fringes. By the 1850s Newark's geography was becoming industrial—the clusters of craftsmen broke up as men sought neighbors of equal wealth and the nonpoor deserted the core of the city.[36] Neighborhood segregation grew more complete later in the nineteenth century when the wealthy deserted the core for the suburbs, but it was the more prosperous journeymen who led the search for new neighborhoods where they could live with those of like means. By

FIGURE 2   Ward System, Newark, 1836 to 1860

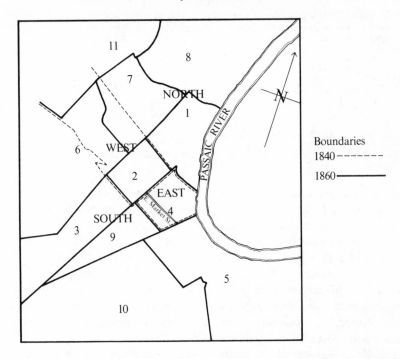

limiting their contacts to others who had roughly the same purchasing power as themselves, craftsmen established apparent control over the products of the economy, although they had lost real control when the chance for self-employment diminished.[37]

In the 1830s Newarkers had not begun to choose their neighborhoods on the basis of industrial values, although the old village center at East Market Street in the East Ward had become Newark's business district (Figure 2), and few families lived there. Rampant speculation in building lots had caused the first split between business and residential areas. In the 1830s, under speculation's "guidance," new streets were opened, old ones straightened and enlarged, new buildings erected, and old ones refitted. Land at the core of the town was built over, and the vegetable and flower gardens of former years disappeared. Land prices rose ever higher, and as building fell behind investing, a severe housing shortage developed. Working people lived under more cramped conditions than formerly, and workers lost the security derived from growing at least some of their food.[38]

Newark's residential pattern remained preindustrial, however, since proportionately more of those in the most prestigious occupations in 1840 still lived in the city's core, the East Ward (Table 33). Of the four existing wards, the East Ward had the lowest proportion of residents employed in manu-

TABLE 33
Occupational Distribution by Ward, 1840[a]

Type of occupation	North	East	South	West
Agriculture	18.6	3.9	4.7	3.5
Commerce	3.8	12.5	3.7	8.2
Manufacturing and trades	73.8	71.6	89.2	84.4
Navigation and mining	1.0	5.8	0.6	1.0
Professions	2.8	6.1	1.9	2.9
Ward's percentage of total population	21.1	24.8	27.5	26.8

[a]From the manuscript of the U.S. Census of 1840. Occupational designations of the U.S. Census Office.

facturing and the trades and the highest in commerce and the professions, occupations of higher social and economic status. The North Ward contained a sizeable number of farmers; it was the last area of settlement and the place agriculture made its final stand within the city limits.

In accord with a preindustrial neighborhood pattern, many chose to live near other members of their craft in the late 1830s. Since each craft included men of varying degrees of wealth, this produced some mixing of economic strata. In terms of the ward boundaries of 1860 (when there were eleven rather than four wards), in the late 1830s three of the eight crafts studied had most of their members living within one ward.[39] Between 1836 and 1840, 68 percent of the trunk makers and 68 percent of the leather makers were living in the area that became the second ward. This area contained the swamp where the tanneries were first located, and although industrialization had begun in leather making, the workmen stayed nearby. The jewelers, whose craft retained its traditional methods in the 1830s, were also clustered, but to a lesser extent—42 percent of them were living in the area that became the ninth ward.

The decisions of the mobile craftsmen changed the physical form of Newark as it grew from a city of 17,000 in 1840 to one of almost 72,000 inhabitants in 1860. The area of the city did not change, but the distribution of people and industries did. Within the city a central business district, the CBD, almost devoid of residences, formed in the fourth ward. It was a typical nineteenth-century American downtown, full of factories, banks, commercial establishments, the railroad depot, churches, and saloons. The homes of the very rich were on Park Place, while some of the poorest laborers found quarters among the industrial buildings.[40] The population moved farther outward from the CBD every decade. The first, second, third, and ninth wards were contiguous to the CBD and the next to be developed. They formed the Old Core (OC) of the city, where most of the population lived in 1840 and where many industries were located. The fifth, sixth, and seventh wards were the next to be settled, and this Inner Ring (IR) was becoming densely populated

TABLE 34
Area of Residency

	CBD	OC	IR	OR
Craftsmen, 1836–40[a]	17.6	75.6	6.0	0.8
Craftsmen, 1850[b]	15.8	60.0	20.3	3.9
Craftsmen, 1860[b]	12.7	36.1	38.6	12.3
Male Newarkers, 1860[b]	11.9	37.6	37.6	13.0

CBD = Central Business District
OC = Old Core
IR = Inner Ring
OR = Outer Ring
[a]Area of first residency for craftsmen listed in city directories.
[b]Area of residency for those listed in U.S. census manuscripts.

by 1860. The eighth, tenth, and eleventh wards, forming the Outer Ring (OR), were only sparsely settled even in 1860.

In the 1840s and 1850s, as the population moved out to the new housing on the outskirts, the CBD and the Old Core lost population proportionately while the Inner Ring and the Outer Ring gained. In the late 1830s, 76 percent of the craftsmen had lived in the Old Core with most of the rest in the CBD (Table 34). By the late 1840s an outward shift of the population had begun; for the craftsmen the movement was mainly from the Old Core to the Inner Ring. At that time 60 percent of the craftsmen were living in the Old Core, while the Inner Ring and the CBD contained 20 percent and 16 percent respectively. In the 1850s the shift of the population center outward occurred at a more rapid rate, and half of Newark's male population and of the craftsmen lived in the ring by 1860.

The dispersal of the population was accomplished in two ways—by new migrants to the city settling in the fringe areas and by older residents moving toward the ring in search of new, more congenial neighborhoods. In the 1830s, the Old Core was, proportionately, the favorite destination for craftsmen who were moving. Of those craftsmen who crossed a ward boundary when they moved, 61 percent either moved into or remained within the Old Core.[41] Twenty-two percent of the craftsmen moved into the CBD, and only 16 percent moved to the ring. In the 1840s, the Old Core remained the favorite destination for those moving (57 percent), but the ring gained in population faster than the CBD (28 percent vs. 16 percent). By the late 1850s, as the attractions of the ring became more powerful, 44 percent were moving to the ring, 44 percent to the Old Core, and only 12 percent to the CBD. To solve the commuting problems caused by this dispersion of the population, preparations for the first horse-drawn omnibuses between Newark and Orange were made in 1860.

TABLE 35
Area of Residence by Value of Property for Male Craftsmen

Value of property	1850[a]				1860[b]			
	CBD	OC	IR	OR	CBD	OC	IR	OR
None	16.2	59.8	20.0	3.9	18.2	37.0	33.9	11.0
$1–500	12.8	46.1	30.8	10.2	3.4	34.6	48.3	13.7
$501–1,000	10.3	41.2	37.3	11.1	2.7	17.5	60.4	19.2
$1,001–1,500	9.8	71.7	18.4	–	4.1	15.8	57.1	23.0
$1,501–3,000	11.0	71.4	16.9	0.6	6.6	40.3	39.3	13.8
$3,001–5,000	21.4	60.7	14.3	3.6	9.7	61.9	22.1	6.3
$5,001–10,000	31.3	65.7	3.1	–	10.3	61.6	18.7	9.3
$10,001+	26.2	69.1	4.8	–	25.8	58.4	12.5	3.4

CBD = Central Business District
OC = Old Core
IR = Inner Ring
OR = Outer Ring
[a]Only real property included.
[b]Real and personal property included.

As a result of these residential choices, the craftsmen and all Newarkers were dividing along class lines by 1860; the industrialized city structure was appearing. Those with the least wealth and those with the most were concentrated in the CBD and the Old Core, while those of middling wealth lived mainly in the ring (Table 35).[42] The journeymen who had managed to amass a little property were the instigators of this residential pattern. The concentration of the wealthy at the core persisted because of the desire of the manufacturers and masters to remain close to their businesses. The self-employed craftsmen were not spread throughout the city as were their employees who were heads of households. In 1840, 93 percent of the self-employed craftsmen lived in the CBD and the Old Core as did 87 percent of the journeymen. But with the expansion of the 1840s, journeymen began to desert the core to find better neighborhoods for their families in the ring; only 69 percent of the journeymen lived in the central areas in 1850, but 93 percent of the self-employed still did. In the 1850s, the self-employed began to desert the core too, but the journeymen were far ahead. In 1860, 74 percent of the self-employed craftsmen but only 40 percent of the journeymen lived in the CBD or the Old Core. It was the more prosperous, but not self-employed, craftsmen with families who began to search for new neighborhoods of uniform affluence first. In the latter part of the nineteenth century, in contrast, the self-employed and the wealthy in general would be the trend setters in suburbanization.

As men began to choose neighbors of equal wealth rather than common occupation, the residential concentrations that had been typical of some crafts broke down. By 1850 most of the leather makers were still in the Old Core, but only 38 percent of them, rather than the 68 percent of 1840, still lived in the second ward. The jewelers and the trunk makers also evidenced some clustering, but they were less concentrated than in 1840; the jewelers remained concentrated in the ninth ward, where 34 percent of them lived, while the trunk makers continued to be concentrated in the second ward (31 percent). By 1860 there were smaller clusters still. Only 30 percent of the jewelers were still residing in the ninth ward, while some trunk makers continued to cluster, but now in the sixth ward (27 percent). Seventeen percent of the leather makers continued to live in the second ward, but another cluster developed in the contiguous seventh ward (24 percent).[43]

By the 1850s the desire for job access and craft solidarity no longer outweighed the status value of wealth. Only those craftsmen who boarded placed job access above other criteria, living predominantly in the CBD and the Old Core. In 1860 only 41 percent of the craftsmen who headed their own households lived in the central areas, and those who lived with their parents were distributed similarly—46 percent in the CBD and the Old Core. But 73 percent of those who boarded or lived with others were centrally located. As in other nineteenth-century cities, the hotels and boarding housings of Newark clustered near the CBD where the widest range of jobs was available for their patrons. Those who boarded with families also demanded job access, and consequently boarding was more common near the center of the city than at the fringe.[44]

The fruits of industrialization—the new class divisions, the status value of wealth, and the lack of cohesive neighborhood life—shaped men's leisure as well as their choice of residence. Craftsmen created a rich world of new social organizations, expressing the complex sources of their consciousness. Outside of work, they sought a sphere for expressing shared values with small groups of like-minded men. In the 1820s the artisan class had dominated the social life as well as the social structure of Newark. In the 1830s incipient industrialization destroyed this class, but some of the old forms of social interaction persisted. In the 1840s and 1850s, Newarkers, like other urbanites, created an entirely new and more complex social life in a plethora of organizations that filled men's leisure hours, some combining pleasure with economic security. These groups were segregated by status based on wealth as well as by ethnicity, race, and religion. There were at least four status groups in Newark: the wealthy elite, the majority of the self-employed, the workers in the crafts, and the chronically underemployed and impoverished. All had separate spheres of activity, and craftsmen moved in different social worlds depending on their wealth and their ethnic or religious background.

Journeymen flocked to join organized leisure activities in the 1840s and 1850s. The volunteer fire companies had been popular with journeymen in the 1830s too, but now militia and guard units, sports teams, benefit societies, and lodges also vied for their attention. The fire houses provided much needed meeting places for men, although the guardians of the city's morality objected to the gambling that took place in them. Besides the socializing at regular meetings, the new organizations sponsored balls, and the guard units organized many excursions each year to compete with teams elsewhere. By the 1850s many guard units were attached to large firms and composed solely of their employees. Some of these units had more than, one hundred members, and they brought coworkers together for pageantry and excursions, continuing the social relations formed on the job into the leisure hours. In Newark, factory-based guard units existed among saddlers, trunk makers, hat finishers, and tanners, and some of the jewelry firms even had company baseball teams. The most class conscious of these workers' social organizations was the Newark Turnverein, which was formed by German workers in 1848. The membership of this gymnastic club was composed primarily of craftsmen, and the club furthered workers' education in socialism as well as physical culture.[45]

Militia and guard units and sports teams were well-suited to the regimentation of time that was a product of industrialization. Workers could no longer take breaks when they wished or leave for a few days fishing when they felt like it, since manufacturers demanded punctuality and punished absenteeism. Evenings and Sundays were reserved for leisure, and groups that met at fixed times were appropriate for those free hours. The character of these groups also reflected the changing nature of production—they were usually quite large, often with fifty or more members, and the team effort was important. The drill of the rifle unit mimicked the nature of mechanized production in which men moved according to the speed of machines and relied on the labor of others.

Within the shadow of team cohesion, however, such organizations provided exercise in the competitive individualism valued so highly by industrial society. The firemen were proud of providing a vital community service, but they also enjoyed the thrill of the fight in which individuals excelled each other in daring. The guard units not only competed as groups, but individuals within each troop were singled out for awards, and prizes such as watches and silver spoons were coveted trophies of individual excellence.[46] The *Newark Daily Advertiser*, the spokesman for manufacturers and industrial values, understood the utility of these social organizations in perpetuating those values:

Commencing with the famous parade last June, our streets have since been enlivened almost daily with the beat of the drum, the sound of brass instruments and the glitter of uniforms, either of militia or fire companies. These parades and receptions are not so useless as some imagine. They supply a necessary appetite for amusements, perpetuate good feeling, and form subjects for thought and emulation among those engaged.... They show private pecuniary prosperity, and only exist in a rapidly expanding community.[47]

Groups such as guard units, fire companies, and sports teams played an important role in industrial society by providing a new arena where average men could use their talents. The essence of craftsmanship was that each producer, the journeyman as well as the master, exercised control and mastery over his work—the application of his rational mind. Industrialization destroyed the space in production for the worker to display his competence and experience mastery. In the 1840s and 1850s, journeymen sought these satisfactions outside of work, and the militia units, sports teams, and fire companies revealed the journeyman's desire to reassert control of the self and experience mastery through accomplishment.

This new round of social activities was a male preserve, and, just as craftsmen attempted to shield their families from the economic world, so they implemented Victorian notions of male and female roles in their leisure activities. Men spent less time with their wives and children since they no longer worked at home, and the leisure activities that were confined to adult or teenage males extended that absence. This increased the isolation of the wife in the home, as those concerned about the quality of family life noted:

The avidity for these organizations and for general amusements, tends too much to a disregard of domestic pleasures, perhaps also to a contraction of the social entertainments in which both sexes can participate; in most of the organizations, public festivals, &c., the ladies being excluded.[48]

Working-class men, no less than others, built a life for themselves outside the home.

Some activities included men of different statuses, but the overlap was never great. Over seven hundred men belonged to Newark's volunteer fire companies by the time they were disbanded in 1854, including some well-known merchants and manufacturers who headed companies. But the vast majority of firemen were journeymen. Some lodges may have had a multi-class membership too, but the self-employed tended to dominate these groups, having become avid "joiners." In the 1840s fraternal groups like the Odd Fellows became important to the social life of the city; by 1847, the Odd Fellows had five lodges and two encampments in Newark with close to nine hundred members.[49] The Odd Fellows and some other fraternal groups provided not only a new outlet for sociability, but financial security as well, for these were also benevolent associations, giving relief to members, allotments to widows and orphans, and burial to the dead. Journeymen, however, often had their own mutual benefit funds through their unions or craft associations. Lists of the charter members of the first two lodges of Odd Fellows formed in Newark reveal a preponderance of the self-employed—merchants, master craftsmen, and manufacturers. Half of the twenty-two charter members who formed Howard Lodge #7 in 1841 could be definitely identified from the city directories as self-employed; at least 61 percent of the twenty-three charter members of Friendship Lodge #11 in 1842 were also self-employed. While these lodges grew with time, their size was limited to a few hundred members and such groups were necessarily exclusive.[50]

Although the self-employed craftsmen and the journeymen usually belonged to different groups, Newark's social life was not simply split along class lines; the status gradations of wealth also limited social interactions. An elite of the self-employed took the lead in organizing the social activities of the town, just as the wealthy dominated social life and social policy in other American cities.[51] This was an entrepreneurial elite to which only a few craftsmen belonged; those who had become manufacturers were accepted, but the average self-employed craftsman was not. An example of the activities of this elite was the Newark Association for Improving the Condition of the Poor, founded in 1849 and patterned on the New York group of similar name.[52] It was the first men's charitable society in Newark except for *ad hoc* committees that had arisen during the depression of 1837; previously, organized charity had been the province of Newark's women. The aim of the Newark Association was the same as that of the New York group: "to discourage indiscriminate almsgiving" by rationalizing the distribution of aid to the poor and by sending visitors to investigate them and give them advice. This group's suspicion of the poor, and their belief in business values, clearly indicates a class consciousness among the wealthy as strong as that of the German workers in the Newark Turnverein. Of the fifty-nine men listed as officers or visitors of the Association in 1849, only four were listed without an occupation in the city directory. (These four may have been wealthy men of leisure, since all did appear in the directory, which tended to overlook those without property.) Of the other members, eight were professionals, five were government officials, nine were manufacturers, sixteen were merchants, five were builders, one was a broker, one was a farmer, and one a gardener. Four were master craftsmen who owned their own stores, and only five were craftsmen who are not known to have been self-employed. Sixty-six percent of Newark's men worked in crafts in 1850, but only nine out of the fifty-nine members were craftsmen. Even though the self-employed craftsman might have stood far above his employees in status, his standing in the community was well below the top.

Had the only divisions in Newark society been those of class and wealth, the working class might have bolstered its awakening consciousness with shared leisure as well as work experiences. But another important component of status by the 1840s and 1850s was ethnic or religious heritage, which cut across class lines. Industrialization had helped to destroy Newark's ethnic and religious homogeneity as European immigrants flocked to the city for newly created jobs. Ancient prejudices and Old World cultures, as well as wealth, came to define social groups and social identity in Newark as in other American cities that experienced large-scale immigration. The major lines of division in Newark were between Protestants and Catholics, and between Americans, Irish, and Germans. Most of the lodges, guard units, fire companies, and other social groups were the province not only of one wealth level, but also of one religion or birthplace. Journeymen sought to express their separate identities as native Americans, Irish, Germans, Protestants, or Catholics outside the work place.

Preindustrial Newark had been overwhelmingly Protestant and native-born, as had its mechanics. Immigration had begun in the 1830s, however, and the city census of 1836 revealed that 18 percent of Newark's population was foreign-born. The newcomers were chiefly Irish, and they brought a new diversity to the cultural and religious life of Newark.[53] In 1829 the first Roman Catholic Church was founded in this previously Protestant city, and the few Germans who began to settle in Newark built the first German Lutheran Church in 1840. By 1860, 37 percent of the population was foreign-born, and there were five Roman Catholic churches, ten German-language churches, and one Jewish synagogue in Newark in addition to the various English-speaking Protestant congregations. Immigration of the Irish, who were predominantly Roman Catholic, and the Germans, perhaps half of whom were Roman Catholic, split the craftsmen at a time when religious hatreds were extreme.[54] The ethnic composition of the crafts suggests that most would have had a sizeable minority of Catholic workers, at least one-third, by 1860 (Table 13). The ethnic and religious diversity within the working class assured that journeymen would be unable to extend any common consciousness they formed on the job into shared social experience.

The cohesion of each ethnic and religious group was based not solely on tradition, but, more fundamentally, on the reality of clashing values; the antagonisms between groups arose from the attempt to implement a single social policy. By the 1830s the Protestant churches could no longer speak for all Newarkers, and the old social code was in jeopardy. Those among the native-born who adhered to the strictest version of the code feared the increase in immigration because they assumed the superiority of their culture to that of the mass of Europeans. They abhorred the customs of some of the newcomers, especially the latter's consumption of alcohol and secular enjoyment of the Sabbath. Although they recognized some immigrants as "respectable," like the Roman Catholic priest, Father Moran, who was a temperance advocate, they condemned most others. When a fire burned down two houses inhabited by Irish immigrants, guardians of the old morality described it as the "natural result" of intoxication and gambling, "the fruits of an Irish wake."[55]

But the cultural proclivities of many native Americans were changing too, compounding even further a complex situation. Sabbath-breaking was common, especially among the young men who played ball. The first public dance ever held in Newark, the Fireman's Ball, was given in 1836, and a decade later there were many held each year.[56] The editor of the *Newark Daily Advertiser,* an advocate of both the old social code and the new economic system, commented:

We are sorry to see any encouragement given to this fashionable vice of fashionable parties, in this city. It's tendency is every way and altogether bad, ... Besides, why should the plain, sober minded, business doing people of Newark ape the follies of the pampered children of Fashion? There is, we believe, now not a fashionable individual, in the accepted meaning of the term, in the town, and long may it be before we are cursed with this fungeous growth of our large cities.[57]

Newark's businessmen were adopting the most stringent form of the old social code, including strict temperance, for themselves, and in the 1830s some of the native-born journeymen began to see the legal enforcement of this code as an imposition of the "rich." One self-styled "mechanic" protested Newark's temperance laws for interfering with "the amusements and refreshments of working classes."[58] The emerging industrial elite in many cities, in league with Protestant ministers, viewed temperance as the key to those virtues like thrift and industry that were necessary to both economic success and religious grace.[59] They added temperance to the code by which artisans had lived and made this morality the cornerstone of worldly success. Members of the working class who rejected this code were, in the eyes of the manufacturers, responsible for their fate and their poverty. Native-born Protestant journeymen could be found on both sides of the temperance issue.

The Protestant ministers and their adherents did not relax their vigilance although many, perhaps most, Newarkers ignored their preachments. They continued to have great influence with Newark's lawmakers, and in the 1850s the police were still arresting Newarkers for working, drinking, or gambling on the Sabbath and for the crimes of adultery and drunkenness.[60] Amusements like theaters, minstrel shows, and circuses became popular with the public despite attempts to outlaw them; the Presbyterians, Newark's special guardians of the old code, viewed the theater as "decoying into evil courses a multitude of youth, and spreading through the community a demoralizing influence."[61] Many of these theaters catered to the broadest audience—the working class. By the 1850s, as rural themes faded, the melodramas offered the workers their own heros, the firemen, who with practical good sense and wholesome sentiments overcame the villains of the "aristocracy."[62]

The major source of contention between natives and foreigners, Protestants and Catholics, was the issue of temperance. Despite the activity of temperance advocates, saloons dotted every neighborhood and formed a regular part of men's leisure activities, especially among the Germans and the Irish. Those native Protestant workers who adhered to the norms of their ethnic group as propounded by the ministers often found themselves at odds with foreign-born or Catholic workers. Newark's Protestant ministers led the temperance crusade, denouncing the city's immorality caused by "grog shops and foreigners," and Protestants made repeated efforts to prohibit the sale of liquor and close the beer halls on Sunday, as well as to use licensing regulations to make Newark completely dry.[63]

In 1853 some Germans held a mass meeting to remonstrate against the laws forbidding Sabbath tippling as denying them self-government and constitutional freedoms. In a petition to the Common Council they protested that the "temperate use of *good* spirituous liquors, such as beer and wine, and also the innocent amusements afforded us in our beer and wine saloons, [are]...indispensable to our well being."[64] It was their custom to dedicate Sunday not only to "pious contemplations, but also to rest, recreations and amusements," since Sunday was the one time a laborer had for relaxation. The Common Council retorted that "a proper degree of modesty, we think, should have restrained them from meddling with this subject until they could have informed themselves properly of the structure of our government." Although the Council admitted that temperance had not been written into the Constitution, it claimed that temperance was a local custom of long duration, and that immigrants ought to adopt it in place of the "corrupt and vitiated habits of Europe."

Although the Protestant social code was the source of much of the animosity between native and immigrant, Protestant and Catholic, "pure" religious intolerance also existed, even among Protestants. This, too, acted to set members of the working class against each other. When they formed a local branch of the Young Men's Christian Association in 1854, for instance, pious young Newarkers debated whether to admit Protestants who were not Evangelicals, like Universalists.[65] No one even suggested admitting Roman Catholics, whom Protestants saw as wedded to an authoritarianism that was un-American. In the early 1850s, the Newark City Tract Society and the Essex County Bible Society sought to convert the immigrant Catholics to Protestantism. The Ninth Annual Report of the Bible Society exemplified their attitude with its call to the faithful:

At a time when a vast foreign population is rushing in upon us like a flood—when infidelity on the one hand, in its protean forms, and Romanism on the other, with its determined and deadly hostility to God's truth, and our free institutions—are assailing those truths, and endeavoring day and night to undermine those truths and those interests which are dear to our hearts, shall we be idle?[66]

The animosities between Roman Catholics and Protestants reached the flash point in Newark in September 1854 during a parade of the American Protestant Association. The A.P.A. was a secret society formed about six months before the riot, and its members came armed to their first public event in Newark. At one point the parade went past a leather factory, and some Irish Catholic workers came out in their work clothes to watch and to heckle. The marchers began shooting guns, and in the ensuing battle one Irishman was shot to death, the German Catholic Church on the corner was ransacked, and only the last-minute intervention of the marshalls prevented the mob from burning the church.[67] According to the local newspapers, both Whig and Democratic, however, the aggressors were not primarily native-born Protestants, but Orangemen continuing the battle that had raged in Ireland for centuries. Neither paper mentioned whether the marchers were journeymen or businessmen, so the precise interaction of class, ethnic, and religious factors in this event are not clear, although all factors contributed.

In the tense atmosphere caused by clashing values, Newarkers seemed to give ethnic as well as religious prejudices free rein, and thus destroyed civic unity. Some Germans complained, for instance, that the Street Commissioners had neglected the sewers and sanitation in their area during a cholera outbreak, and that one had said, "I don't care if all Dutchmen die in one heap."[68] In November 1854 there was a small riot between a crowd of Irishmen and the native-born police after the latter tried to arrest two Irishmen. Ethnic hostilities also surfaced over welfare facilities. In January 1855, some Germans opened a soup kitchen to feed the indigent of all backgrounds, but, during the depression following the panic of 1857, many natives refused to donate to the city-wide Relief Association because it gave help to foreigners. Believing that Germans often were professional beggars and not the "worthy poor," natives preferred to give to their own churches to support their fellow parishioners, few of whom were foreign-born. At the same time the Germans of the sixth ward wanted to form their own relief association, since they had no voice in the dispensing of funds and were being slighted by the Association. Clashes between immigrants were common, too; Irish and Germans sometimes fought each other, as when some Irishmen set upon the German Turnverein Society. The hatreds between the English and the Irish were particularly intense, causing some violence in Newark. The Irish also formed a group of Repealers in 1846 to aid the cause of Irish independence. The social order was in ruins by the 1850s, and even "sacred" symbols of common purpose could not bring unity. In 1854 there were three separate Fourth of July celebrations in Newark—one for "Americans," one for Germans, and one for Irish.[69]

The bitterness between natives and foreigners, Protestants and Catholics, caused each group to withdraw into itself outside the work place. Where they could, immigrants sought to build their own communities and develop their own institutions to protect and maintain their customs and values. The prejudices of the natives encouraged them, since natives demanded assimilation but practiced segregation. The ethnic churches were among the earliest of the separate institutions, but there were also German-language newspapers, both German and Irish mutual benefit societies, and German and Irish guard units. The Germans also formed many musical associations and began to hold an annual two-day *Volksfest* in 1856. But, the children were the key to cultural separatism, and German and Irish Roman Catholics labored to start parochial schools for them. There were also 192 pupils in a secular German-English School.[70]

The growth of ethnic ghettos in Newark, as elsewhere, bolstered this withdrawal and further divided workers from each other. In both 1850 and 1860 proportionately more foreign-born craftsmen than native-born lived in Newark's ring.[71] Eighty-three percent of the natives lived in the core in 1850, but only 66 percent of the foreign-born. In 1860, 62 percent of the native-born craftsmen lived in the central areas, but only 40 percent of the foreign-born. This core/ring dichotomy based on birthplace was characteristic of the population as a whole as well as of the craftsmen. Sixty-six percent of native-born male Newarkers lived in the core in 1860, but only 36 percent of the foreign-born did. The sixth ward of Newark became known as a German area, while the seventh was becoming an Irish one. Thirty-five percent of Newark's German males over fourteen lived in the sixth ward in 1860, while 18 percent of the city's Irish males over fourteen lived in the seventh ward. Indeed, the concentrations of craft groups that remained in 1860 were less a function of craft identity than of ethnic cohesion. As more Germans became trunk makers, the concentration of trunk makers shifted from the second ward to the sixth; in the same way, the concentration of leather makers shifted from the second to the seventh wards as more Irishmen entered this craft. In the 1850s the trend toward segregation by wealth, however, cut across craft and ethnic lines and separated members of the working class as effectively as ethnic hostilities.

In the 1840s and 1850s, workers in Newark were beginning to grapple with the complexity of industrial society, as others would later in the century when industrialization set its stamp on most of urban America. Newark's journeymen were conscious of their new class position, but also of the differences between them in wealth, ethnicity, and religion. To acknowledge all their interests, they assigned them priority in separate spheres—workers who united on the job to fight their bosses often went home to segregated neighborhoods and spent their leisure in segregated clubs. Since the beginning of the industrial age, American workers have had to cope with this multiplicity of allegiances. As immigration from Europe reached epic proportions, and later as black Americans left agriculture for the opportunities of urban life, workers dealt with increased diversity as Newark's journeymen had. Their attempts to unionize or to strike against exploitation sometimes foundered on their mutual suspicion, but even when class consciousness asserted itself on the job, neighborhoods often remained segregated and socializing was limited. Although large-scale immigration ceased in the 1920s, the white working class has not lost its ethnic roots, and, in the last decade especially, working-class ethnics have forcefully asserted their claims for recognition and respect in the public arena. Today, unlike the early nineteenth century when industry was strictly segregated, black and white often work together. But even when they stand united, as in the automobile industry in Detroit, they go home to separate neighborhoods and activities.[72]

CHAPTER 6

Ethnic Politics
and Craft Unionism

The craftsmen's conflicting class, ethnic, and religious allegiances shaped not only their social life and their residential choices, but also their attempts to gain power in the community. Newark's journeymen recognized that they had a common interest in opposition to their employers, and their class consciousness found expression in their creation of craft unions dedicated to job control and higher wages. But Newark's workers, like Americans elsewhere, also sought to assert and protect their ethnic or religious interests, and by the 1850s politics had become their chosen arena for cultural combat. Journeymen, for the most part, struggled on the job for economic power, and for ethnic or religious dominance in politics, reinforcing the separation of work and "life" that facilitated the balancing of multiple loyalties. In Newark, as elsewhere, an ethnic politics and a narrow craft unionism resulted from the compromise workers made between their countervailing allegiances.

The dominant pattern of working-class action was rooted in the turbulence of the 1830s, before mass immigration began. During the first throes of industrialization, journeymen and employers in Newark and other Eastern cities became conscious of their new antagonism, but some of the ties of artisan institutions and world view still bound them together. As work was revolutionized, journeymen created new institutions, craft unions, to regain their lost power on the job. But the impact of industrialization in the 1830s was not so overwhelming as to call into question the entire artisan heritage, and Newark's political tradition, which asserted the identity of interests between employer and employee, found continued support among men of all classes. In the 1830s, when Newarkers and most Americans sought a political solution for economic problems, they framed the issues in terms of the opposition between the aristocracy and all producers—employers and em-

109

ployees alike—and not in terms of the antagonism between the two new classes that were forming. This political consensus derived from the mechanics' ideology held sway for the next thirty years as a prop for laissez-faire capitalism, and thus the major political parties ignored the realities of industrial class strife.

To regain control of their work and its profits, Newark's journeymen began to apply economic pressure to their employers by forming craft unions and conducting strikes. Between 1834 and 1836 most of the journeymen's unions formed a city-wide labor council, the Newark Trades Union, to further their goals, and they joined with unions in New York, Philadelphia, Boston, and several other cities in the National Trades Union. The Newark Trades Union was a strong organization and an active one, containing 1,168 members in sixteen societies at its height in February 1836. The Journeymen Carpenters Union was one of the few that does not appear to have belonged to the Newark Trades Union; since carpentry was not industrializing, its members did not face the same problems as those journeymen in crafts which were. The Newark Trades Union was quick to help unions elsewhere, raising hundreds of dollars to aid the striking hand loom weavers of Philadelphia, the Journeymen Hatters of New York, and the Journeymen Saddlers, Harness Makers, and Trimmers of Philadelphia.[1]

The National Trades Union envisioned such cooperation between unions in different cities as the way to effect uniformly high wage levels in all areas of the country. One of the three recommendations adopted at the annual convention of the National Trades Union in August 1834 was to promote the formation of Trade Unions all over the country, so that journeymen could engage in concerted action to enforce standard wage rates.[2] The concern with wages also appeared in the recommendation that encouraged the member trades unions to take action within their states to halt the use of state prison labor in craft production, since it was "highly injurious to the working classes": competition from cheap convict labor depressed the wage rates of regular craftsmen.

Industrialization was only in its first stages in the 1830s; significant mechanization lay in the future, and consequently the distribution of profits—the level of wage rates—was the major focus of worker discontent and the primary expression of class antagonism. From 1834 to 1836 many of Newark's unions went on strike at least once, usually for wage increases to keep up with inflation.[3] Some of the unions won increases without striking. The hostility created by the journeyman's loss of control over his wages was most clearly expressed by the Journeymen Boot Fitters, who complained that "the project of *grinding the poor* to overflow the pockets of the rich, has of late years succeeded to an extent, alarming in its magnitude and ruinous in its consequences."[4] No other issue loomed as large as the distribution of the profits being produced. Along with other trades unions, the Newark Trades Union also sought the ten-hour day, but it was introduced without much opposition among outdoor mechanics and in many fields, including shoe manufacture, harness making, coach trimming, and currying.[5]

The shoemakers were the best organized of all craftsmen in the 1830s, not only in Newark but nationally, and their concerns illustrate those of journeymen experiencing the first stage of industrialization. The shoemakers' unions in all the East Coast cities held a convention in March 1836 to form a general organization, which would have been the first craft union of national scope.[6] It never held another convention, however, as the shoemakers' union died in the depression of the following year. By March 1836 the unions of shoemakers in all cities had held successful strikes for wage increases, but wages were not uniform. The convention surveyed wage rates and proposed recommendations to make them identical across the country. The shoemakers' unions also sought to restrict the number of apprentices an employer could hire, in order to limit the substitution of cheap child labor for that of adult men during task differentiation. The male shoemakers encouraged the women's shoemaking unions to strike for wage increases, and they also supported efforts to ban the importation of shoes from abroad.

The National Trades Union emphasized economic rather than political action, but it also sought a "superior and uniform system of Public Education, by means of Manual Labor Schools, patronized by the Legislature."[7] These were to teach rudimentary academic subjects as well as skills and were intended to replace the dying apprenticeship system. Journeymen were worried about their sons' futures and sought to perpetuate the old type of mechanic—skillful and educated—through new institutional supports.

To attain its goals in education and prison labor, the Union chose to act as a pressure group on all politicians, rather than to form a political party or to attempt to take over an existing party. Union members eschewed a political path, saying "the present political parties of the day we have nothing to do with." The leaders of the Union movement worried that any overt political action would divide their members, who had a variety of political loyalties, and jeopardize united action for uniform wage levels. The Newark Trades Union, in an effort to insure that the members were not needlessly at odds with each other, voted to have no political or religious questions debated.[8] One of Newark's delegates to the 1834 national convention even desired that the word "political" be removed from a resolution:

The proceedings of the Unions, he said, were watched, narrowly watched, and although he believed that in reality the term implied nothing improper, it was misunderstood by many, and might prove fatal to the interests of the Unions by arraying against them the force of one or other of the political parties.[9]

Other convention delegates suggested that the word "politics" was used as a bugbear by the "aristocracy," who wished to pass legislation inimicable to the interests of the majority, and reiterated the right of the "working classes" to review all measures with an eye to their effects on the majority of citizens. The opponents of the trades unions frequently branded them as a new variety of political party or as unfair fronts for one of the major parties.

Union leaders viewed politics with suspicion because, had they advanced a new politics based on the class interests of journeymen, they would have destroyed the old consensus molded by artisans and incurred the enmity of the rest of the community. The artisan political heritage emphasized the split between the "producers" and the "aristocracy." The producers—masters and journeymen together—were to stand firm, countering any aristocratic attempts to gain special privileges and to undermine the economic and political freedom all enjoyed. Newark's mechanics believed in limited government, although they applauded state and federal support of manufactures and sponsorship of internal improvements, arguing that such activities were useful to the entire community rather than a single "class." But in general they relied on private individuals to create the collective good, and in the 1820s Newark's master craftsmen had run its government on this model.

Within this consensus there had been as much factionalism among Newark's Jeffersonian Republicans as there was among Republicans nationwide. By 1828 Andrew Jackson had become the overriding political issue, with men aligning themselves for or against him, and by the mid-1830s two political parties, the Jacksonians and the Whigs, had formed. In Newark the Jacksonians were a small minority with little to differentiate them from the Whigs on economic issues. Unlike Jacksonians elsewhere, Newark's Jacksonians supported federally sponsored internal improvements and the protective tariff just like the Whigs; they joined the majority of their party only to support Jackson in his war on the Bank of the United States. While nationally Jacksonians emphasized the anti-monopoly issue, New Jersey Jacksonians were instrumental in chartering the state's most lucrative monopoly by giving the Camden and Amboy Railroad and its "junior partner," the Delaware and Raritan Canal Company, sole railroad rights between New York and Philadelphia. New Jersey Jacksonians encouraged this monopoly because they courted rural voters, who preferred that the state rely on revenue from the monopoly rather than on general taxation. Nationally, the Whigs and the Jacksonians framed their differences in terms of the old consensus, the fear of aristocracy. The Whigs attacked Jackson as a tyrant because of his military past and his "arbitrary" actions that enlarged the scope of the Executive, while the Jacksonians attacked the Whigs as anti-democratic Federalists in disguise and supporters of "the money power."[10] In Newark this rhetoric served as the sole distinguishing feature of the two parties.

Most Newarkers adhered to the Whig Party because nationally and locally it championed the mechanics' program of the 1820s, appealing to journeymen and employers alike on the basis of support for industry, especially through the tariff. By the late 1830s, New Jersey's Jacksonians were also supporting an inflexible hard currency, which to Newarkers seemed to favor agrarian interests over commercial and industrial prosperity.[11] Thirteen percent of Newark's craftsmen took an active role in politics between 1836 and 1840, and two-thirds of them were Whigs.[12] They served on ward committees and nominating committees, as convention delegates and candidates, as pollwatchers, and in city government. The craftsmen's social organizations often drew them into Whig politics. Newark's volunteer fire companies became political clubs and political pressure groups just as they did in other cities; they functioned in this manner for the Whigs as they did for the Jacksonians in cities like New York and Philadelphia.[13] Many of Newark's largest manufacturers were prominent Whigs, but to have dominated city politics so thoroughly the Whigs must have had significant support from journeymen too.

In the 1830s few, even among union leaders, saw the limitations of the old political consensus. The majority of Newark's union leaders in shoemaking, hatting, carpentry, saddle making, and leather making were not active in local political parties, and the 37 percent who were active in both union and political affairs led no crusade for a new politics for journeymen.[14] The artisan tradition has molded them all; responding to the factionalism within that consensus, some were Whigs and some Jacksonians. Others belonged to the third party movement of Mechanics and Workingmen, who were probably the strongest supporters of the mechanics' ideology, championing the proposals that mechanics began to articulate in the 1820s, such as the abolition of imprisonment for debt and the creation of a public education system.

Workingmen's Parties, variously entitled, appeared in most manufacturing cities in America between 1829 and 1836, reflecting the dislocations of early industrialization. Each party responded to local concerns and situations, but all had a common grounding in the mechanics' ideology; they attracted those who desired a society in which there were broad opportunities for small capitalists.[15] The Newark movement began in 1830 with a ticket of Mechanics and Workingmen championing free public education, improved assistance for the poor, and ballot rather than voice voting. This group refused to take a stand for or against Jackson, confining itself to mechanics' issues that were appropriate for the local or state level. In appealing to mechanics they swept the town meeting, and a few months later a group of Farmers, Mechanics and Workingmen formed on the county level to advocate further reforms in taxation and qualifications for office holding. The local Jacksonians also supported this ticket, and it was successful.

The men involved in the mechanics' movement in Newark maintained no concerted party effort, however, focusing instead on keeping their demands before the public.[16] As in other cities, the Newark Mechanics and Workingmen included men of various occupations, both employer and employee, and even a few trade unionists—held together only by their concern for the vulnerability of the mechanic. In 1834, 1835, and 1836 they formed separate tickets again to advocate their traditional concerns along with an antimonopoly position, but they were not successful. By this time the Mechanics and Workingmen were closely allied with the local Jacksonians, and that union adversely affected their popularity; in addition their issues had been adopted by both the major parties. By 1838 the state legislature had passed weak laws on public education, judicial reform, monetary reform (allowing small bills), and fairer representation for the counties. It abolished imprisonment for debt in 1842 but denied requests for mechanics' lien laws. Newark's Whig city government responded by passing a local mechanics' lien law in 1847. The New Jersey prison system continued to engage in direct competition with free labor through convict labor in weaving, shoemaking, chair making, and cooperage, but the mechanics had won substantial recognition for their interests by the mid-1830s.[17] Although their proposals found broad support, after 1830 the Mechanics and Workingmen as a party never won the votes of more than a handful of Newarkers, for most citizens remained transfixed by the major parties and their policies.

Because they did not perceive their struggle against the manufacturers in political terms, Newark's journeymen did not rush into politics to unseat their employers. In the 1820s the master craftsmen had formed the backbone of local political movements and had been the candidates for local offices, and in the 1830s the self-employed continued to dominate local politics. In the period from 1836 to 1840, 51 percent of the self-employed craftsmen in the eight trades took an active part in politics, but only 9 percent of the journeymen did.[18] In the traditional crafts dominated by self-employed artisans, political participation was particularly common; for instance, 25 percent of Newark's jewelers and 32 percent of its trunk makers were active in party affairs in the late 1830s.

Property qualifications for both office-holding and voting bolstered the political dominance of the self-employed. In 1836 the suffrage qualifications in the city included the provision that one had to have paid taxes, held a freehold, or rented a tenement with a yearly value of $5 or more. Property qualifications for voting were abolished in 1844, but those for jury duty and county office-holding remained until 1851. Since almost all men, including bachelors, paid taxes, the property qualifications probably kept only a few men from the polls.[19] Such laws were symbolic, however, of the prestige of the propertied.

While the property qualification probably did not depress political participation by journeymen, the residency requirement for voting may have. The city demanded residency of six months within its boundaries, and the state demanded residency of one year. The average craftsman in the eight trades were so mobile, staying only three years in Newark in the late 1830s, that, if the law was enforced, many were without the franchise much of the time.

Other factors besides apathy, status considerations, and voting restrictions may have affected the degree of political involvement among journeymen. Some journeymen charged that their employers tried to dictate their votes, as in 1834 when a few journeymen complained that they had been discharged for their political opinions. Among them was a man who worked for the largest saddle making firm and who, his fellow employees charged, "spent hour after hour reading and talking to journeymen and apprentices on political subjects, hindering their work" and destroying "all regularity and good order."[20] The fired journeyman was a Jacksonian, while his employer was one of the city's foremost Whigs. The same year a call was issued to all *"Whig* Saddlers, Harness Makers and Coach Trimmers" to meet in preparation for the Fourth of July celebration.

The continuing appeal of the mechanics' ideology to both employers and journeymen meant that the bourgeoisie could dominate local politics and further their economic goals while politicians claimed that no class interests were being served. The manufacturers, unlike the masters in the 1820s, did not share a common interest with the journeymen, and thus the continuation of the old routines worked to their benefit. The notion of limited government, in particular, was detrimental to workers and the poor, but good for wealthy taxpayers. The journeymen's vision of uniting to secure their best interests did not widen to become a social vision for the whole community. Until conditions became intolerable, Newarkers did not think to achieve a common good through united (governmental) action. Out of the boosterism that accompanied economic development, Newarkers sought incorporation as a city in 1836, but the city government instituted much needed services, like street paving and lighting or a water system, only slowly and on the most limited basis consistent with underfinancing.

Newark's reaction to the depression of 1837 was symptomatic of the hegemony of the old ideals and their impact on the working class. The traditional system of poor relief—which provided an undifferentiated almshouse, stressed the role of intemperance, and distinguished between the worthy (widows and orphans) and the unworthy (everyone else)—could not deal with the massive unemployment that accompanied the depression. Despite pleas by the poor, the city government failed to expand its programs, limiting itself to giving road work to more men by hiring them all on a part-time basis. The bulk of the relief effort was private. Many groups held concerts and fairs to raise money, and businessmen set up ward committees, which solicited donations and gave relief to those who had exhausted their own resources, although each family was expected to fend for itself for as long as possible.

The Common Council did not respond to the needs of industrial workers, but it did respond to the needs of "mechanics" by trying to solve the currency shortage that was stifling business. It issued the $20,000 worth of loan certificates for the water supply system in small sums of under one dollar each in value to provide the small change necessary for business, and thus employment, to continue. But when the Council wanted to issue $30,000 more, Mayor Halsey refused, not wanting government to usurp what was recognized as the function of private banking.[21] Although the private effort was not sufficient to meet the needs of the unemployed, the dominant ideology would accept no other.

In their search for power in the 1840s and 1850s, journeymen built on the experience of craftsmen in the 1830s—their creation of a craft unionism and their adherence to a preindustrial political ideology—but they faced new issues emanating from the development of deep ethnic and religious divisions within the community. Journeymen along with other Newarkers and Americans elsewhere began to look to the political process to channel the severe cultural conflicts that were rupturing the social order. At the same time, journeymen were ever more conscious of their dwindling control over their work as industrialization proceeded, and they attempted to overcome their ethnic and religious antagonisms within the framework of trade unionism that had been created in the 1830s. Beset by the counterclaims of class and ethnic group, journeymen confined their struggles for power to craft unionism and ethnic politics. The major political parties remained blind to the grievances of the working class, and the mechanics' ideology, however archaic, was the major point of consensus in Newark's political arena.

By the late 1840s, the foreign-born were an important element in the labor force of many crafts and already were a majority in leather making (Table 13). Paradoxically, this diversity encouraged the continuation of the forms of worker action that had evolved among native craftsmen in the 1830s. Journeymen of various backgrounds found it easier to agree on a limited program of higher wages and elimination of female and child job competition than on any broader proposal to reform society, which would necessarily involve questions of religious belief or moral value. The economy began to revive again in 1843, and as full-scale production resumed, journeymen organized once more for wage increases. While the city-wide and national assemblies of unions remained dormant, journeymen revived local craft unions when inflation again made the division of profits seem particularly inequitable. The journeymen shoemakers, curriers, carpenters, and masons all formed unions as they had in the 1830s, and the journeymen tailors organized for the first time in Newark. Most of the strikes called by unions in the 1840s and 1850s were for higher wages, and the shoemakers, whose union extended into the surrounding areas, attempted to institute the closed shop and gain union recognition to achieve control over wages. But not all journeymen joined the unions, and employers often found scabs. Hostility between fellow craftsmen could become intense in such situations. Several shoemakers were arrested during the 1850 strike for attacking a scab, but they insisted they had been assaulting him verbally, not physically, and they were released.[22]

The continuity of the forms and issues of working-class action among carpenters was not unexpected since most of them were native-born, but there were many immigrants in shoemaking, hatting, and leather making, and journeymen in these crafts followed the same traditions.[23] Craft unionism held sway even though few of the union leaders of the 1830s were still involved in local activities in the 1840s. At most, one-fifth of the union leaders of the 1830s were still journeymen in Newark in the late 1840s; some had died, others had become self-employed or changed their occupations, most had moved elsewhere.[24] New leaders arose, but journeymen built on the tradition of craft unionism, because it represented the core of class consciousness, emanating from the work situation, on which those of various ethnic and religious backgrounds could agree—that the laborers were being "robbed of their hire."

Journeymen overcame their ethnic and religious antagonisms enough to form craft unions and conduct strikes for limited objectives, but most did not go further and protest industrialization or mechanization itself. Workers in industrializing crafts acquiesced to the loss of tools, and Newark's curriers even struck one shop where the owner made them buy an implement with their own money.[25] The class consciousness of most of Newark's journeymen had not expanded to a critique of society as a whole, and few expressed any overt interest in the visionary, utopian, and socialist schemes that George Evans, Robert Owen, and others were propounding elsewhere.[26] The lone anti-capitalist experiment in Newark occurred in 1849 when there was a meeting to form a *"Protective Union* of the producing classes, both *male and female,* for the purpose of bettering their condition as to their rightful share of the results of their labor." This group formed an Association of Producers, with an initiation fee of $5, which constituted one share of capital stock. The Association sold one hundred shares of stock, and established an 8¢ per week sick benefit fund. It also invested in a grocery, a consumers' cooperative which, while open to all, would give a discount to members. If more funds could be collected, the Association hoped to invest in some "mechanical department." They wished to aid all working men to become self-employed so that they would not be "compelled to submit to the numberless exactions of those whose only occupation consists in interposing themselves between the producer and consumer." They complained that:

The condition of the workingman is daily becoming worse. Mechanics have resorted to different methods to relieve themselves from unnecessary burdens without success. Trades Unions and strikes have had their day, and it has been demonstrated that when labor contends with capital, labor must in the end succumb. Mechanics have discovered also that neither of the political parties can reach their case, and they begin to feel to a limited extent that the remedy is in their own hands.[27]

But "the remedy," which hearkened back to a Newark of the 1820s, was not attractive to many, and the grocery and the Association disappeared quickly, inspiring no others in Newark to attempt cooperative experiments to reclaim their "independence."

While the major effect of immigration was to exacerbate ethnic conflict and thus to reinforce the limitation of working-class action to craft unionism, immigration was also responsible for bringing a more radical critique of industrial capitalism to Newark. In the 1850s a more extreme labor "radicalism" appeared among a segment of German immigrants to Newark who espoused a socialism influenced heavily by Marx. By 1850 one hundred Germans in Newark had formed an *arbeiterverein* (German Trades Union) that allied with groups in other cities and sent representatives to the first national convention of German workingmen held in Philadelphia in that year. Within a few years some German workers in Newark were supporting Joseph Weydemeyer's brand of Marxian Socialism and attempting to meld political action with trade union work. From 1853 to 1858, Fritz Anneke, a German immigrant, published the *Newarker Zeitung*, which supported the labor movement and followed the socialism expounded by Weydemeyer. The *Newark Daily Advertiser*, the voice of the manufacturers, called these Germans "radicals," and few, if any, native-born journeymen became educated about their beliefs. Nonetheless, in 1859 some Germans again formed a Workingmen's Union that cut across craft and industry lines "to secure good wages, afford mutual relief in sickness, etc."[28] While the number of Germans involved in this more radical labor activity was probably quite small, Anneke's paper was nevertheless influential in the German community because it also championed German cultural forms against the nativist onslaught.

The traditions of most journeymen—immigrants and natives—did not lead them to accept or understand the socialists' notions of joining economic and political action or of creating unions that ignored craft lines. In the 1850s, Newark's journeymen and American workers in general strengthened the craft union movement, laying the foundations for most working-class action for the rest of the century. In Newark, previously unorganized workers—the jewelers, the stone cutters, the building laborers, and the hod, brick and stone carriers—formed craft unions and demanded higher wages in the 1850s. Other workers, like the female hat trimmers who struck P. W. Vail over the low wages he paid, were active although they formed no permanent organizations. The older unions like the Journeymen Carpenters and the Journeymen Shoemakers continued their attempts to set wage rates. Employers usually reduced wages in bad times like the winter of 1857–58, and the unions always demanded increases when good times returned. The Journeymen Shoemakers may not always have been successful in raising wages, but they continued their struggle by reaching out for solidarity with shoemakers elsewhere. In 1853, Newark's shoemakers attempted to form a National Association of United Cordwainers with men from Boston, New York, and other cities. In 1860 they sent aid to those shoemakers who were on strike for higher wages in Massachusetts's cities; according to the Newark shoemakers, the striking Lynn shoe operatives received but half the wages they did. Not surprisingly, Newark shoe manufacturers also supported the Lynn strike, however much they resisted local ones; if the price of labor in Massachusetts rose, Newark's products would be competitive nationally, and Newark manufacturers might reclaim the Southern shoe market.[29]

Those craftsmen who had organized earlier sought to extend their power in the 1850s through imposing union work rules, building union treasuries, and reviving the idea of country-wide unity among craftsmen. The Newark Hat Finishers Association, representing those engaged in one of the last skilled tasks left in hatting, pushed the employers hard and struck frequently in the late 1850s to secure union shops. Although it tried to set wages, the union's main goal was to restrict the number of apprentices per shop to counter manufacturers' attempts to cut wages through the use of unskilled workmen. The Association, unlike earlier unions, realized the necessity of a strike fund, and it was giving $4 per week to each striker in order to bring all the hat factories and shops under union rule. The union was at least partially successful in its attempts, some firms becoming "fair" and others remaining "foul." The hat manufacturers tried the usual union-busting tactics, including advertisements for strike breakers in papers as far away as Danbury, Connecticut, but the workers countered by joining hatters elsewhere to form the United States Hat Finishers Association in 1854.[30] American craftsmen in four other trades—printers, stone cutters, molders, and machinists—were organized sufficiently to form national unions in the 1850s; in other crafts, such as shoemaking, the ideal of national unity provided the foundation for a stronger craft union movement in future decades. The Hat Finishers Association also foreshadowed the future, however, in that it included only the most skilled workers in the field. The unions of the 1830s and 1840s had included all workers, but the extension of mechanization and of the division of tasks destroyed craft solidarity and laid the basis for the split between skilled and unskilled workers that rent the American labor movement for decades.

In the 1840s and 1850s, while journeymen were developing craft unions for economic action, they also sought expression for their ethnic and religious values; industrial class conflict did not intrude into the political arena, but ethnic conflicts did. To a large extent ethnic politics was as much a product of Newark's working class as were the craft unions: journeymen joined with others in their ethnic or religious group to pressure the politicians to represent their viewpoint in the law. Temperance became the rallying cry of native Americans of all classes; of nearly equal importance to them was the wholesale pre-election naturalization of foreigners whether or not they met the legal requirements for citizenship. The Germans and the Irish abhorred temperance, and Roman Catholics of all nationalities wanted aid for parochial schools, an anathema for Protestants.

Cultural conflict did not become intense in Newark until the early 1850s; Whig control of the city in the 1840s rested on some apathy among voters, on the dominance of the native-born among the electorate, and on the continued belief by journeymen and employers alike in their common political interests.[31] Four-fifths of those craftsmen who took an active part in politics in the 1840s were Whigs, and many journeymen supported the Whigs because they feared foreign competition as much as their employers did.[32] National currents, especially the growing discord over slavery, influenced Newarkers, but the foremost political issues were those generated by local economic conditions and the mechanics' tradition. In the 1840s, when the Free Soilers became active in the city, they found their greatest support among the blacks, who could hold meetings but were not allowed to vote under state law.[33] As long as Newarkers were more concerned about economic development than ethnic and religious tensions, the Whig Party received their votes.

Whig control rested not only on continued support for the tariff, which was sacred in Newark, but on meeting the demands that "mechanics" had made in the 1830s and paying some attention to those made by workers in the industrial sector. By 1849 even the *Newark Daily Advertiser* agreed with the workingmen of Trenton who were trying to obtain the ten-hour day, insisting that it was necessary to keep labor respectable and stop the process of making men into machines.[34] Too much toil they said, was not good for physical or intellectual health, and children under twelve years of age should not work at all. In 1851 the state legislature acted on a plethora of such demands: abolishing the property qualification for county office-holding and jury duty, putting a $200 exemption on debt collection, providing a free public school system, outlawing the labor of children under ten years of age in factories, and legislating the ten-hour day in factories. Violations of the factory act were punishable by a $50 fine, which hardly acted as a deterrent to noncompliance, but even toothless acts were a recognition of the felt needs of the industrial work force and of the importance of the mechanics' ideology.

But Whig attempts to overcome ethnic tensions and appeal to all groups failed in the long run. As early as 1840 the Whig Party included a German-speaking branch, but as the decade wore on the Party, locally and nationally, was increasingly identified with the strict, native-born Protestant morality propounded by businessmen and ministers. Although the Whig Party was usually victorious in local elections in the 1840s, splinter tickets were sometimes formed and Democrats sometimes elected in challenges to the strict Whig tavern licensing policy designed to encourage temperance.[35]

During the early 1840s the Democrats had been such a permanent minority that they rarely put up candidates of their own for city office, and the only positions they acquired were obtained by federal appointment. But as immigration increased, and with it the degree of ethnic and religious tensions, the Democratic Party gained strength. The Irish, most of them working class, were strongly attracted to the Democratic Party, but some of the Germans were Democrats too. The *New Jersey Staats Courier*, the German-language newspaper published in Newark in 1850, was pro-Democratic. In 1849 the Democrats ran a full slate of candidates for local office for the first time and carried the fifth ward as well as several at-large contests.[36] By 1853 the Democrats had a majority on the city council, which was elected on a ward basis, and in 1857 the first Democratic mayor was elected.

The local Whig Party was beset with the image of corruption that often afflicts those long in power, and this further aided the Democrats in their bid for power. In the state elections of 1849 an anti-monopoly group was formed from members of the Whig Party to protest the power of the Camden and Amboy Railroad in the party and in the state government. Voters began to suspect the aims of local Whig control, too; in 1850 the staunchly Whig *Newark Daily Advertiser* was even printing letters asking, "Where is the public act of it's [Newark's] government that is not tinctured more or less with some private interest or lack of justice?"[37]

While on the national level both parties were racked by the sectional conflict over slavery, on the local level throughout the North, the Whig Party foundered on the rock of ethnic conflict.[38] In Newark the Whigs had claimed support among all craftsmen, but by 1854 the Whig Party had succumbed to the pressure of native Americans who believed that immigrant Catholic voters were subject to an authoritarian dictation that threatened American republicanism. Some old Whigs objected, but in 1854 the Whig Party of Newark was a cover for the Know Nothings, the secret society that was attempting to use the political process to purge America of immigrant and Catholic influences. In the elections that year the Whigs, following the lead of the Know Nothings, attacked the Democratic candidate for mayor for favoring aid to parochial schools and sought to run union tickets in the sixth and seventh wards "to oppose the ultra tendencies of the foreign-born citizens and residents who seek to control those wards, and elect men to the Common Council pledged to support their peculiar anti-American doctrines."[39] This did little to endear Whigs to the many immigrant craftsmen. The Democrats were proimmigrant and antitemperance, and they countered the Whig appeal to craftsmen on the tariff by arguing that since most of Newark's trade was with the South, the Democratic policy of appeasement of Southern interests was vital to Newark's continued economic health.

The Democratic Party did not inherit the Whig hegemony of the past, however, because social unity had disappeared. In late 1854 the Know Nothings came above ground in many states and cities, and in Newark they formed the American Party, since some Whigs were not giving their wholehearted support to anti-immigrant and anti-Catholic positions. As the Whig Party died, the Republican Party also formed in Newark in 1856, two years later than it emerged elsewhere. All three parties—Democrats, Republicans, and Americans—vied for control of the city government in the next few years, and all had large bases of support, but none had a majority. The Democrats failed to create a unified voting bloc among immigrants. Within the Democratic party, Irish and German Democrats in the sixth ward fought incessantly over ethnic representation and often put up splinter tickets. And in 1854 at least part of the German community split with the Democrats over the issue of slavery, and led by their newspaper, the *Newarker Zeitung*, many joined the Republicans in 1856.[40]

The parties were in great disarray in the 1850s; many people were switching from one to another, and almost everyone running for office was formerly a member of another party. The craftsmen who were active in politics in the 1850s favored no one party, and many moved from one to another searching for the best expression of their ethnic allegiances and their views on national issues, especially slavery.[41] In these three-way races, the Democrats could win city-wide elections, but they did little to increase their support among the electorate.[42] In 1857 the Democratic city clerk was forced to resign after embezzling city funds, and the Democrats no longer had a monopoly on the corruption issue. They also cut school appropriations drastically for 1858, upsetting many parents and community leaders. In 1858 the Democrats even bowed to temperance pressure and outlawed the sale of liquor on Sunday and closed the beer halls, alienating more German voters. A united opposition in the fall of 1858 beat back the Democratic city ticket and reduced the number of Democratic aldermen.

By 1860 the American Party was dying, but political chaos still reigned. The Constitutional Union Party appealed for support both to the Americans and to "Old Line Whigs." The Democrats were split between Douglass and Breckinridge; the importance of southern markets to many of Newark's industries gave Breckinridge much support among leading industrialists and made his candidacy viable in this northern city. The Republicans were also in the fight, and they won the at-large city elections of 1860, while the Democrats retained control of the Council. Together, Douglass, Breckinridge, and Bell outpolled Lincoln in the presidential election.

Throughout the political calm of the 1840s and the chaos of the 1850s only one constant remained—the artisan political tradition. While both journeymen and employers advanced their ethnic allegiances and their views on slavery in the political arena, they never questioned the old consensus on economic issues. Manufacturers, viewing themselves as producers, found perfectly comfortable the tradition that limited government spending and regulation, supported manufactures, and lauded the self-employed. Native journeymen continued to respond to appeals to the mechanics' heritage. As they had in the 1830s, both Whig and Democratic Parties paid homage to the mechanic—the independent, self-made man—but so too did the Americans and the Republicans. In 1853 the Whigs nominated Joel Haywood, a blacksmith and "fellow mechanic" for governor of New Jersey, and groups entitling themselves Young Mechanics Associations formed to support him.[43] The American Party also appealed to voters on the basis of this rhetoric, and their newspaper, the *Newark Daily Mercury*, included many a peaen to the mechanic, little different from those heard thirty years before:

However Snobdom may scorn and snear, the mechanic is the very blood and muscle of society. Remove him and you strike out of existence the pivot element upon which all the machinery of society depends.[44]

Such editorials went on to assure the voters that self-reliant, independent men should be their leaders. The Republican Party throughout the North echoed the same sentiments: America was a nation of small entrepreneurs, workers and employers united as the "producing classes." Men succeeded by their own abilities and failed by their own shortcomings, and those who labored for wages all their lives had not seized their opportunities.[45]

While championing ethnic interests, both native and foreign-born politicians socialized immigrants to an American politics that ignored current class realities. The Democratic Party, especially, helped to instill this view of the range of permissible political issues in the immigrant. In 1854 the *Newarker Zeitung*, with its interest in a new class politics, attacked the local Democrats' advocacy of the rights of workingmen as insincere. The response of the Democrats revealed the strength of the mechanics' ideology. The Democratic candidate in the sixth ward said, "I am at a loss to understand how the interests of the workman can be opposed to the manufacturer; it looks to me when properly understood, that they are parallel and identical."[46] The Democrats understood the rights of workingmen to mean equal opportunity in the political arena to run for office and in the economic arena to become a success. They were proud of having candidates "who recognize no class prejudices, but regard alike the interest of the mechanic and the millionaire."[47]

The only active threat to the belief in the common political interests of employer and employee appeared in the 1840s from the National Reform

Association, which tried to harness the discontent of journeymen to a program of land reform that would liberate industrial workers from wage labor. In 1846 about forty Newarkers established a local branch of the National Reformers, and the group remained active in the city through 1850. Newark's National Reformers included both natives and Germans, but they had no success at the polls, and few of the politically active craftsmen joined them.[48] As in the 1830s, most journeymen did not perceive politics as a way to solve their economic problems nor to alter power relations between classes. Their heritage kept them focused on the old distinctions between Whigs and Democrats rather than on new conceptions of political action. In the 1850s, the salience of ethnic tensions overcame any questioning of the mechanics' ideology that journeymen might otherwise have undertaken. The political rhetoric continued to laud the entrepreneur, even after most of the craftsmen had no chance for self-employment within their trades. The survival of this archaic ideology in the industrial age effectively forestalled the development of a working-class political consciousness based on economic grievances. It also helps explain the ability of the bourgeoisie to dominate local government and promote laissez-faire capitalism while politicians pledged to eschew class legislation.

The prestige of wealth and the journeymen's reluctance to fight their employers through the political process combined to leave Newark's government in the control of the self-employed in the 1840s and 1850s. Rich manufacturers and others who sought tariff protection and low taxes headed the Whig Party of Newark in the 1840s; these men had clear economic motives for political participation, and they expected others to defer to them because of their prestige. Manufacturers often acted as a united group, such as when the leather manufacturers and the hatters of the city called meetings to arrange for a Whig parade in 1844.[49] In the 1850s, as manufacturers began to worry about their relations with their Southern customers, more of them joined the Democratic Party. As in the 1830s the journeymen were less prone to active participation in party affairs. Between 1846 and 1850, 35 percent of the self-employed craftsmen in the eight trades but only 5 percent of the journeymen were involved in local politics.[50] In the period 1856–60, 26 percent of the self-employed and 5 percent of their employees were politically active. Though small in numbers, the self-employed craftsmen were very influential in the political life of their city, and the effect of wealth on political activism was equally impressive. In 1850 the correlation between the ownership of real estate and increased political participation was strong (Table 36): three-fourths of those craftsmen who owned real property valued at more than $10,000 were involved in party affairs, while but 6 percent of those with no real property took part. In 1860 there was also a positive correlation between the ownership of property, real or personal, and political participation.

TABLE 36
Percentage Participating in Politics by Value of Property for Male Craftsmen[a]

Value of property	1846–50	1856–60
None	5.8	6.9
$1–500	10.2	6.9
$501–1,000	5.9	4.0
$1,001–1,500	7.2	9.4
$1,501–3,000	23.4	16.2
$3,001–5,000	34.9	17.1
$5,001–10,000	57.1	19.3
$10,001 +	78.1	47.4
	$\gamma = .6307$	$\gamma = .3558$

[a]Data derived from the manuscripts of the U.S. Censuses of 1850 and 1860 and lists published in newspapers of candidates, committees, delegates, and poll watchers.

Money was not a prerequisite for political participation, since in 1850 44 percent of those craftsmen who were involved in party affairs owned no real property, and in 1860, 26 percent owned no property, real or personal. But political activity was much more prevalent among the rich, and the propertied dominated local government. The coincidence of political and economic elites was common in American cities at that time, and in Newark the local political elite was the industrial elite of self-made men. The industrial elite filled many positions in the city government; several prominent manufacturers were aldermen, and they and allied business supporters dominated the mayoralty. From 1836 to 1860, manufacturers and business promoters occupied Newark's mayoralty for seventeen years, lawyers for four years, and men of unknown occupation for four years.[51] That the rich wanted to be in the government or to control it in order to protect their interests is understandable, but it is also clear that no other group in society actively challenged their control.

The mechanics' ideology and the deference to wealth were not the only reasons for the lack of active political participation by journeymen, however. Although property qualifications for voting were removed in the early 1840s, residency and citizenship requirements remained. As the proportion of craftsmen who were foreign-born increased, fewer craftsmen could participate legally in politics. According to the law, the foreign-born had to be residents for five years before becoming citizens, and consequently relatively few of them were involved in party affairs before 1860. In the period 1846 to 1850, 13.3 percent of the native-born craftsmen, but only 3.7 percent of the foreign-born took part in politics.[52] Ten years later the differential still existed; 15.8 percent of the native-born, but only 4.3 percent of the foreign-born participated.

Residency requirements could also keep many journeymen from voting.

Residency restrictions may have been ineffective however; election frauds, especially voting by those who were ineligible, were considered common in this era. But the effects of rootlessness on participation were strong, nevertheless. Long-term residents were bound to be more involved in the life of the community and more likely to take leadership, sooner or later, in its affairs, and more manufacturers than journeymen were long-term residents. The contentment of the wealthy and the self-employed with having found the "main chance" in Newark would lead the city to concentrate ever harder on economic development that proceeded from and catered to the individual. On the other hand, the lack of a long-resident poor population would reduce the claims of the lower classes for consideration. They were interlopers unless they settled.

Yet, despite all their obvious advantages, the self-employed and the wealthy did not have as much control over local politics as they would have liked. In an effort to gain that control, manufacturers continued to try to coerce their employees into voting for prescribed candidates. In 1844 a worker stated that "at a large Saddle Factory in Newark, upon the morning of the day of the election for President in 1840 every voter was handed a Whig ticket, which he was to vote upon penalty of being thrown out of employment if he refused."[53] In the presidential election of 1860, when so many manufacturers saw ruin for themselves in a victory for Lincoln and a consequent secession of the South, workers also charged that employers were trying to influence their votes and were even discharging some employees.[54] The extent and effect of coercion of workers is unclear; employers always denied these charges. But the fact that manufacturers resorted to coercion at all testifies to their desire for power, and to their understanding of how useful political power was to the maintenance of their position.

Because journeymen accepted the mechanics' ideology, expressing in politics their ethnic but not their economic allegiances, government, both nationally and locally, was unresponsive to their plight as workers. While only the federal government could have controlled industry successfully in a national economy, journeymen in industrial areas could have made greater use of state and city government to ameliorate their condition. New Jersey's laws of 1851 against child labor and for the ten-hour day in factories previewed the protective legislation on wages, hours, safety, and unemployment that American workers won in the twentieth century from state, and later the federal, government. Had New Jersey's journeymen more often sought to use politics for economic ends, they might at least have made sure that the 1851 acts were enforced. City government could also have regained for workers some of the profits of their labor by providing, from the taxes paid by industry and land owners, a healthier, safer, and more enjoyable environment. Only in 1883, when a "labor" candidate, Joseph Haynes, was elected mayor did Newark begin to provide services for improving the workers' standard of living, such as an adequate water system, a free public library, and a city hospital.[55] Not until the ascendence of the Progressive Movement in the early twentieth century did urban Americans in general come to accept the notion of city government responsibility for the welfare of the community.

Before 1860, however, the dominance of the mechanics' ideology in Newark reinforced the tradition of limited government, to the detriment of the working class and the community as a whole. The dearth of corporate action caused by the political support for low taxes and "individual initiative" continued, leaving those with fewer resources at a distinct disadvantage in dealing with the problems generated in the industrial city. But the lack of services for the poor was not the only problem; even matters of "civic pride" were overlooked.[56] Newarkers neglected their public spaces; the parks and Common were allowed to deteriorate, overrun by hogs, dogs, and boys. While individual owners sometimes paved or cleaned the streets in front of their houses, the city government's street commission confined its operations to patching, not improving. At most times the streets were rivers of mud strewn with refuse, and the city only began installing gas lamps for street lighting in 1853.

Further, Newark's government took little positive action to improve the health and safety of the populace.[57] In 1846 the laying of pipes for the water system was completed in the older, more commercial part of town. The residents of the ring and of the more residential areas still had to rely on prayer and luck in case of fire and hope that their wells provided pure water. The Council ignored complaints about industrial pollution, whether they involved the stench from the varnish factories, the building of a leather factory in a residential area, or the filth of the tanneries; decomposing animal matter from the tanneries flowed through open sewers and filled cellars whenever the sewers overflowed. Since Newark lacked an adequate sewer system, the waterways always carried raw sewage, and cholera could not be prevented. Newark was built on and near swamps, and consequently malaria was also a constant health problem. While the rich could be cared for by family physicians, the poor waited until 1859 for the city to establish a dispensary for them. Although Newark was an uncomfortable and fairly dangerous place to live, the cumulative death rate was not particularly high. At 18.16 per 1000 from 1841 to 1855, it was significantly below that of the nation's four leading cities. This may have been a function of Newark's size, since smaller cities were healthier in general than larger ones.

Although the city government failed to respond to the needs of the community and of the poor, the wealthy also neglected their humanitarian role. While they resisted tax increases, thus limiting government expenditures, the rich failed to contribute meaningfully in the private sphere. Agitation for a library and a hospital went on for years, before the subscription was sufficient for either, the private library opening in 1848 and a private hospital in the 1860s. Newarkers compared their city, and other American cities, unfavorably to English ones. While critics thought that laborers lived better in Newark than they could in an English city because of higher wages in America, they also said that the community as a whole fared worse. The older English cities had managed to establish amenities, both public and private, which Newark had not. A corporate tradition existed to balance the capitalist one, and to provide necessary city services. In Newark, according to critics, the "general rage for wealth" meant that the whole population was overworked and that the moral and intellectual powers were totally neglected. It also meant that any nonprofit enterprise requiring the cooperation of many, like a hospital or library, was unlikely to make much headway.[58]

Ultimately, then, cultural consolidation, not change, was characteristic of the industrial city. The values of private enterprise and limited government had reigned supreme in the town as well as the city. But with growth the by-products of the implementation of these values could not be so easily controlled and were especially injurious to the working class and the poor. The pursuit of wealth brought dissimilar groups together, causing friction. Most were agreed, however, on the main goal—economic improvement. The "stingy" city government reflected this continuing emphasis on private values.

Newarkers even met the great increase in crime and violence, which may have been the most disturbing problem for the community, with niggardly appropriations for constables and the night watch. Law enforcement was ineffective in the face of mass indifference, and a general lawlessness seemed to prevail, especially in the 1840s. The problem ran the gamut from wild drivers injuring and killing people to idle gunplay that struck down innocent bystanders. It was dangerous for little children to go to school alone, as they might be robbed or run over on the way. Vandalism, incendiarism, and robbery were a plague on the city. Finally in 1857 the Council instituted a day police force of twenty-one men to replace the ward constables—hardly adequate for a city of 64,000, but all that the government would support. Only in comparison to big cities such as New York did Newark seem to be a safe place. Contemporaries attributed this to the fact that it was a manufacturing city where "labor [was] more regular and legitimate" than in commercial centers.[59]

Since the government did so little to solve the problems caused by economic development and population growth, situations rarely occurred in which the contradictions between the political ideology of the mechanic and the reality of the industrial city became manifest. These contradictions surfaced once in 1857, during the severe economic recession, when a journeyman was caught stealing meat. The police ascertained that he had been a conscientious workman, but that his wife and children were starving since he had become unemployed. The journeyman, in keeping with the value placed on self-reliance, said he would rather steal than beg. The police released him with the meat and a small collection, and a local newspaper commended the police for their action and the man for his spirit![60] It is doubtful, however, that this disregard for the "sanctity" of private property would have continued if any large number of unemployed journeymen had decided to be similarly self-reliant.

When the city government did recognize the problems of the poor, it kept its solutions within traditional boundaries. In 1857 Newark's government instituted three industrial primary schools, run by charitable women with city funds to supplement the regular primary and grammar schools.[61] In these, poor or beggar children who would not otherwise go or be allowed by their parents to go to school could learn the three R's and make money by part-time work. The school provided one meal a day, supplies, and clothing if needed. The girls learned to sew; some of the things they made were given back to them as wages and the rest were sold to support the school. Employment was sought also for the boys. All these children, 593 in 1860, were less than ten years of age. They were being readied for their station in the industrial world, where their survival depended on hard work and self-reliance.

The political choices journeymen had made were most devastating during depressions, when politicians conducted business as usual. During the panic of 1857, Newark's journeymen faced serious unemployment. In January 1858, for instance, only 98 people were actively employed in jewelry making, whereas previous to the panic 1,076 had been. Employment picked up later in the year, but unemployment of this magnitude could obliterate a worker's savings and the resources of the city's charities. While workmen could help each other in normal times—by taking up a collection for the widow of a fellow worker, for example—in a depression they were all helpless. In such perilous times journeymen called for more from their government, and in the winter of 1857–58 over one thousand men—Irish, Germans, and natives—rallied to demand jobs on public work projects. But with tax revenues down, the city government refused to extend its operations and placed its faith in private efforts. Indeed, some manufacturers paid in stores when they could get no cash or tried to keep men on part-time.[62] The resurgence of business in the spring brought steady employment again, and journeymen did not apply the lessons of the winter in an effort to make the political parties respond to their needs as workers.

In response to industrialization and the tensions caused by large-scale immigration, Newark's journeymen fashioned different modes of action to achieve their goals as workers and as members of various ethnic and religious groups. In the 1850s they completed the foundations of craft unionism and ethnic politics. To retain power on the job, journeymen wanted permanent societies that could successfully set work rules and organize strikes for higher wages; this was their first line of defense against lowered wages and overwork. Because employers were so powerful, however, journeymen in the most skilled tasks found it easier to be successful if they excluded the less skilled in their industries from the unions. Craft unionism was an expression of journeymen's class consciousness, but it was also tending to become an exclusive movement. On the other hand, to achieve their goals as members of ethnic and religious groups, journeymen, like other Americans, used the political system as an arena for cultural conflict. Those who advocated combining economic and political action usually found little support among the electorate, and Marxian socialism was confined to a small segment of the German community. This pattern of working-class action evolved in many manufacturing cities, and it formed a major tradition upon which American workers drew in the latter part of the nineteenth century.

After the Civil War, manufacturers instituted mechanization on a much wider scale, immigration made the American working class even more ethnically heterogeneous, and class conflict became both more violent and more thoroughly organized. But the forms of action workers took to expand their power in the late nineteenth century reflected the choices made by earlier generations of journeymen. The most common form of worker action remained the combination of journeymen within one industry on the local level for higher wages and job control, using the strike as their primary weapon. To enhance their effectiveness these unions then reached out within each industry to form national organizations and across industry lines to form local labor councils. The tendency of the skilled to exclude the unskilled from their unions remained, and the craft unions that formed the American Federation of Labor in 1886 followed the example set by the hat makers, among others, in the 1850s. But in the late nineteenth century many trade unionists also looked beyond their immediate interests to those of the entire working class, and to implement these goals they typically extended, rather than scrapped, their unions. In 1866, some trade unions, including Newark's curriers' union, extended their scope by forming the National Labor Union, which acted as a political lobby for workers, urging the eight-hour day and monetary reforms. After the death of the N.L.U., workers' criticisms of the economic system fostered the Knights of Labor and its program of education and cooperation. In many manufacturing centers like Newark, the Knights of Labor was the predominant labor organization in the 1870s and 1880s, and much of its support came from trade unionists whose greater class consciousness led them to attempt to unify the skilled and the unskilled.[63]

Workers' attempts to use the political system for economic ends foundered in the late nineteenth century as they had earlier, however, because of the vitality of ethnic conflict and the belief that class politics was un-American. Groups who advocated a working-class politics—organizations as diverse as the National Labor Reform Party and the Socialist Labor Party—

failed to inspire more than a small number of workers to vote for them. Until the 1890s, few outside the German community were interested in Marxian socialism, even in Newark where the Socialist Labor Party was formed in 1877. Manufacturers continued to appeal to the political traditions that were so helpful to them, hearkening to a past in which workers and employers had similar interests—Newark's Manufacturers' Association, for instance, entitled its newspaper the *Newark Artisan*.[64] The widening scope of immigration in the late nineteenth century also blocked a working-class political movement by extending the hold of ethnic politics in America. The urban political machine organized immigrant working-class voters into ethnic blocks, socializing them to an American politics that gave them symbolic achievements (the first Irish mayor or Italian alderman) as well as personal aid as individuals. The machine bosses were self-made men, tied by corruption to the business community, who shuddered at the thought of an assault on capitalist privilege. When workers advocated political action for economic change they encountered deep resistance from the machines and their followers as well as from the manufacturers and their supporters.[65] New conditions and new ideas broadened the scope of working-class action in the late nineteenth century, but the traditions of craft unionism and ethnic politics continued to shape workers' struggles for power well into the twentieth century.

CHAPTER 7

Conclusion

The most far-reaching changes in the average man's expectations, in the nature of his work, and in his power in the community and over his job occurred during the initial stages of industrialization. From its inception, American industrialization depended on large-scale immigration from Europe for an expanded supply of unskilled and semiskilled workers, so that ethnic and religious antagonisms as well as class conflicts racked the social order. Journeymen had, thus, to reconcile the cultural diversity and conflict in their own ranks with their attempts to maintain power over their work and to perpetuate artisan values and customs. Although the mix of industries and ethnic groups varied from city to city, by the 1850s the emerging working class had created common patterns for structuring the competing claims of its artisan heritage, of ethnic diversity, and of industrial capitalism.

Industrialization proceeded slowly in some crafts and fast in others, bypassing a few altogether, but in Newark and many other Northeastern cities it had almost completely destroyed household production, traditional skills and work rhythms, and the old relationship between master and journeyman by the mid-nineteenth century. Furthermore, the factory system fostered a split between work and "life" by separating production from the home and by mandating specific hours for labor. Urban journeymen used this dichotomy to create autonomy from the capitalist class: in "life"—the sphere of leisure and the family—they could perpetuate the values of their artisan heritage and of their ethnic and religious groups. Journeymen began to build this sanctuary in the home by keeping their wives and children isolated from the world of production and dependent on their support whenever possible. The artisan's authority within his household had rested on his position as the leader of the domestic production unit; journeymen could likewise dominate their families as the sole breadwinners. Americans,

Germans, and Irish followed similar patterns of family structure and formation; they married relatively late, their children were comparatively few, and their households were rather small and without a production function.[1] Within these limits, however, the family preserved cultural traditions, and workers, both native and immigrant, clung to their family values against appeals for change from feminists, reformers, and revolutionaries.[2]

Journeymen also wished to extend their sphere of autonomy beyond the home, and in the process they reshaped the cities in which they lived. To create greater scope for personal independence and for feelings of mastery, they sought new neighborhoods and social groups that were uniform in wealth or ethnicity. In every major city, segregated organizations—fire companies, guard units, benevolent associations, and the like—proliferated in the 1840s, and by the 1850s ethnic ghettos and wealth-graded neighborhoods were evolving too.[3] Among their peers, journeymen found the freedom, the equality, and the respect for their own values that the world of industrial work denied them.

To create this life style, journeymen had to challenge capitalist domination at work. Against the united opposition of their employers, journeymen waged a difficult struggle to preserve some control over their jobs and over the profits of their labor. By creating craft unions, journeymen minimized female and child labor, kept their wages high enough to support their families, and confined their work to sixty hours per week, thereby acquiring some leisure. Journeymen often found unity difficult to achieve, however, because of their ethnic and religious differences. By the 1850s, journeymen frequently were overcoming their prejudices at work and were forming unions at the same time that they were extending their isolation from one another outside the work place in segregated neighborhoods and social groups.[4] Separating work and "life" enabled journeymen to unite on the job without homogenizing their ethnic and religious differences and even without losing their prejudices.

The journeymen's challenge to their employers was sufficient to sustain their autonomous life style but not to overturn their subordinate position at the work place and in social relations. The growing power of the industrial elite and the lack of political mechanisms to redistribute wealth or even to create sufficient community facilities characterized every manufacturing city. At first journeymen made no political challenge to capitalist industrialism because they retained the artisan political ideology that coupled the defense of equal opportunity to the belief that employers and employees had identical interests vis-a-vis the state. By the 1850s, ethnic and religious conflict was so bitter that a journeyman usually chose his political allegiance to bolster the values and the power of the ethnic or religious group to which he belonged.[5] Journeymen rarely used the political process to further their class interests, and their political activities divided them against themselves. The modes of action that journeymen created—craft unionism and ethnic politics—were more successful at bolstering a private life within an ethnic community than at maintaining workers' control over the means and methods of production.

The first generation of industrial workers thus bequeathed to the American working class a legacy that centered the search for autonomy—for the expression of values and the exercise of mastery and independence—primarily outside of work in the family, the social group, and the neighborhood. Until the 1920s, American industrialization continued to be dependent on large-scale immigration, and beginning in the 1880s millions of Eastern and Southern Europeans swelled the populations of the old manufacturing cities in the Northeast and of the new industrial centers in the Midwest. With the constant influx of immigrants of diverse nationalities and religions, many of whom came from preindustrial cultures, the main focus of working-class life remained the attempt to retain preindustrial and ethnic values within the urban, industrial world.[6] In the late nineteenth and early twentieth centuries, workers followed the example of their forebears, using the family to preserve older traditions and creating segregated social worlds through leisure institutions. In every city ethnic ghettos grew more extensive, and wealth-graded neighborhoods became the fixed pattern of urban residence.[7] If anything, the search for satisfactions outside of work became even more intense; further mechanization destroyed the meaningful content of most jobs, and workers' attempts to regain control of their work were largely unsuccessful. The strike and unionization remained the workers' chief weapons, but, as the partnerships of earlier decades gave way to corporations that enlisted the coercive force of government and police, the ability of manufacturers to combine against their employees and overpower them increased. The consequent defeat of many union movements in the late nineteenth century ingrained a preference for narrow craft unions, which had had the greatest staying power, among skilled workers.[8] Although class-conscious political movements became more numerous, most workers continued to view the political process as a road to symbolic achievement for their ethnic or religious groups, and industrial capitalists still wielded tremendous political power under the banner of equal opportunity and free enterprise.

In the twentieth century, American workers have faced new challenges, but they have met these by modifying rather than by replacing old ways of life and modes of action. Since World War II, American workers have achieved a new level of affluence because of widespread unionization, increased productivity, and expanded consumer credit. Workers have been able to create a more comfortable and expressive "life" away from work at the very time that their jobs have become more deadening because of automation and efficiency drives.[9] Thus new conditions—affluence and automation—have encouraged workers to continue to seek independence, mastery, and the realization of their values primarily off the job in the family and leisure.

In maintaining cultural continuity, the contemporary working class has remained family-centered and wedded to traditional family roles.[10] Like journeymen in the 1840s who looked askance at utopians and socialists seeking to destroy the patriarchal Victorian family, most workers have been shocked by the attack of the young and the New Left on traditional sex roles, by the demand for sexual freedom, and by experiments with alternative family and household patterns in the past decade. Most working-class men want to be the "providers" for their families and desire wives whose first allegiance is to their homemaking role, although many wives take paid jobs to help maintain or to raise the family's standard of living. Workers view consumer goods, the fruit of the new affluence, as a vehicle for creating a "good life" for their families as well as for implementing values that find no expression on the job. They desire home ownership, for example, because they believe it is supportive of family life, but also because it gives them independence from the landlord—an independence they would like to have from their bosses. The working-class focus on family extends beyond the nuclear family, as workers confine their socializing to relatives and kin more often than others do.

Increased leisure has accompanied growing affluence in this century, but the content of leisure has changed. Working-class men have shown relatively less interest in the all-male social groups common previously and more interest in family activities and mass entertainment. At least in part, suburbanization has furthered this trend; the acquisition of the family-supportive home breaks up the old neighborhood. Suburbanites spend less time forging social ties to other workers in neighborhood bars or at ethnic lodges and fraternal orders and more time at home in front of the television or with their families.

This decline in structured social life among workers has occurred at the same time that the working class has become more homogeneous culturally.[11] Since the cessation of large-scale immigration in the 1920s, the mass culture disseminated through the media and consumerism has replaced the distinctions of ghetto culture among broad segments of the working class. Ethnic allegiances remain alive for some, surfacing in the loyalty shown to inner-city neighborhoods in the face of every attempt at urban renewal, highway construction, or desegregation, but antagonisms have abated.[12] The decline of ethnic and religious conflicts has not heralded an age of unity among workers, however. Since the 1920s, black migration from the rural South has met the need for more industrial labor, and blacks have become an important component of the urban working class. There are striking parallels between the interactions of white and black workers today and those of native and immigrant workers in the past. Racial antagonisms inhibit collective action, and even when white and black workers unite on the job, they go home to segregated neighborhoods and separate social worlds.[13]

In the twentieth century the vast expansion of bureaucratic management and the growth of the service sector of the economy have created another kind of heterogeneity within the working class.[14] The nineteenth-century working class was composed of manual laborers, while those in white collar jobs were usually self-employed. The rise of the corporation has created not only managers who are not capitalists, but also a large number of workers whose jobs, though in offices, approximate the conditions of industrial labor. Clerical workers, for instance, suffer routinization, mechanization, and close supervision, and they lack avenues for advancement. Service workers, such as cleaners, bellhops, and hospital orderlies, also experience these working conditions. Today, many white collar and service workers are the wives and children of blue collar workers, and they share a common world view and life style. As white collar and service workers follow forms of working-class action—creating unions to attain better wages and conditions—this new heterogeneity becomes less divisive of working-class unity.

Despite new conditions, the working class has only modified, not discarded its traditional modes of action: unions are stronger than ever, and strikes are prevalent. Workers support their unions as their first line of defense for their "good life." They view their new affluence as a collective achievement, and they find scabbing morally repugnant.[15] Although many unions have moved beyond narrow craft lines to include whole industries, and a few include workers from many industries, American unions have continued to concentrate on securing high wages and leisure to enable their members to find satisfaction off the job rather than controlling working conditions or the means of production. In the twentieth century, automation has taken mechanization far beyond the dreams of nineteenth-century manufacturers, and the expansion of bureaucratic management has narrowed even further the scope of the worker's freedom, initiative, and equality. The multitude of wildcat strikes since the 1950s and the reform caucuses within unions all attest to the job dissatisfaction that is growing as more and more workers are better educated and desire personal freedom and creativity in their work. But most leaders seem unable to imagine a system of industrial work that does not degrade workers, and although workers grumble, they have yet to invent new modes of action to restructure the work place.[16]

The long tradition of an unpoliticized working class also has been breached but not broken. Workers and their unions have begun to use the political process in a more sustained fashion since the 1930s, but trade union goals have defined the limits of political action. Workers unite politically primarily to safeguard gains to be made through strikes and collective bargaining. They support laws that strengthen unions or make it easier to organize them and welfare measures, like unemployment insurance and social security, which provide an underpining for their standard of living.[17] While ethnic politics has been fading along with ethnic antagonisms and allegiances, racial and cultural issues, like anti-busing or anti-"hippie" crusades, still dominate the political landscape. The continuing concentration on the private sphere of autonomy with its attendant racial segregation sustains a politics that divides the working class against itself. Since 1970, workers have seen their "good life" in jeopardy because of inflation, unemployment, the energy crisis, and the deterioration of the environment. Perhaps because they have no long tradition of class politics, workers have not created a strong political movement to use government to alleviate these problems, much less to gain more control over their jobs or over the economy.

The roots of the American working class lie in workers' first confrontations with industrialization early in the nineteenth century. At that time, craftsmen in the Northeast confronted the reality of new methods of production, of diminishing economic power, and of unprecedented ethnic and religious heterogeneity within an ideological and political framework that esteemed independence and the self-made man. In cities like Newark, skilled and unskilled workers, natives and immigrants, struggled to maintain their cultures and their independence and in the process created a life style and modes of action that shaped workers' lives for the next half century and influence the working class even today.

Appendix A
The Number of Craftsmen

Table 4 was constructed as follows:

1826: The figures were compiled by Isaac Nichols, assessor, for the Census of Newark, 1826. Published in *The First Jubilee of American Independence, Newark* (Newark: M. Lyon and Co., 1826).

1836: A census was taken for the city of Newark from June to August 1836, and published in the *Newark Daily Advertiser* of 15 September 1836. A Dr. Jabez Goble took an industrial census earlier in the year and it was published in the *Journal of the American Institute of the City of New York* 1 (New York: T. B. Wakeman, 1836). The City Census counted 294 blacksmiths, 433 carpenters, 258 hatters, 27 jewelers, 169 leather makers, 527 saddlers, 543 shoemakers, and 35 trunk makers. Dr. Goble did not count blacksmiths, carpenters, or trunk makers. He did count 610 hatters, 100 jewelers, 150 leather makers, 590 saddlers, and 734 shoemakers. An article accompanying the city census stated that some of the largest workshops, especially those in hatting, were nearly closed during the summer when the census was taken. Thus the city census grossly underestimated employment in some industries, and Dr. Goble's figures may well be more reliable. The figures given by the city census were used except those for hatters, jewelers, and shoemakers. Dr. Goble's figures for these craftsmen were used.

1845: The figures were taken from the city census of 1845, which was published in the *Newark Daily Advertiser* of 6 January 1846.

1850: The numbers of employees in crafts in 1850 can be derived from two sources: the manuscripts of the Census of Manufactures for 1850 and those of the federal population census of 1850. The population census of Newark does not list the occupations of women, and thus their numbers are known only from the Census of Manufactures. For males a comparison of the sources can be made. As shown in Table 37, the sources agreed closely only on the numbers of jewelers, leather makers, and saddlers. For hatting and trunk making more workers are found in the Census of Manufactures than in the population census. Since these two crafts were industrializing quickly, these "extras" may have been unskilled workers who would not have called themselves hatters or trunk makers. The extremely poor coverage of black-

TABLE 37
Number of Male Workers in 1850

Source	Black-smithing	Carpentry	Hatting	Jewelry making	Leather making	Saddle making	Shoe-making	Trunk making
Population census	301	515	554	482	542	453	860	144
Census of Manufactures	44	141	681	505	562	448	533	248
% difference between them	+593.2	+265.2	−18.6	−4.6	−3.6	+1.1	+61.4	−41.9

smiths and carpenters by the Census of Manufactures would likewise seem to be a function of their traditional structure of small shops and self-employment. The Census of Manufactures did not include shops with a capital investment of less than $500. The same reasoning might explain why more shoemakers were found in the population census—the craft was reverting to the small shop form. Thus the figures in Table 4 were derived as follows: (a) those for blacksmiths and carpenters are the number found in the population census; (b) those for hatters, jewelers, leather makers, saddlers, and trunk makers are the number of men and women given in the Census of Manufactures; (c) the number of shoemakers is the sum of the number of male shoemakers found in the population census and the number of females reported in the Census of Manufactures.

1860: The figures for 1860 were also derived from the manuscripts of the population census of that year and the Census of Manufactures. Though occupations for females were given in the population census, for no group do the numbers found approach those given by the Census of Manufactures (Table 7). Thus as in 1850 the Census of Manufactures was the source for the number of female employees in each craft. The relationship between the numbers of males in each craft given by the two sources was the same in general in 1860 as it had been in 1850 (Table 38). Blacksmiths and carpenters were grossly underrepresented in the 1860 Census of Manufactures. Fewer shoemakers and more hatters and trunk makers were to be found in the 1860 Census of Manufactures than in the population census of that year. But in 1860 the two sources agreed closely only on leather makers. The Census of Manufactures seems to have made a severe undercount of jewelry making firms in 1860, which is reflected in the low employment figures. But, the 1860 Census of Manufactures counted many more saddle makers than the population census did. This could signify an increase in unskilled workers in this trade. The figures for Table 4 were derived then as follows: (a) those for blacksmiths and carpenters are the number found in the population census; (b) those for hatters, leather makers, saddle makers,

TABLE 38
Number of Male Workers in 1860

Source	Black-smithing	Carpentry	Hatting	Jewelry making	Leather making	Saddle making	Shoe-making	Trunk making
Population census	425	794	1022	723	883	757	1089	312
Census of Manufactures	108	33	1215	485	951	1011	657	645
% difference between them	+293.5	+2306.1	−15.9	+49.1	−7.1	−35.0	+65.8	−51.7

and trunk makers were taken from the figures for males and females in the Census of Manufactures; (c) those for jewelers and shoemakers were derived as the sum of the number of males found in the population census and the number of females given in the Census of Manufactures.

Appendix B
Classification of
Newarkers' Occupations

The occupations of Newark's white males over fourteen years of age who appeared in the samples taken from the 1850 and 1860 population censuses were classified as follows:

I. No occupation or student

II. Unskilled or service:
      boatman
      canalman
      hostler
      laborer
      seaman
      waiter
      watchman

III. Semiskilled:
      barber
      beer, brewer
      carman
      cartman
      coachman, coach driver
      cutter
      enameled cloth
      file cutter
      glue factory
      india rubber
      japanner
      oilcloth
      paper factory
      polisher of metals
      sash and blind
      stair rod maker
      stone rubber

    teamster, stage driver
    varnish factory

IV. Skilled (many of these were being industrialized):
    (a) building trades
        carpenter
        mason
        painter
        slater
    (b) metal
        blacksmith
        cutler
        engraver
        gunsmith
        ironmoulder
        jeweler
        locksmith
        machinist/millwright
        pattern maker
        rule maker
        silver plater
        spring maker
        tinsmith
        tool maker
        watchmaker
    (c) leather
        carpet bag maker
        currier
        harness maker
        morocco dresser or finisher
        patent leather
        saddler
        shoemaker
        tanner
        trunk maker
    (d) wood
        boat builder
        bow maker
        cabinet maker
        cane maker
        chair maker
        coachsmith, carriage maker, coach trimmer, coach maker
        cooper

      moulder
      woodturner

(e) cloth or clothing
      hatter
      muff maker
      rope maker
      sail maker
      silk twist maker
      tailor
      upholsterer
      weaver (fringe, carpet, lace, and no specification)

(f) other
      baker
      butcher
      chemical works
      comb maker
      confectioner
      cigar maker
      engineer, boiler making
      lamp maker
      looking glass frame maker
      paper box maker
      printer
      quarryman
      stone mason, cutter
      tallow chandler

V. Petty Proprietors:
      boardinghouse keeper
      butter dealer
      farmer
      gardner
      grocer
      inn keeper
      milkman
      miller
      peddlar
      stable

VI. Clerical, sales:
      bookkeeper
      clerk
      express agent

VII. Semi-professionals:
     clairvoyent
     musician
     music teacher

VIII. Proprietors, Managers, Officials:
     broker
     builders, contractors, architects
     finding store
     insurance
     iron dealer
     leather dealer
     merchant
     store (dry goods)

IX. Professionals:
     druggist
     lawyer
     physician

Appendix C
Classification of Occupations
for Craftsmen
Who Changed Jobs

The occupations held by members of the eight crafts either before they joined a craft or after they left one were classified as follows:

I. Unskilled or Semiskilled:
  - blockcutter
  - box maker
  - brick maker
  - carman
  - carpet weaver
  - carter
  - chair seat maker
  - composition boiler
  - cracker baker
  - express
  - file maker
  - glue factory
  - hostler
  - india rubber
  - iron railing
  - laborer
  - lager beer
  - lamp maker
  - market man
  - oilcloth
  - railroad conductor
  - rectifier liquor
  - saddletree riveter
  - sawyer
  - skinner
  - varnisher
  - watchman

II. Skilled:
  - baker
  - blacksmith
  - boot or shoemaker
  - brass finisher .
  - butcher
  - cabinet maker
  - carpenter
  - carriage trimmer
  - coach smith
  - composition roofer
  - cutler
  - cutter
  - daugerrotypist
  - die sinker
  - edge tools
  - engine turner
  - engineer
  - foreman
  - furrier
  - harness maker
  - hatter
  - iron turner
  - jeweler
  - lace weaver
  - lapidary
  - leather currier or tanner
  - locksmith

machinist
mason
moulder
painter
patent pumps
pilot
saddler
scissors maker
ship carpenter
steam and gas fitter
step maker
tailor
tinsmith or tinner
tool maker
trunk maker
turner

III. Nonmanufacturing proprietorships:
artist
barrel dealer
clothing
coal dealer
confectioner
dry goods
exchange stable
fancy store
fishmonger or dealer
fruiterer
grocer
hotel keeper
lime and brick merchant
lumber merchant
meat store
merchant
oil dealer
oyster house

porter house
refectory
saloon
second-hand furniture
tavern
tobacconist
undertaker

IV. Other White Collar:
accountant
attorney or lawyer
bank president
boarding house keeper
broker
clerk
colporteur
dentist
express
fire department
manufacturer
paint mill owner
penny post
physician or doctor
police
political officeholder
railroad agent
sales
teacher

V. Other:
cultivator of mulberry trees
dairyman
farmer
fisherman
florist
gardener
sexton

Notes

Introduction

1. Lewis Mumford provides an excellent description of the effects of industrialization on the physical environment in *The Culture of Cities* (New York: Harcourt Brace Jovanovich, Inc., 1970).

2. John R. Commons, *et al., History of Labour in the United States* (New York: Augustus M. Kelley, 1966), 1: introduction.

3. Carter Goodrich and Sol Davison, "The Wage Earner in the Western Movement," *Political Science Quarterly* 50 (1935): 161–85 and 51 (1936): 61–116; Helene Zahler, *Eastern Workingmen and the National Land Policy, 1829–1862* (New York: Columbia University Press, 1941).

4. Stephen Thernstrom and Peter R. Knights, "Men in Motion," *Journal of Interdisciplinary History* 1 (1970): 7–37.

5. Stuart Blumin, "Mobility and Change in Ante-Bellum Philadelphia"; Herbert Gutman, "The Reality of the Rags-to-Riches Myth"; Stephen Thernstrom, "Occupational Mobility in Boston," in *Nineteenth Century Cities,* eds. Stephen Thernstrom and Richard Sennett (New Haven: Yale University Press, 1969). Also, Stephen Thernstrom, *Poverty and Progress* (Cambridge: Harvard University Press, 1964).

6. Norman Ware, *The Industrial Worker, 1840–1860* (Gloucester, Mass.: Peter Smith, 1959).

7. William A. Sullivan, *The Industrial Worker in Pennsylvania, 1800–1840* (Harrisburg, Pa.: Pennsylvania Historical and Museum Commission, 1955). The same general interpretation can be found in Edwin C. Rozwenc, *Cooperatives Come to America* (Mt. Vernon, Iowa: Hawkeye-Record Press, 1941).

8. Arthur Schlesinger, Jr. made the original formulation in *The Age of Jackson* (Boston: Little, Brown and Co., 1945).

9. Lee Benson, *The Concept of Jacksonian Democracy* (Princeton: Princeton University Press, 1961); Joseph Dorfman, "The Jackson Wage-Earner Thesis," *American Historical Review* 54 (1948): 296–306; Walter Hugins, *Jacksonian Democracy and the Working Class* (Stanford: Stanford University Press, 1960).

10. Stanley Lebergott, *Manpower in Economic Growth* (New York: McGraw-Hill Book Co., 1964), pp. 137–54; Jeffrey G. Williamson, "American Prices and Urban Inequality since 1820," *Journal of Economic History* 36 (1976): 303–33.

11. Sam Bass Warner, Jr., *The Private City* (Philadelphia: University of Pennsylvania Press, 1968), chap. 4.

12. Bruce Laurie, "'Nothing on Impulse': Life Styles of Philadelphia Artisans, 1820-1850," *Labor History* 15 (1974): 337-66 and "Fire Companies and Gangs in Southwark: The 1840's" in *The Peoples of Philadelphia*, eds. Allan F. Davis and Mark H. Haller (Philadelphia: Temple University Press, 1973), pp. 71-88.

13. Paul Faler, "Cultural Aspects of the Industrial Revolution: Lynn, Mass., Shoemakers and Industrial Morality, 1826-1860," *Labor History* 15 (1974): 367-94.

14. Herbert Gutman, "Work, Culture and Society in Industrializing America, 1815-1919," *American Historical Review* 78 (1973): 531-88.

15. Alan Dawley, *Class and Community: The Industrial Revolution in Lynn* (Cambridge: Harvard University Press, 1976).

16. Herbert Gutman, "Class, Status, and Community Power in Nineteenth-Century American Industrial Cities—Paterson, New Jersey: A Case Study" in *The Age of Industrialism*, ed. Frederick C. Jaher (New York: Free Press, 1968), and "The Worker's Search for Power" in *The Gilded Age*, ed. H. Wayne Morgan (Syracuse: Syracuse University Press, 1963).

17. For instance, studies of municipal institutions, such as the school and the police, describe their development as a response to the changing class structure. According to the new monographs, such "city services" were created to impose discipline on the poor and the working class and quiet the fears of the upper and middle classes. Works in this vein include James Richardson, *The New York Police* (New York: Oxford University Press, 1970); Michael Katz, *The Irony of Early School Reform* (Cambridge: Harvard University Press, 1968); and Stanley Schultz, *The Culture Factory* (New York: Oxford University Press, 1973).

18. Michael Feldberg, "The Crowd in Philadelphia Perspective," *Labor History* 15 (1974): 323-36.

19. E. P. Thompson, *The Making of the English Working Class* (London: Victor Gollancz Ltd., 1963), preface.

20. John Coolidge, *Mill and Mansion* (New York: Russell and Russell, 1942); Hanna Josephson, *The Golden Threads* (New York: Duell, Sloane, & Pearce, 1949); Vera Shlakman, *Economic History of a Factory Town: A Study of Chicopee, Mass.* (Smith College Studies in History, Vol. 20, No. 464, Oct. 1934–July 1935); Caroline F. Ware, *Early New England Cotton Manufacture* (Boston: Houghton Mifflin Co., 1931); Norman Ware, *The Industrial Worker, 1840-1860*.

21. Warner, *The Private City;* Jeffrey G. Williamson, "Antebellum Urbanization in the American North East," *Journal of Economic History* 25 (1965): 592-608; Jeffrey G. Williamson and Joseph A. Swanson, "The Growth of Cities in the American North East, 1820-1870," *Explorations in Entrepreneurial History*, 2nd series, vol. 4, no. 1, Supplement (1966): 1-79.

22. See Sullivan, *The Industrial Worker in Pennsylvania*, for comparison of textile and iron workers.

23. United States, Census Office, *Statistics of the United States in 1860* (Washington, D.C., 1866), p. xviii.

24. "Leather makers" included tanners, curriers, morocco dressers, patent leather makers, and japanners. "Shoemakers" included bootmakers, while "saddlers" included harness makers and bridlemakers. Carpet bag makers were included in "trunk makers" and capmakers in "hatters."

25. The figure for 1826 is derived from the industrial and population census

taken by the town assessor in that year and published in *The First Jubilee of American Independence, Newark* (Newark: M. Lyon and Co., 1826). The figure for 1860 is derived from the manuscripts of the U.S. Census of Population and the U.S. Census of Manufactures for 1860 and the *Statistics of the United States in 1860,* p. xviii.

Chapter 1

1. William H. Shaw, *History of Essex and Hudson Counties, New Jersey* (Philadelphia: Everts and Peck, 1884), 1: 550–53.
2. Ibid., p. 560.
3. "A Cobbler's 'Ten Footer,'" *Newarker,* 15 April 1936, p. 34.
4. *The First Jubilee.*
5. "Sheldon Smith, His Influence on Newark Manufactures," *Newark Daily Advertiser* (hereafter *NDA*), 25 September 1863.
6. Samuel H. Popper, "Newark, New Jersey, 1870–1910: Chapters in the Evolution of an American Metropolis" (Ph.D. dissertation, New York University, 1952), p. 28.
7. All figures for population and industries in 1826 cited in the following paragraphs are derived from the town census printed in *The First Jubilee.*
8. Ibid. This figure represents the number of people per house. It is not adjusted for multiple dwellings, though these were probably rare.
9. Edmund S. Morgan, *The Puritan Family* (New York: Harper and Row, 1944).
10. *Sentinel of Freedom,* Newark, 16 November 1819 and 7 December 1819.
11. *Sentinel,* 29 April 1828.
12. John Cunningham, *Newark* (Newark: New Jersey Historical Society, 1966), p. 46.
13. Henry Clarke Wright, *A Human Life* (Boston: Bela Marsh, 1849), pp. 85, 106–7, 109.
14. *Sentinel,* 16 November 1819; 19 September 1826; 3 April 1827; 12 June 1827; 17 February 1829.
15. Ibid., 7 December 1819.
16. Rev. William A. Hallock, *The Life and Labors of the Rev. Justin Edwards, D.D.* (New York: American Tract Society, 1855), pp. 44–48.
17. When conditions changed in the 1830s many comments were made on how worried rural parents were about the influence of the city on their sons' characters. See, for instance, *NDA,* 5 March 1834.
18. *Sentinel,* 20 June 1826 and 27 June 1826.
19. Ibid., 27 June 1826.
20. Commons, *History of Labour,* 1: 83–85.
21. *Records of the Town of Newark, N.J., 1666–1836,* Collections of the New Jersey Historical Society (Newark: New Jersey Historical Society, 1864), vol. 6.
22. *Sentinel,* 21 September 1819; 5 December 1826; 19 December 1826.
23. Ibid., 24 April 1821.
24. Jackson Turner Main, *The Social Structure of Revolutionary America* (Princeton: Princeton University Press, 1965), pp. 77, 80–81.

25. Charles S. Olton, *Artisans for Independence* (Syracuse: Syracuse University Press, 1975), pp. 12–13.

26. Carl Bridenbaugh, *The Colonial Craftsman* (New York: New York University Press, 1950), pp. 105–7, chap. 5; Dawley, *Class and Community*, pp. 45–46.

27. *Sentinel*, 28 June 1825.

28. John Albee, *Confessions of a Boyhood* (Boston: R. G. Badger, 1910), p. 150; Wright, *A Human Life*, p. 127.

29. Bridenbaugh, *The Colonial Craftsman*, p. 129.

30. Wright, *A Human Life*, p. 38.

31. Lucy Larcom, *A New England Girlhood* (Cambridge: The Riverside Press, 1889), p. 9.

32. Wright, *A Human Life*, p. 20.

33. Ibid., p. 129.

34. *Records of the Town of Newark*.

35. E. P. Thompson, "Time, Work-Discipline, and Industrial Capitalism," *Past and Present* 38 (1967): 56–97; Merritt Roe Smith, *Harpers Ferry Armory and the New Technology* (Ithaca, N.Y.: Cornell University Press, 1977), pp. 66, 255, 270.

36. Wright, *A Human Life*, p. 128; Bridenbaugh, *The Colonial Craftsman*, p. 130; Indenture of James Brady... to Ambrose Tompkins, MG1, #I107, New Jersey Historical Society.

37. *Sentinel*, 14 July 1829.

38. Dawley, *Class and Community*, p. 36.

39. A good example of the preindustrial mix of work and leisure can be found in the diary of a young merchant: Zephaniah W. Pease, *Life in New Bedford A Hundred Years Ago* (New Bedford, Mass.: George H. Reynolds, 1922).

40. Bruce Sinclair, *Philadelphia's Philosopher Mechanics* (Baltimore: The Johns Hopkins University Press, 1974).

41. Newark Mechanics Association, *Constitution and Bylaws of the Newark Mechanics Association for Mutual Improvement in the Arts and Sciences, 1828*, New Jersey Historical Society.

42. *NDA*, 8 January 1833; 5 February 1833; 25 March 1833.

43. Indenture of James Brady... to Ambrose Tomkins. Cunningham, *Newark*, pp. 83–84. *Sentinel*, 19 December 1820; 16 April 1822; 30 August 1825.

44. Cunningham, *Newark*, pp. 50–51.

45. *The First Jubilee; Sentinel*, 20 June 1826 and 11 July 1826.

46. Frank J. Urquhart, *History of Newark, New Jersey* (New York: Lewis Publishing Company, 1913), 1: 466, 479, 480, 488.

47. Olton, *Artisans for Independence*, pp. 52–53.

48. *Sentinel*, 7 July 1829.

49. Howard Mumford Jones, *O Strange New World* (New York: Viking Press, 1964), pp. 212–14.

50. *Sentinel*, 7 December 1819.

51. Olton, *Artisans for Independence*, pp. 32, 93.

52. Carl Prince, *New Jersey's Jeffersonian Republicans* (Chapel Hill: University of North Carolina Press, 1964), pp. 79, 252.

53. *The First Jubilee*, pp. 28–30.

54. *Sentinel*, 27 May 1828; Walter R. Fee, *The Transition from Aristocracy to*

Democracy in New Jersey, 1789–1829 (Somerville, N.J.: Somerville Press, 1933), pp. 259–68.

55. *Sentinel,* 5 September 1826; 12 September 1826; 19 September 1826; 3 October 1826; 7 November 1826; 21 November 1826.

56. Urquhart, *History of Newark,* 1: 486.

57. *Sentinel,* 12 September 1826.

58. Ibid., 7 November 1826.

59. Frank T. De Vyver, "The Organization of Labor in New Jersey before 1860" (Ph.D. dissertation, Princeton University, 1934).

60. *Sentinel,* 19 September 1826.

Chapter 2

1. *NDA,* 30 July 1835; 9 July 1836; 20 September 1836.

2. Derived from statistics given in the *Journal of the American Institute of the City of New York* 1 (1836): 475–79 and 2 (1837): 418–19.

3. *NDA,* 21 January 1835 and 13 April 1835.

4. Census of Population, 1836 taken by the city government and printed in B.T. Pierson, *Directory of the City of Newark, 1837–38* (Newark: Daily and Sentinel Office, 1837), p. 24.

5. Shaw, *History of Essex and Hudson Counties,* 1: 561.

6. *NDA,* 5 May 1836.

7. Wheaton J. Lane, *From Indian Trail to Iron Horse* (Princeton: Princeton University Press, 1939), p. 249; Shaw, *History of Essex and Hudson Counties,* 1: 561.

8. *NDA,* 7 December 1836.

9. Thomas F. Gordon, *A Gazetteer of the State of New Jersey* (Trenton: Daniel Fenton, 1834), p. 191; *Journal of the American Institute of the City of New York,* 1 (1836): 475.

10. *NDA,* 7 February 1837.

11. Ibid., 14 August 1834; 18 November 1834; 19 November 1834; 27 October 1836; 23 November 1836; 25 November 1836.

12. Shaw, *History of Essex and Hudson Counties,* 1: 561.

13. *NDA,* 17 January 1846; 19 March 1846; 26 January 1849. B. T. Pierson, *Directory of the City of Newark, 1841–42* (Newark: Aaron Guest, 1841), p. 204.

14. Williamson and Swanson, "The Growth of Cities in the American North East," p. 48; manuscript of the U.S. Census of Population, 1840.

15. *NDA,* 18 August 1846 and 17 December 1846.

16. B. T. Pierson, *Directory of the City of Newark, 1846–47* (Newark: Aaron Guest, 1846), p. 251; *NDA,* 2 December 1846 and 18 March 1847.

17. *NDA,* 9 January 1849.

18. Ibid., 10 August 1847; 1 September 1847; 1 April 1850.

19. Ibid., 10 December 1856 and 19 October 1857.

20. Calculated from the manuscript of the U.S. Census of Manufactures, 1860.

21. Ibid. ($8,667 vs. $7,475).

22. Ibid.

23. Ibid. ($85,000 vs. $8,667).

24. William Haber, *Industrial Relations in the Building Industry* (Cambridge: Harvard University Press, 1930), pp. 274–75. *NDA,* 12 September 1835. For all crafts, information on apprenticeship was taken from the want ads of the *Newark Daily Advertiser.* Apprenticeship was assumed to be existing in its traditional sense if ads appeared for runaways and/or for new apprentices wanted and no controversy arose that pointed to disruptions of the system.

25. *NDA,* 27 January 1853.

26. Alex W. Bealer, *The Art of Blacksmithing* (New York: Funk & Wagnalls, 1969), p. 24; U.S. Census Office, *Manufactures of the United States in 1860* (Washington, D.C., 1865), p. cxcvi.

27. *NDA,* 8 December 1854.

28. Ibid., 5 September 1835 to 12 September 1835; 4 February 1836; 18 February 1836; 5 March 1836 to 11 March 1836; 22 December 1849; 28 May 1851.

29. Shaw, *History of Essex and Hudson Counties,* 1: 561. Advertisements for apprentices continued to appear in *NDA.*

30. Dawley, *Class and Community,* p. 26.

31. *NDA,* 11 October, 1850 and 2 April 1859.

32. Ibid., 22 June 1854.

33. Gordon, *Gazetteer of the State of New Jersey,* p. 189. *NDA,* 23 May 1835.

34. *NDA,* 26 July 1850.

35. Ibid., 25 May 1835; 31 March 1836; 6 April 1836; 26 April 1836.

36. Dawley suggests this for shoemakers in Lynn. See Dawley, *Class and Community,* pp. 45–46, 62.

37. In 1850, male shoemakers in Lynn averaged $20 per month. Wages in Newark were 10 percent higher. Dawley, *Class and Community,* p. 53.

38. Shaw, *History of Essex and Hudson Counties,* 1: 561. Gordon, *Gazetteer of the State of New Jersey,* p. 189. *NDA,* 11 October 1834; 17 December 1835; 16 March 1850; 23 December 1854; 15 September 1860.

39. Peter C. Welsh, *Tanning in the United States to 1850,* U.S. National Museum Bulletin No. 242 (Washington, D.C., 1964), p. 21. Welsh, among others, describes tanning as remaining unchanged until the late nineteenth century. This was not the case in Newark, nor in Delaware. See Lucius F. Ellsworth, "The Delaware Leather Industry in the Mid-Nineteenth Century," *Delaware History* 11 (1964/65): 261–81.

40. *The First Jubilee; Journal of the American Institute,* 1 (1836): 475–79; *NDA,* 31 May 1850.

41. *NDA,* 28 October 1846.

42. *NDA,* 18 May 1835 and 9 September 1848. John R. Commons, *et al., Documentary History of American Industrial Society* (Cleveland: Arthur H. Clark Co., 1910), 6: 182.

43. Main, *Social Structure of Revolutionary America,* pp. 80–81.

44. *NDA,* 24 March 1836.

45. Ibid., 27 January 1858.

46. The indenture of Isaac Champenois to Isaac A. Alling dated 23 April 1844 and reprinted in "Newark, the City of Gold and Platinum and Precious Stones," *The Keystone* (May 1925), p. 163.

47. *NDA,* 21 November 1856; 12 July 1859; 15 July 1859. *Newark and its Lead-*

ing Business Men (Newark: Mercantile Publishing Co., 1891), p. 74. Industrial accidents were reported periodically in the newspapers, but no statistics on accident rates are available for the pre–Civil War period.

48. *NDA*, 10 February 1855; 19 November 1856; 27 January 1858; 25 March 1859. Indenture of David Dodd to Aaron Carter, 19 October 1853, New Jersey Historical Society. B. T. Pierson, *Directory of the City of Newark, 1856–57* through *Directory of the City of Newark, 1860–61* (Newark: Aaron Guest, 1856–1860).

49. *NDA*, 10 March 1846; 23 November 1846; 5 April 1850; 13 February 1856. Manuscript of U.S. Census of Manufactures, 1850.

50. B. T. Pierson, *Directory of the City of Newark, 1856–57* through *Directory of the City of Newark, 1860–61.*

51. *NDA*, 6 July 1860 and 1 September 1860.

52. Ibid., 24 March 1836; 27 March 1848; 3 May 1850; 20 July 1855; 3 October 1856. *National Trades Union,* 10 October 1835.

53. Shaw, *History of Essex and Hudson Counties,* 1: 561. *Sentinel,* 30 May 1826. *NDA*, 14 May 1835; 19 June 1835; 15 September 1836. *National Trades Union,* 19 March 1836. Milton J. Nadworny, "Jersey Labor and Jackson" (unpublished typewritten manuscript), New Jersey Historical Society, p. 26.

54. *NDA*, 26 September 1850.

55. Ibid., 16 March 1850; 19 September 1856; 9 June 1860.

56. *Newark and Its Leading Businessmen,* p. 129. *NDA*, 18 June 1860.

Chapter 3

1. *Newark Monitor,* 15 July 1834. *NDA*, 13 August 1846 and 3 September 1846. *Newark Daily Eagle,* 25 January 1854.

2. See Leon F. Litwack, *North of Slavery* (Chicago: University of Chicago Press, 1961), for the caste position of blacks in the antebellum Northern cities. Statistics on black craftsmen are from the manuscripts of the Censuses of Population of 1850 and 1860.

3. Josephson, *The Golden Threads;* Shlakman, *Economic History of a Factory Town;* and Caroline Ware, *Early New England Cotton Manufacture.*

4. Women's work in manufacturing was confined mainly to textile production in Europe too. Joan Scott and Louise Tilly, "Women's Work and the Family in Nineteenth-Century Europe," *Comparative Studies in Society and History* 17 (1975): 36–64, and Louise Tilly, Joan Scott, and Miriam Cohen, "Women's Work and European Fertility Patterns," *Journal of Interdisciplinary History* 6 (1976): 447–78.

5. *NDA*, 11 October 1834 and 15 September 1836.

6. Ibid., 23 September 1858 and 9 October 1858.

7. Ibid., 17 September 1839 and 10 July 1840.

8. Edith Abbott, *Women in Industry* (New York: D. Appleton and Co., 1910), p. 319.

9. *NDA*, 12 January 1838 and 25 September 1840. *Newark Daily Eagle,* 27 October 1854.

10. Calculated from the *Manufactures of the United States in 1860.* This figure is probably a little high, since it includes the wages of the few male workers in the field.

11. Barbara Welter, "The Cult of True Womanhood," *American Quarterly* 18 (1966): 151–74.

12. *NDA,* 25 August 1836.

13. All demographic statistics on women in the crafts were derived from the manuscript of the U.S. Census of Population for 1860.

14. George E. Barnett, *The Printers—A Study in American Trade Unionism* (Cambridge: American Economic Association, 1909), pp. 318–19.

15. The total numbers of trunk makers in 1850 and 1860 and saddle makers in 1860 in the population censuses were far smaller, however, than those reported for these trades by the Censuses of Manufactures. It might be that many of the male workers in these two crafts who were not reported in the population censuses were children under fifteen. The proportion of fifteen- to twenty-year-old trunk makers in 1850 was high compared to other crafts, but by 1860 the trunk makers listed were no longer abnormally young. Who was being left out of the population census is thus difficult to tell for either year. It could be older workers in 1850 and the teen-agers in 1860, or the child labor in both years. Or, it could be those, regardless of age, who gave imprecise occupational information. In 1860 a larger proportion of the saddle makers were teenagers than were other craftsmen, and thus child labor may have been more prevalent in saddle making too.

16. *NDA,* 17 October 1856 and 8 November 1858.

17. Derived from the population statistics given in U.S. Census Office, *Fifth Census* (Washington, D.C., 1832).

18. *NDA,* 30 July 1835 and 20 September 1836.

19. U.S. Bureau of the Census, *Historical Statistics of the United States, Colonial Times to 1957* (Washington, D.C., 1960), p. 71.

20. *NDA,* 22 September 1836 and 17 May 1839.

21. Paul H. Douglass, *American Apprenticeship and Industrial Education* (New York: Columbia University, 1921), p. 80.

22. *NDA,* 26 September 1836.

23. "Newark, the City of Gold and Platinum and Precious Stones," p. 163; Indenture of David Dodd to Aaron Carter; *NDA,* 22 February 1859.

24. *NDA,* 13 June 1839 and 21 November 1839.

25. Barnett, *The Printers,* pp. 177–206.

26. B. T. Pierson, *Directory of the City of Newark, 1837–38,* p. 24.

27. Derived from U.S. Census Office, *Population of the United States in 1860* (Washington, D.C., 1864); U.S. Census Office, *Compendium of the Seventh Census* (Washington, D.C., 1854); and U.S. Census Office, *The Seventh Census of the United States: 1850* (Washington, D.C., 1853).

28. Oscar Handlin, *Boston's Immigrants* (New York: Atheneum, 1968), pp. 55, 72–83.

Chapter 4

1. To some degree this viewpoint informs works as diverse as: Fredrich Engels, *The Condition of the Working Class in England* (Stanford: Stanford University

Press, 1968), pp. 145, 160–66; Neil J. Smelser, *Social Change in the Industrial Revolution* (Chicago: University of Chicago Press, 1959), chap. 9; E. P. Thompson, *The Making of the English Working Class,* pp. 306–8, 340, 416–17.

2. Michael Young and Peter Willmott, *The Symmetrical Family* (London: Routledge and Kegan Paul, 1973) demonstrate that in the English case, work and economic necessity alone do not determine "the family." It responds as well to values and new ideas like feminism, and the time span for its evolution is measured in centuries.

3. Ibid., p. 73. The same was true in England.

4. Manuscript of the U.S. Census of Population, 1860, Newark, Ward 2.

5. Philip J. Greven, *Four Generations* (Ithaca, N.Y.: Cornell University Press, 1970), pp. 33–34; Paul C. Glick, *American Families* (New York: John Wiley and Sons, Inc., 1957), p. 54.

6. Conrad and Irene Taeuber, *The Changing Population of the United States* (New York: John Wiley and Sons, Inc., 1958), p. 68.

7. William J. Goode, *World Revolution and Family Patterns* (New York: Free Press of Glencoe, 1963), p. 49.

8. Robert V. Wells, "Demographic Change and the Life Cycle of American Families," *Journal of Interdisciplinary History* 2 (1971): 275.

9. The relationship between age of oldest child and age of father was also strong for all Newarkers: for 1850, $\gamma = .8808$ and for 1860, $\gamma = .8626$.

10. Susan E. Bloomberg, *et al.*, "A Census Probe into Nineteenth-Century Family History: Southern Michigan, 1850–1880," *Journal of Social History* 5 (1971): 33; Glick, *American Families,* p. 40; David Kennedy, *Birth Control in America* (New Haven: Yale University Press, 1970), pp. 42–45; Robert E. McGlone, "Suffer the Children: The Emergence of Modern Middle-Class Family Life in America, 1820–1870" (Ph.D. dissertation, University of California, Los Angeles, 1971), p. 154.

11. Manuscript of the U.S. Census of Population, 1860, Newark, Ward 6.

12. Wells, "Demographic Change," p. 276.

13. Manuscript of the U.S. Census of Population, 1860, Newark, Ward 6.

14. Ibid.

15. *NDA,* 24 June 1836.

16. Bloomberg, *et al.*, "A Census Probe," p. 33; John Modell and Tamara K. Hareven, "Urbanization and the Malleable Household: An Examination of Boarding and Lodging in American Families," *Journal of Marriage and the Family* 35 (1973): 469.

17. Manuscript of the U.S. Census of Population, 1860, Newark, Ward 2; manuscript of the U.S. Census of Manufactures, 1860, Newark.

18. Manuscript of the U.S. Census of Population, 1860, Newark, Ward 8; Election list, *NDA,* 1857.

19. Wells, "Demographic Change," pp. 278–79.

20. *NDA,* 29 January 1835.

21. Wells, "Demographic Change," p. 280.

22. Commons, *Documentary History* 5: 240.

23. *Newark Daily Eagle,* 29 July 1854.

24. *NDA,* 8 September 1849.

25. There were 37,026 women in Newark in 1860, approximately 36 percent of whom were under fifteen (ie., 36 percent of the women in Essex County were under

fifteen). The Census of Manufactures reported 5,168 female hands employed in Newark, meaning 22 percent were employed. This accords with the figures for Essex County in which 18 percent of the women over fourteen were employed.

26. The census enumerated the occupations of women for the first time in 1860, and coverage was very incomplete. Unmarried teenage women were most likely to have an occupation listed for them. That the percentage of craftsmen with dependents working did not rise appreciably between 1850 and 1860 suggests that they either needed no help from teenage daughters in supporting the family or, like other Victorians, were loath to admit it.

27. *NDA,* 30 July 1835 through 15 August 1835.

28. Ibid., 27 March 1848; *Manufactures of the United States, 1860,* p. 336.

29. The inaccuracies produced by the inadequate coverage of firms would make these figures from the Censuses of Manufactures suspect, but wage information from other sources generally confirms the wages they reported. See *NDA,* 22 December 1849; 5 April 1850; 7 June 1850; 27 January 1858 and De Vyver.

30. *NDA,* 8 January 1846 and 11 December 1847.

31. Reprinted in George R. Taylor, *The Transportation Revolution, 1815–1860* (New York: Holt, Rinehart and Winston, 1964), p. 296.

32. *NDA,* 7 May 1850; Board of Health, *Report of the Health Physician of the City of Newark, 1860* (Newark: Evening Journal Office, 1861), pp. 19-20.

33. This budget allotted approximately 50 percent for food, 25 percent for shelter (rent, fuel, furniture), and 18 percent for clothing. At least the expenditures for food and clothing would diminish if there was one less child in the family, and $360 represents a deduction in the budget of one-fifth in the food and clothing allowances.

34. This ignores the problem of seasonal or spotty unemployment. Although it is clear that factories shut down in slow seasons, and that for many crafts this included part of the summer, there is insufficient information to gauge the extent of such unemployment and its effect on yearly wages.

35. In 1850 the percentage of males in each craft who were married was: 57 percent, carpenters; 58 percent, blacksmiths; 66 percent, shoemakers; 45 percent, saddlers; 37 percent, jewelers; 31 percent, trunk makers; 53 percent, leather makers; and 49 percent, hatters.

36. *NDA,* 11 December 1847.

37. Ibid., 18 September 1847.

38. Ibid., 17 June 1857.

39. For the Newark sample, $\gamma = .6578$ for age by value of property in 1850 and $\gamma = .6298$ in 1860.

40. Alvin H. Hansen, "Factors Affecting the Trend of Real Wages," *American Economic Review* 15 (1925): 32; Jürgen Kuczynski, *Short History of Labor Conditions under Industrial Capitalism* (London: Frederick Muller, Ltd., 1943), 2: 43; New Jersey, Bureau Statistics of Labor and Industries, *Ninth Annual Report* (Trenton: John L. Murphy Publishing Co., 1886), pp. 18-20; Taylor, *The Transportation Revolution,* p. 331.

41. In *Youth and History* (New York: Academic Press, 1974), chaps. 2 and 3, John Gillis shows that industrialization in Europe also made boys more dependent on their parents and increased coresidence of parents and teenagers.

42. *NDA,* 28 November 1833; 14 December 1836; 14 December 1838; 13 June

1839; 21 October 1839; 21 November 1839.

43. Ibid., 14 December 1836 and 24 December 1847.

44. Ibid., 9 August 1848.

45. Ibid., 5 March 1834.

46. Ibid., 14 February 1838; 1 June 1838; 28 December 1839; 31 December 1839; 19 February 1840; 27 January 1846; 22 September 1846; 26 September 1846; 5 October 1846; 3 November 1846; 3 November 1847; 12 November 1849; 19 November 1849; 12 March 1856; 11 May 1859.

47. Ibid., 29 September 1846; 1 October 1853; 3 June 1856.

48. Ibid., 9 August 1848.

49. Ibid., 28 September 1853.

50. *Newark Daily Eagle,* 17 May 1854 and 25 May 1854.

51. Ibid., 22 March 1854.

Chapter 5

1. Historians and sociologists have long chronicled the problems of organizing workers of different ethno-religious backgrounds and the lack of common ground outside the work place even when strong unions exist. See, for example, David Brody, *Steelworkers in America* (New York: Harper and Row, 1960); Peter Friedlander, *The Emergence of a U.A.W. Local, 1936–1939* (Pittsburgh: University of Pittsburgh Press, 1975); Milton Gordon, *Assimilation in American Life* (New York: Oxford University Press, 1964).

2. Lynn shoemakers had a similarly low level of upward mobility after 1830. Dawley, *Class and Community,* p. 55.

3. According to the Newark city directories from 1836 to 1840, 91 percent did not change occupations, 6 percent left their craft, 2 percent joined a craft, and 1 percent passed through a craft. Between 1846 and 1850, 89 percent did not change, 6 percent left, 4 percent joined, and 1 percent passed through. Between 1856 and 1860, 91 percent did not change, 4 percent left, 4 percent joined, and 1 percent passed through.

4. Derived from the Newark city directories.

5. Derived from the manuscripts of the U.S. Censuses of Population of 1850 and 1860.

6. *NDA,* 5 August 1834 and 8 September 1834.

7. Ibid., 2 August 1834.

8. Mentioned in De Vyver, "The Organization of Labor in New Jersey before 1860," and *NDA.*

9. *NDA,* 27 September 1834.

10. *National Trades Union,* 7 February 1835.

11. *NDA,* 4 February 1835.

12. Maurice Neufeld, "Realms of Thought and Organized Labor in the Age of Jackson," *Labor History* 10 (1969): 32 and *NDA,* 30 June 1838.

13. Commons, *History of Labour* 1: 96–98 and *NDA,* 20 January 1835; 23 January 1835; 6 February 1835; 9 February 1835.

14. *National Trades Union,* 31 January 1835.

15. *NDA*, 22 March 1836; 6 April 1836; 26 April 1836. *New Jersey Eagle*, 1 July 1836.

16. *NDA*, 22 January 1836 and 27 January 1836.

17. *Third Annual Report of the Newark Mechanics' Association*, New Jersey Historical Society. *NDA*, 8 January 1833; 5 February 1833; 25 March 1833; 1 August 1833; 6 May 1835; 19 June 1835; 30 June 1835; 28 July 1835. *Newark Monitor*, 7 June 1831 and 4 December 1832.

18. *NDA*, 28 July 1835; 30 July 1835; 3 August 1835; 8 August 1835; 10 August 1835; 12 August 1835; 15 August 1835.

19. Ibid., 13 June 1833; 17 June 1835; 1 July 1835; 6 July 1835.

20. Ibid., 11 May 1837.

21. Ibid., 7 June 1837; 26 June 1837; 19 December 1838; 19 April 1839; 31 May 1839; 14 March 1846.

22. Ibid., 5 July 1836; 5 July 1837; 16 June 1838; 25 June 1840; 3 July 1847.

23. Jones, *O Strange New World*, pp. 221–26.

24. *NDA*, 3 November 1847.

25. Ibid., 22 March 1858.

26. *Newark Daily Eagle*, 11 January 1854; *NDA*, 6 July 1860.

27. *NDA*, 19 October 1837; 30 June 1838; 3 July 1838; 14 July 1838.

28. Thernstrom, *Poverty and Progress*, chap. 3; *NDA*, 18 June 1860.

29. Glenn Porter and Harold C. Livesay, *Merchants and Manufacturers* (Baltimore: Johns Hopkins Press, 1971), p. 63. Information available on the founders of Newark's craft-based industries suggests conclusions similar to those which Herbert Gutman reached in his analysis of the manufacturers of Paterson, New Jersey, "The Reality of the Rags-to-Riches Myth." An example is "Old Banister Shoe Plant on Washington Street Sold," *Sunday Call*, Newark, 27 May 1923.

30. Popper, "Newark, New Jersey, 1870–1910," pp. 28, 30–31.

31. Photostat of Account Book of Carter, Pennington and Doremus, New Jersey Historical Society. *NDA*, 13 November 1847. "Newark, the City of Gold and Platinum and Precious Stones," p. 175.

32. *NDA*, 28 January 1847.

33. The extent of geographical mobility in nineteenth-century America has been one of the most important finds of the new quantitative historians. Peter Knights first documented this for urban Americans and revealed the usefulness (as well as the limitations) of city directories in his book, *The Plain People of Boston, 1830–1860* (New York: Oxford University Press, 1971). City directories are searched to find out how many people stayed in the city as well as how often they moved about within the city. This technique really measures how long part of the population are listed in the directories, and not how long they stayed in the city. Given the biases found in the Newark city directories, a craftsman who was native-born, middle-aged, head of a household, and did not change residences within the city had the best chance both of being in the directory and of staying in it as long as he lived in the city. Although the biases of the directories seriously threaten the accuracy of estimates made from them, the information deduced from the Newark directories is presented for purposes of comparison with the results other scholars have obtained for other cities. It must be realized, however, that if these estimates have any validity it is only for a group of the craftsmen—those who were over thirty years of age and were heads of households.

34. *NDA,* 24 March 1835 and 2 April 1849.

35. Thernstrom, *Poverty and Progress,* chap. 3.

36. Gideon Sjoberg, *The Preindustrial City: Past and Present* (New York: Free Press, 1960), pp. 97–100; Robert E. Park and Ernest W. Burgess, *The City* (Chicago: University of Chicago Press, 1967), pp. 50–58.

37. This interpretation for the impetus for residential segregation is developed by John Foster, *Class Struggle and the Industrial Revolution* (London: Weidenfeld and Nicolson, 1974), pp. 4–5.

38. *NDA,* 21 November 1835; 25 May 1836; 28 October 1836.

39. Statistics derived from information on addresses and occupations in the Newark city directories of 1836 to 1840.

40. *NDA,* 24 June 1857.

41. Derived from Newark city directories 1836–40, 1846–50, 1856–60.

42. Area of residence by value of property for Newark males in 1860 yielded a similar, if slightly stronger, pattern of wealth and poverty in the core and the "middle class" in the ring.

43. The changing age distribution of the crafts was not responsible for the clustering of members of some crafts nor for the destruction of those aggregations, since these were not a function of apprentices or others living in factory dormitories. The jewelry makers, trunk makers, and leather makers who were heads of households had clustered in the same wards as the other members of those crafts. In 1840, 54 percent of the trunk makers who were heads of households lived in the second ward as did 62 percent of the leather makers, while 40 percent of the jewelers lived in the ninth ward. In 1850, 38 percent of the trunk makers and 31 percent of the leather makers were in the second ward, while 44 percent of the jewelers were in the ninth. In 1860, 37 percent of the trunk makers were in the sixth ward, 22 percent of the leather makers were in the seventh ward, and 24 percent of the jewelers were in the ninth.

44. Modell and Hareven, "Urbanization and the Malleable Household," pp. 472–73.

45. *NDA,* 4 December 1847; 20 October 1853; 22 October 1853; 5 November 1853; 7 November 1853; 5 December 1853; 6 December 1853; 2 October 1854; 4 September 1858. William F. Kamman, *Socialism in German American Literature* (Philadelphia: Americana Germanica Press, 1917), p. 58.

46. *NDA,* 6 December 1853.

47. Ibid., 22 October 1853.

48. Ibid., 3 November 1853.

49. *NDA,* 22 September 1847 and 25 January 1854; *Directory 1837–1838, Directory 1846–47,* and *Directory 1853–54.*

50. Shaw, *History of Essex and Hudson Counties,* 1: 533. Newark Lodge #7 of Masons had a membership under 40 up to 1843, but had 204 members by 1860.

51. Edward Pessen, "The Social Configuration of the Antebellum City: An Historical and Theoretical Inquiry," *Journal of Urban History* 2 (1976): 280–93.

52. B. T. Pierson, *Directory of the City of Newark, 1849–50* (Newark: Aaron Guest, 1849).

53. B. T. Pierson, *Directory of the City of Newark, 1835–36* (Newark: Newark Daily Advertiser, 1835) and *Directory 1837–38,* p. 24.

54. See, for instance, John Higham, *Strangers in the Land* (New York: Atheneum, 1965), passim. There are no exact figures on the religious affiliation of immigrants. It is thought that most of the Irish and approximately half of the Germans were Roman Catholic.

55. *NDA,* 19 October 1835; 20 October 1835; 25 August 1836. Shaw, *History of Essex and Hudson Counties,* 1: 508–9.

56. *NDA,* 26 March 1839 and 6 February 1846.

57. Ibid., 10 March 1837.

58. Ibid., 12 September 1833.

59. Laurie, "Nothing on Impulse," pp. 350–54 and Faler, "Cultural Aspects of the Industrial Revolution," pp. 368–69.

60. *Newark Daily Eagle,* 22 March 1854; 22 May 1854; 3 July 1854.

61. Ibid., 21 April 1854.

62. David Grimsted, *Melodrama Unveiled* (Chicago: University of Chicago Press, 1968), pp. 192–93.

63. *NDA,* 10 December 1850; 6 January 1855; 12 July 1858.

64. Newark, N.J., Common Council, *The German Petition to the Common Council of the City of Newark* (Newark: Daily Mercury Office, 1853).

65. *NDA,* 26 June 1854.

66. Essex County Bible Society, *Ninth Annual Report, 1855,* p. 5, Nelson Collection, Princeton University Library.

67. *NDA,* 5 September 1854 and 6 September 1854. *Newark Daily Eagle,* 6 September 1854 and 11 September 1854.

68. *NDA,* 29 July 1854.

69. Ibid., 2 February 1846; 6 March 1847; 6 June 1854; 24 July 1854; 20 November 1854; 13 January 1855; 20 January 1855; 2 April 1855; 1 December 1857; 16 January 1858.

70. *Newark Weekly Journal,* 15 June 1858.

71. Derived from the manuscripts of the U.S. Censuses of Population for 1850 and 1860.

72. Stanley Feldstein and Lawrence Costello, *The Ordeal of Assimilation* (Garden City, N.Y.: Anchor Books, 1974); John C. Leggett, *Class, Race, and Labor* (New York: Oxford University Press, 1968); Michael Novak, *The Rise of the Unmeltable Ethnics* (New York: The MacMillan Co., 1971).

Chapter 6

1. *National Trades Union,* 20 December 1834; 1 August 1835; 14 November 1835; 2 January 1836; 13 February 1836.

2. Ibid., 30 August 1834.

3. Ibid., 13 February 1836 and 19 March 1836, and *NDA,* 5 May 1835; 12 September 1835; 24 March 1836.

4. *NDA,* 6 April 1836.

5. *National Trades Union,* 22 August 1835 and 10 October 1835.

6. Ibid., 26 March 1836.

7. Ibid., 30 August 1834.

8. Ibid., 22 November 1834 and *NDA,* 27 September 1834.

9. *National Trades Union,* 13 September 1834.

10. Herbert Ershkowitz, "New Jersey Politics during the Era of Andrew Jackson, 1820–1837" (Ph.D. dissertation, New York University, 1965), and Stanley Kutler, *Privilege and Creative Destruction* (New York: J. B. Lippincott Co., 1971), pp. 69–71.

11. Walter R. Fallaw, Jr., "The Rise of the Whig Party in New Jersey" (Ph.D. dissertation, Princeton University, 1967).

12. Calculated as the percentage of those craftsmen in Newark's city directories who were listed in local newspapers as involved in some aspect of politics or government.

13. *NDA,* 13 June 1839.

14. Thirty-seven percent of the 68 craftsmen in the Newark city directories and identified as union leaders were listed in local newspapers as active in politics as candidates, convention delegates, poll watchers, etc.

15. There is a large literature on the Workingmen's Parties, but especially informative are Hugins, *Jacksonian Democracy and the Working Class,* and Edward Pessen, "The Workingmen's Party Revisited," *Labor History* 4 (1963): 203–26.

16. Milton J. Nadworny, "New Jersey Workingmen and the Jacksonians," New Jersey Historical Society, *Proceedings* 67 (1949): 185–98.

17. *NDA,* 15 November 1837; 14 February 1838; 17 April 1838; 1 July 1847.

18. See footnote 12.

19. Richard P. McCormick, *The History of Voting in New Jersey* (New Brunswick, N.J.: Rutgers University Press, 1953), pp. 100–34.

20. *NDA,* 23 June 1834; 24 September 1834; 11 October 1834.

21. Ibid., 22 June 1837 and 26 August 1837.

22. Ibid., 5 June 1847; 29 August 1849; 22 December 1849; 11 October 1850; 12 October 1850; 16 October 1850.

23. Ibid., 11 October 1850 and 29 March 1859, specifically mention interethnic mixing in the shoemakers' union.

24. Of the 68 union leaders listed in the Newark city directories in the 1830s, at least nine and at most fourteen were still listed as journeymen in the directories of the late 1840s. Another seven were listed as self-employed or with another occupation.

25. *NDA,* 9 September 1848. Smith, *Harpers Ferry Armory,* p. 139 states that few American workers engaged in Luddite protest or opposed new technologies *per se.*

26. See Norman Ware, *The Industrial Worker,* chap. 11.

27. *NDA,* 20 June 1849 and 23 October 1849.

28. Kamman, *Socialism in German American Literature,* pp. 17, 24, 41–42; Hermann Schlüter, *Die Anfange der deutschen Arbeiterbewegung in Amerika* (Stuttgart: J. H. M. Dietz, 1907), pp. 131, 139, 168; *NDA,* 28 September 1854; *Newark Weekly Journal,* 22 March 1859.

29. *NDA,* 20 March 1856; 18 April 1856; 15 March 1859; 19 March 1859; 22 March 1859; 25 March 1859; 29 March 1859; 1 April 1859; 2 April 1859; 8 April 1859; 13 April 1859; 22 April 1859; 1 October 1859; 11 February 1860; 23 March 1860; 27 March 1860; 14 April 1860. Schlüter, *Die Anfange,* p. 135.

30. *NDA,* 3 June 1858; 10 June 1858; 16 April 1860; 8 June 1860; 18 June 1860; 20 June 1860.

31. Charges of apathy by voters circulated freely. See *NDA*, 12 October 1836 and 10 April 1849.

32. Of the 8.2 percent who engaged in some political activity between 1846 and 1850, 6.8 percent were Whigs, 0.9 percent Democrats, and 0.5 percent belonged to other parties or more than one.

33. *NDA,* 29 September 1848 and 8 November 1848.

34. Ibid., 8 September 1849.

35. Ibid., 10 October 1840; 13 April 1846; 14 April 1846. Benson, *The Concept of Jacksonian Democracy,* pp. 198–207.

36. *NDA,* 10 April 1849; 4 November 1850; 6 November 1850.

37. Ibid., 9 October 1849 and 31 May 1850.

38. Michael F. Holt, "The Politics of Impatience: The Origins of Know Nothingism," *Journal of American History* 60 (1973): 309–31.

39. *NDA,* 28 September 1854; 7 October 1854; 23 October 1854; 25 October 1854.

40. Ibid., 28 September 1854; 8 October 1857; 5 October 1859.

41. Ibid., 24 September 1856. The 7.1 percent of craftsmen who took part in politics between 1856 and 1860 were distributed as follows: 0.1 percent Whig, 1.9 percent Republican, 0.7 percent American, 2.2 percent Democratic, and 2.2 percent other or more than one party.

42. *NDA,* 5 September 1857; 12 July 1858; 13 October 1858.

43. Ibid., 26 October 1853.

44. *Newark Daily Mercury,* 16 January 1854.

45. Eric Foner, *Free Soil, Free Labor, Free Men* (New York: Oxford University Press, 1970), chap. 1; David Montgomery, *Beyond Equality* (New York: Alfred Knopf, 1967), chap. 1.

46. *Newark Daily Eagle,* 30 September 1854.

47. Ibid., 21 August 1854.

48. *NDA,* 20 May 1846; 3 June 1848; 17 October 1848; 29 October 1850. Only three of the politically active craftsmen belonged to the National Reformers.

49. *Tariff Advocate,* 29 October 1844.

50. Data derived from Newark city directories for those years and lists of candidates, convention delegates, committees, and poll watchers published in newspapers.

51. Urquhart, *History of Newark,* 2: 645–49. Cunningham, *Newark,* pp. 118–21. Business promoter means owners and promoters of banks, utilities, and railroads. Note the similarity to Robert Dahl's picture of New Haven in *Who Governs?* (New Haven: Yale University Press, 1961), pp. 25–31, and Pessen's in "The Social Configuration," pp. 294–95.

52. Data derived from published lists of activists and manuscripts of U.S. Censuses of 1850 and 1860.

53. *Tariff Advocate,* 7 September 1844.

54. *NDA,* 1 November 1860.

55. Cunningham, *Newark,* pp. 223–26.

56. *NDA,* 24 July 1840; 26 March 1846; 30 March 1846; 8 May 1846; 9 April 1847.

57. Ibid., 11 July 1846; 31 May 1850; 31 May 1858. Stuart Galishoff, "Public Health in Newark, 1832–1918" (Ph.D. dissertation, New York University, 1969), pp. 7–8.

58. *NDA,* 11 July 1836; 27 August 1836; 15 November 1839; 24 September 1846; 9 April 1847.

59. *NDA,* 10 June 1847 and 1 September 1857; *Newark Weekly Journal,* 6 July 1858.

60. *NDA,* 26 October 1857.

61. Ibid., 31 May 1858. *Regulations of the Board of Education of the City of Newark, 1861* (Newark: Francis Starbuck, 1861), Report for 1860.

62. *NDA,* 7 November 1857; 9 November 1857; 11 November 1857; 14 November 1857; 27 January 1858; 8 February 1859.

63. Melvin Dubofsky, *Industrialism and the American Worker* (New York: Thomas Y. Crowell Co., 1975), chap. 2, and Leo Troy, *Organized Labor in New Jersey* (Princeton, N.J.: D. Van Nostrand Co., 1965), pp. 42–61.

64. Kamman, *Socialism in German American Literature,* pp. 26–28. Copies of the *Newark Artisan,* 1876, are in the New Jersey Historical Society.

65. The literature on ethnic politics and the political machine is voluminous. A good introduction is Alexander B. Callow, Jr., ed., *The City Boss in America* (New York: Oxford University Press, 1976).

Chapter 7

1. See also Laurence A. Glasco, "The Life Cycles and Household Structure of American Ethnic Groups," *Journal of Urban History* 1 (1975): 339–64.

2. Robert Ernst, *Immigrant Life in New York City 1825–1863* (Port Washington, N.Y.: Ira J. Friedman, Inc., 1949), pp. 178–80.

3. Ibid., chaps. 4, 11–13; Clyde Griffen, "Workers Divided," in Thernstrom and Sennett, *Nineteenth-Century Cities,* pp. 88–92; Knights, *The Plain People of Boston,* chap. 4; Bruce Laurie, "The Working People of Philadelphia, 1827–1853" (Ph.D. dissertation, University of Pittsburgh, 1971), chap. 7.

4. Ernst, *Immigrant Life,* chap. 9; Laurie, "The Working People of Philadelphia," chap. 8.

5. Ernst, *Immigrant Life,* chap. 14; Handlin, *Boston's Immigrants,* chap. 7; Warner, *The Private City,* chaps. 5–7.

6. Gutman, "Work, Culture, and Society," p. 540.

7. Margaret Byington, *Homestead: The Households of a Mill Town* (Pittsburgh, Pa.: University of Pittsburgh, reprint 1974); Tamara Hareven, "The Laborers of Manchester, New Hampshire, 1912–1922," *Labor History* 16 (1975): 249–65; Sam B. Warner, Jr., *The Urban Wilderness* (New York: Harper and Row, 1972), chap. 4.

8. Dubofsky, *Industrialism and the American Worker,* chap. 2.

9. Harry Braverman, *Labor and Monopoly Capital* (New York: Monthly Review Press, 1974), Parts I–III.

10. From the voluminous sociological literature of the contemporary working class see especially: Bennett Berger, *Working-Class Suburb* (Berkeley: University of California Press, 1960); Mirra Komarovsky, *Blue-Collar Marriage* (New York: Random House, 1962); Lee Rainwater, "Making the Good Life," in Sar Levitan, *Blue-Collar Workers* (New York: McGraw-Hill, 1971), pp. 204–29; Arthur Shostak and William Gomberg, *Blue-Collar World* (Englewood Cliffs, N.J.: Prentice Hall, 1964).

11. The creation of a mass culture through consumerism and the media has not obliterated differences in value and behavior between classes, but it has homoge-

nized ethnic distinctions. Berger, *Working-Class Suburb,* chap. 5; Shostak and Gomberg, *Blue-Collar Workers,* pp. 37–39.

12. For instance, Herbert Gans, *The Urban Villagers* (New York: The Free Press, 1962).

13. John Bracey, August Meier, and Elliot Rudwick, *Black Workers and Organized Labor* (Belmont, Calif.: Wadsworth, 1971); Florette Henri, *Black Migration* (Garden City, N.Y.: Anchor Press, 1976). Whether racial antagonisms will abate as ethnic ones have is not at all clear, however. There seems to be a qualitative difference between racial and ethnic prejudice and in the roles blacks and European immigrants have played in American society.

14. Braverman, *Labor and Monopoly Capital,* Parts IV, V; C. Wright Mills, *White Collar* (New York: Oxford University Press, 1951).

15. Berger, *Working-Class Suburb,* p. 39; Stanley Aronowitz, *False Promises* (New York: McGraw-Hill Book Company, 1973), chap. 4.

16. Aronowitz, *False Promises,* chap. 8; Braverman, *Labor and Monopoly Capital,* Parts I, II. Current dissatisfaction with the content of work is forcefully expressed in Studs Terkel, *Working* (New York: Avon, 1975).

17. Rainwater, "Making the Good Life," pp. 220–21; Aronowitz, *False Promises,* chap. 8.

Index

Adams, John Quincy, 12
American Federation of Labor, 130
American Party, 122–23
American Protestant Association, 105–6
Andover, Mass., Moral Society, 6
Anneke, Fritz, 118
apprenticeship, 8–10, 44–46, 74–75
artisan. *See* mechanic
artisan class, 7–8, 10–11, 78, 84–89; political ethic of, 11–12, 109–10, 112, 123

Baldwin and Company, 32
blacks, 6, 37–38, 120, 136–37
blacksmithing, 21, 24–26, 35, 91; wages in, 26, 67, 69, 71
blacksmiths, 25, 43, 47–50, 61, 66, 69, 72, 79; organizations of, 27, 87
boarding, 60–61, 66, 74, 99
bootmakers. *See* shoemakers
Boston, Mass., 50, 110, 119
bourgeoisie. *See* capitalist class
Boyden, Seth, 20
Brady, John, 76
Breckinridge, John C., 122
building trades, except carpentry, 84, 111, 116, 118

Camden and Amboy Railroad, 112, 121
capitalist class, composition of, 82–84; consciousness, 86–87, 102; ideology of, 86, 89–90, 104, 127–28, 131; politics of, 114–15, 122–26
carpenters, 11, 25, 43, 47–50, 61, 66, 69, 72, 79, 117; House Carpenters and Masons Benevolent Association, 87; unions of, 27, 84, 88, 90, 110, 113, 116, 119
carpentry, 21, 24–25, 35, 45, 71, 91; wages in, 26–27, 67, 69
carpet bag making. *See* trunk making
carriage, coach, and wagon making, 3, 16, 20, 89, 111
Carter, Aaron, 91

Carter, Pennington, and Doremus, 91–92
child labor, 41, 65, 120
class, xv–xvii; structure, 10, 78
Clay, Henry, 12
Clinton Works, 20
Combs, Moses, 10
Commons, John R., xiv
Constitutional Union Party, 122
convict labor, 110, 114
cooperatives, 86–87, 117–18
cordwainers. *See* shoemakers
cost of living, Newark, 67
craftsman. *See* mechanic
currying. *See* leather making

Danbury, Conn., 119
Dawley, Alan, xvi
Delaware and Raritan Canal Co., 112
Democratic Party, 112–15, 121–24
Detroit, Mich., 58, 108
Douglass, Stephen, 122

economic depressions, 19, 21, 88, 129
Elizabeth, N.J., 19
Essex County, N.J., 19, 67
Essex County Bible Society, 105
ethnicity, 77–78, 102–3; and group conflict, 105–6; and residential segregation, 107
ethnic politics, 109, 120–23, 131
Evans, George, 117

Faler, Paul, xvi
family, 5, 53, 136; and children, 57–60, 63–64, 71, 75–76; composition of, 60–63; and ethnic differences, 55–57, 62; formation of, 54–57; and production, 60, 64–66, 71–72; and sex roles, 54, 64–66, 101; Victorian ideal of, 54, 60, 62
Feldberg, Michael, xvii
Field and Keep, 62
fire companies, 88, 99–101, 113
Free Soil Party, 120

167

women in production, 27–29, 32–35, 38–41
work, value of, 8–9
working class, xiii–xiv, 78, 83, 133–35, 138;
and unions, 84–85, 88–89, 109–10, 116–18,
129–30, 137; composition of, 82–84, 103,
137; consciousness, xiv–xv, 84, 88, 92, 110,
117; effect of heterogeneity on, 77–78,
107–9, 116; ideology of, 85–86, 89–90; politics, 109–15, 120, 123–26, 129–31, 137–38
working conditions, 32–35, 111
Wright, Henry Clark, 8–9

Young Men's Christian Association, 105